The Way
of the
Enneagram

The Way
of the
Enneagram

Our Return to the Golden World

Robert Bruce

Second Edition

Published by Enneagram Academy

enneagramacademy.com

Copyright © Robert Bruce 2022
First edition 2022
Second edition 2023

ISBN 978-0-646-85837-1

Cover, text design and typesetting by Akiko Chan
Diagrams by Silvia Roos, Graphic Insight V2

IN GRATITUDE TO ALL MY GUIDES ALONG
THE WAY, BUT PARTICULARLY

Russ Hudson
Carl Jung
Joseph Campbell
Eckhart Tolle
Pema Chödrön

Contents

PART I

THE WAY OF
THE ENNEAGRAM

Introduction

When I was forty-three, my father whom I loved very much, was dying. My marriage of eighteen years was coming to an end. I was confused and overwhelmed. I would cry for hours at a time without knowing why. I told myself that none of this had much to do with me; it was just a difficult combination of life's circumstances. I didn't know what to do; I just wanted to get my "old life" back again.

As I came to know later, this was a fairly normal and well-timed midlife crisis. I had been unhappy for many years, but I believed my unhappiness was manageable. I had developed strategies to cope with it. I made up stories to explain away my unhappiness or blame it on others. I had become protected and isolated. It was like living in a little hut, with the walls there to protect my heart and to help me survive. I was trying to make the protection as strong as possible. But now the walls were beginning to tremble and the disturbance was coming from beneath the floor. Attempts to keep the walls in place were failing. There was nothing I could do.

In retrospect, I can see it had taken two big shocks, particularly the death of my father, to shake me out of my unhappy trajectory. Without a crisis, there would have been no need to change. The challenges of relationships, family, career, and financial needs over many years had slowly drawn me into a downward spiral of unhappiness and perceived adversity. I had come to believe that I was living in a difficult world, without much prospect for joy and happiness. At some level, I knew there must be a better way to live, so I became curious about my role in my unhappiness.

What followed were many years of searching: a trip to India, Jungian therapy, countless workshops, and many inspiring books. Each offered a little kernel of truth. Each step along the way gave me enough encouragement to take the next step. Occasionally, there were moments of inspiration and truth when I knew something much bigger was at play. These were the little winks from the universe that kept me going. While these inspiring experiences were encouraging, they didn't provide a consistent framework to help me live a more joyful and fulfilling life. Eventually I was introduced to the Enneagram and then I knew I had found the guidance and wisdom for which I had been searching.

A Reluctant Discovery

My discovery of the Enneagram was slow and reluctant; I found reasons for not embracing it. I didn't want to hear what it was revealing; it was too confronting. There was a precision to its insights. It felt like they were spoken by someone who had known me for a lifetime. It was both embarrassing and liberating. It described how I protected myself, offering insights that were undeniably accurate. It also showed how limiting these protective strategies had become.

But its greatest gift to me was its explanation of how I had been drawn into the downward spiral of unhappiness and perceived adversity. It explained the tendency to protect myself from suffering and, in doing so, to move further away from an authentic connection with others and myself. And even more importantly, it offered a way to re-trace my steps and as I did, my life began to improve. I was less disturbed by the challenges I encountered. I began to see the intrinsic beauty around me and to realise I was living in a benevolent world.

As I began to use the Enneagram, I was impressed with its compatibility with other teachings. It sits comfortably beside almost any field of personal exploration: from spirituality to psychology, from mythology to religion and from relationship theory to mindfulness.

Not only is it compatible, it seems to provide an overarching framework that adds depth and clarity to many teachings.

For me, the strongest testament to the transformative power of the Enneagram came from my ageing mother. After I had been working with the Enneagram for a couple of years, she could see that something in me had changed. I was happy for no particular reason. In a very matter-of-fact way, she offered me the greatest affirmation she had ever spoken, "I wish your father could see you now."

*   *   *   *

Our Way Back to the Golden World

Now, more than anything, I want to share the richness and versatility of the Enneagram with its wonderful blend of ancient wisdom and modern psychology. But before doing this, we need to understand how we lose connection with our true nature. This is the subject of Chapter One. We will then apply the insights and wisdom of the Enneagram to navigate our way back to our true nature and our return to the Golden World.

In Chapter Two we explore the origins and history of the Enneagram. It also includes an overview of the nine Enneagram types and the psychological forces that lead to their formation. The exploration of the types continues in Chapter Three with some frameworks and questions which may help you identify which type you are.

A fundamental tenet of Enneagram teaching is that at some deep level in our unconscious there is an all-pervading sense of separation and loss. This underlying sense of separation manifests in nine different fearful beliefs about ourselves, the nine Basic Fears. Each of the nine Enneagram types develops as a coping strategy to compensate for, or cover over, our Basic Fear. This is the focus of Chapter Four, What Each Enneagram Type Tries to Conceal.

As we become familiar with of our Basic Fear, the need for coping strategies falls away. We no longer have to protect ourselves and we can behave in ways that are not limited by our Enneagram type. This movement away from the limitations of type, and the influence of Basic Fear, allows us to become psychologically healthier, less self-absorbed and more open to the joys of life. In the Enneagram this is described as moving up the Levels of Health. The teachings around the Levels of Health are covered in Chapter Five. They are one of the most important parts of the Enneagram; they provide us with our path to freedom.

The Levels of Health also reveal how, in the way we respond to life's challenging circumstances, we can move down the levels. We become more self-absorbed and more psychologically unhealthy. In each moment when we are triggered, we have a choice in how we respond. We can react negatively, reinforcing our protective and habitual behaviours, which takes us further into our Enneagram type. Or we can stay with the uncomfortable feelings that are arising. Chapter Six shows how our attempts to get away from pain takes us down the levels; it also shows how we can learn to do the opposite. Being with our own discomfort becomes our doorway to freedom.

Chapter Seven explores how we can become aware of our habitual behaviours and begin to dismantle the protective shells we have developed to keep us safe. The protective shells include the thoughts and beliefs we develop about ourselves. They become a 'false self', and we mistakenly believe that this is 'who we are'. Our challenge is to allow the protective shells, and with them our 'false self', to be dismantled. But this is not possible until we bring the difficult contents of the unconscious, including our Basic Fear, into our awareness. Finding the aspects of ourselves that we have been trying to conceal for a lifetime is a difficult task. How we do this, using the Enneagram, is the focus of the remaining chapters of the book.

For most of us, relationships are the most challenging part of our lives. In Chapters Eight and Nine we use the difficulties arising in our relationships to access the underlying content in our unconscious. The gift of relationships is that they supply an almost endless source of discomfort. We can use the discomfort to dismantle our protective shells.

In Part II we undertake a journey into the unconscious, the hero's journey. Like the mythical heroes of the past, we are seeking something of great value. In our terms, it is freedom from the limitations of our Enneagram type and the return to the Golden World. Before we embark on our journey, we need a map of the difficult terrain through which we will pass. In Chapters Ten and Eleven we explore the unconscious, and the challenging aspects of ourselves we might find there. In Chapter Twelve we discover the redemptive qualities of the psyche and the inherent urge within all of us to move towards wholeness and freedom. In Chapter Thirteen the journey begins.

The journey follows the stages of the hero's journey, outlined by Joseph Campbell in The Hero With a Thousand Faces. It begins with the Call to Adventure, an unsettling, but life-changing message from the unconscious. Often, our inclination is to refuse the call and distract ourselves with the challenges of everyday life. Our doubts about accepting the call arise again when we encounter the Threshold Guardians and the Clashing Rocks.

In Chapter Fourteen we cross the threshold into the unconscious and move along the Road of Trials. There will be difficulties and threats along the way. If we can surrender to what is happening, help will be provided, often from unexpected sources. This takes us to the lowest and deepest point of the journey, where the opposing forces of the psyche are allowed to meet and be united. This is the moment of the Sacred Marriage when the opposing forces within the psyche come together. They give birth to a new "third thing", our changed perspective of ourselves and the world. This is our entry into the Golden World. Within the Golden World the structures of the 'false self' fall away and we experience the beauty of what has always been there.

In Chapter Fifteen, we recognise the hero's quest has been accomplished, but the hero must still return to the world with his life-restoring trophy. Chapter Sixteen describes a practical process, Prospecting for Gold, which has its roots in the hero's journey. It provides a simple way to explore the contents of the unconscious. In Chapter Seventeen, we undertake the most difficult round of all, where we use the Passions of the Enneagram to access and reveal the grief around our Basic Fear.

And finally, in Chapter Eighteen, when we have completed the challenging rounds of the hero's journey, we can take our prize. We have done our work to reclaim the contents of the unconscious. We are free from our unconscious pain; there is nothing to conceal or protect. We return to our true nature. The Golden World becomes a consistent and continuing part of our experience.

CHAPTER 1

The Three Centres

May you take time to celebrate the quiet miracles
that seek no attention. —John O'Connell

There is a fundamental life-force energy in all of us that keeps us alive. It guides us intelligently through life and connects us to the profound nature of existence. While it is present throughout the body, it is most evident in three centres: the Head, the Heart and the Gut. These three centres are sometimes called energy centres or centres of intelligence. Together, these three centres are where we experience the source of life within us. They are where we feel the essence of our being and the spark of creation that keeps us alive.

When we are connected to these centres, we have a very different experience of life.

- At the Head Centre, we experience a deep sense of knowing, trust, and wisdom. We have all had experiences of this, even if just glimpses. We don't have to think about what to do: we just know what to do. It is our connection to our own deep inner guidance. We know we are supported and there is a flow to life.

- At the Heart Centre, we experience a deep compassion and intimacy with everything. We feel deep compassion or gratitude around the heart. It can arise when we are with someone we love or when we experience a moment of beauty in nature. Nothing else seems important. It seems to arise in a space of universal oneness when the idea of self falls away.

- At the Gut Centre, we experience the intense aliveness of life. We are not just a body, but are part of something much bigger. When we connect with this bigger possibility, the body feels alive, vibrant, and unlimited.

Most of us, at some time, have had experiences that touch into this much bigger experience of life. Often, they are moments of overwhelming beauty which we experience through no effort of our own. It may be moments in nature such as the early morning song of a bird; it may be a moment in meditation; it may be with people we love; or it may be a smile from a stranger.

These moments may be arising more frequently than we realise. Sometimes they are there for just a second; it might be a splash of beauty in a passing landscape. We are not even sure we saw it, but the heart is touched, and we can feel something happened. As we get into the habit of noticing these moments, they can become bigger and more frequent. We become grateful for the abundance that surrounds us and we realise we are living in a benevolent world.

We have all felt these moments at some time in our lives, even though it might have only been for a few seconds. When they occur, it is clear how deeply they affect us. The body relaxes and surrenders; there is an absence of any need for action and the familiar boundaries of the body disappear. Our thinking stops and there is a knowing that everything is alright. We are being held and supported so there is nothing to fear. We relax into our own wisdom. And of course, the heart is happy beyond measure; it is overwhelmed by its intimate connection with life. We have connected with the three centres. We have returned to the Golden World.

These experiences are profoundly important and hopeful. They are proof, that almost all of us, have already had, at some time, experiences which are beyond the limitations of our daily lives. We have already experienced the beauty of the three centres and entered, sometimes just for a moment, the Golden World. This gives us direction in our journey with the Enneagram. We are not aspiring to some unknown or esoteric experience; we simply want more of an experience that is already known to us. We want 'to celebrate the quiet miracles that seek no attention", and we want these celebrations to be a bigger and more regular part of our lives. We aspire to a more consistent connection with the three centres and the experience of the Golden World.

The possibility of experiencing the Golden World in our daily lives was confirmed by Jesus when he said:

> **The kingdom of heaven is spread across the earth**
> **but people do not see it** (1)

Moving Away from the Golden World

We can live our lives unaware of the inspiring moments that take us to the Golden World. They come into our lives, but we don't pay attention; we look away. Our tendency is to discount such experiences. We are pre-occupied with the challenges of the world, hoping that one day we will find our own source of meaning and joy. We don't realise that we continue to walk past the very thing we desire.

With time, the hope of finding meaning turns to disappointment. We want to protect ourselves from further suffering and our hearts become closed. We become disconnected from the joys and the aliveness of life. Our experience becomes narrow and bitter. We react negatively to other people because we have come to believe they are the cause of our suffering. We put up barriers to protect ourselves and those barriers cut us off from the possibility of love. This is the inner torment we have created for ourselves. From this limited and tormented perspective, we are unable to see the inspiring moments that might be available to us.

We look for distractions or sedation to relieve our suffering. Our discontent gives birth to greater adversity and the struggle with life becomes even more challenging. We look at the world and can only see its deficiencies and shortcomings. Fear begets fear. We have been drawn into a downward spiral of adversity and struggle. It is a path that leads away from everything we desire and ends in a narrow realm of suffering. Our attempts to alleviate our suffering keep moving us further away from connection with the three centres.

Using Discomfort and Adversity to Enter the Golden World

We don't have to wait for inspiring moments of beauty to allow our entry to the Golden World. These moments will be there, but they are irregular, and sometimes infrequent. It is best to see these spontaneous occurrences simply as a reminder that this different experience, and this different world, are available to all of us. They are the encouraging little gifts to remind us what is on offer ... just in case we had forgotten.

A more consistent opportunity to enter the Golden World is available in our moments of discomfort and adversity. In fact, discomfort and adversity provide a steady path to the Golden World, if we are able to use those opportunities wisely. Difficult moments are occurring many times each day so we don't have to wait long for something with which to work. And if we can be present with the difficult emotions as they arise, and don't react, then something different will occur. Our automatic reaction is to find relief from the discomfort with any strategy that might work; blame, self-pity, defence, withdrawal, distraction and so on. These reactions might give some kind of short-term relief, but then the discomfort returns, usually stronger than before. If we can be still and feel the difficult emotions as they arise, then, with time, they will pass. A different psychological process has happened. In allowing the unwanted emotions to be there and to be felt, the discomfort has helped dismantle a part of our protective structures. As this happens, we move gradually towards the three centres. By being present with our discomfort, and not trying to get away from it, we take small steps towards the Golden World ... and we can do this many times each day.

The Protective Shells

We have built protective shells around each centre to protect ourselves from the challenges of life. The shells consist of thought patterns, emotional strategies and instinctive responses that keep us safe. But they cut us off from our own inner energies. We become disconnected from what is happening within, and strangers to our own souls. The shells prevent us being aware of the profound beauty within all of us. They also block our awareness of the beauty in the world.

Over time these protective shells become more solid, and we become invested in keeping them in place. We are then constrained to a narrow world and think that is all there is.

- At the Head Centre, we develop narrow and repetitive patterns of thinking based on limited belief structures. We construct stories about ourselves and the world that reinforce our fearful perceptions. These stories become the basis of our identity. It is a false and constructed identity, but we start to believe this is who we are and defend it vehemently. We reject anything that falls outside of these fixated thought patterns, and we lose connection with our inner guidance and wisdom. We think we need to manage everything ourselves and become fearful when we can't.

- At the Heart Centre, we develop emotional strategies around the heart to prevent it from being touched by grief, sadness, or sorrow. We find distractions and problems that allow us to stay in a state of emotional turmoil or self-created anxiety to keep us away from our real feelings. They protect the heart from difficult feelings, but they also prevent the heart from being touched by the richness of life. We become skilled in developing strategies that keep our true feelings away. We don't want to cry; we don't want to show our vulnerability to ourselves or to others. We are content to soldier on through life, and when feelings arise, we scramble to keep them 'under control'. Or we create our own emotional crises, which although painful, keep us distracted and away from our own deeper pain.

• At the Gut Centre, we have instinctive responses to physical or emotional challenges. Our stomachs are activated and contracted, our muscles tighten, and adrenalin flows to defend ourselves from the perceived threat. We lose connection with the natural flow of the energy through the body. We may feel alive, but it is in a very narrow, defended way. We are cut off from our life-force energy and we are no longer in a state in which nothing needs to be defended. We think our created identity is real and that, instinctively, we need to protect it.

The protective shells, the habitual patterns of thinking and behaving, are our coping strategies. They protect us from the challenges of the world, and also from the pain we feel within. These habitual behavioural patterns are the basis of our Enneagram personality types. Our Enneagram-type behaviours protect us from pain and discomfort, but at enormous cost. They cut us off from the three centres and take us away from the experience of the Golden World.

In the diagram below, the protective shells are the shaded rings that surround each of the three centres:

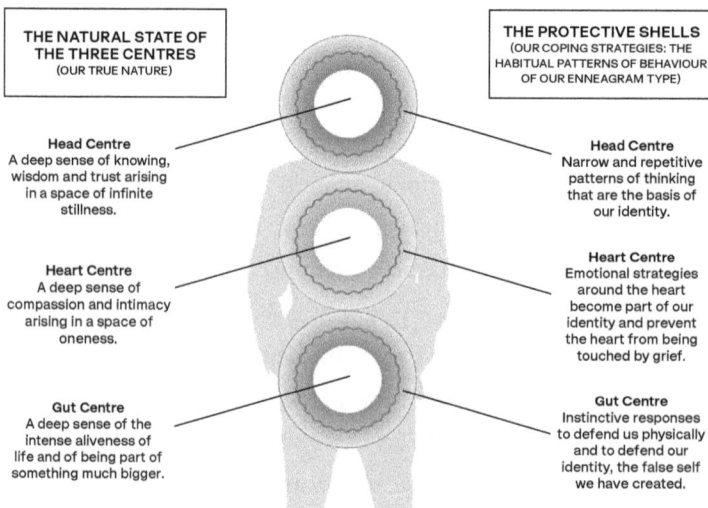

THE NATURAL STATE OF THE THREE CENTRES (OUR TRUE NATURE)

THE PROTECTIVE SHELLS (OUR COPING STRATEGIES: THE HABITUAL PATTERNS OF BEHAVIOUR OF OUR ENNEAGRAM TYPE)

Head Centre
A deep sense of knowing, wisdom and trust arising in a space of infinite stillness.

Head Centre
Narrow and repetitive patterns of thinking that are the basis of our identity.

Heart Centre
A deep sense of compassion and intimacy arising in a space of oneness.

Heart Centre
Emotional strategies around the heart become part of our identity and prevent the heart from being touched by grief.

Gut Centre
A deep sense of the intense aliveness of life and of being part of something much bigger.

Gut Centre
Instinctive responses to defend us physically and to defend our identity, the false self we have created.

How do these protective shells develop?

We come into the world as babies and are confronted with many experiences that are threatening. The birth process itself is overwhelming, with its physical challenges and the separation from our mothers. The experience is made even more challenging by the bright lights, the noise, and our entry into a foreign world. As we progress through early childhood, school years and then into adult life, we continue to be assailed by challenges, losses, grief, injustices, abuse and sometimes trauma. We develop ways to protect ourselves from the full impact of these confronting experiences. None of us would be here today if we hadn't successfully developed effective coping strategies to protect ourselves in the developmental years, and even in adult life.

A three or four-month-old baby has an innocence and an openness that allows them to explore everything with great curiosity. They look at strangers without any need to protect themselves. This changes if something happens that causes discomfort: a loud noise, for example, or too many things happening at once. The baby moves out of that openness and starts to cry or seeks the comfort of the mother. It is unable to cope with the full magnitude of the challenges arising. This is the beginning and early development of its coping strategies. Without these coping strategies, the challenges being experienced would be too much, and the baby itself would struggle to survive.

The Impact of Trauma

When the challenges are overwhelming and traumatic, both for babies, children, or even adults, they have a devastating influence on our development.

Some insightful words from depth psychology highlight the profound impact of trauma, particularly in childhood:

With trauma, play ends, and vigilant self-care begins.

Children exposed to trauma lose their trust in existence. They no longer believe the world is a safe or benevolent place. Therefore, they must take care of themselves — vigilant self-care. For them, vigilant self-care involves the premature development of strong coping strategies that cut them off from normal connections with the world and from the joys of life. Protecting themselves from further trauma becomes their priority and their protective shells become strong. They become disheartened and dispirited; isolated from their feelings and from the three centres. They are far removed from the experience of the Golden World.

The same dynamic occurs for all of us with the day-to-day challenges of life. They might not be as challenging as severe childhood trauma, but the result is similar albeit to a lesser degree. Vigilant self-care becomes our primary concern and we build coping strategies to protect ourselves.

Our Over-reliance on Coping Strategies

As we grow older, we can become over-reliant on our coping strategies. Often, we will see threats that really aren't that threatening; they may just be situations that would be uncomfortable for us. However, just to be sure, and to protect ourselves from potential discomfort, we continue to rely on, and reinforce our coping

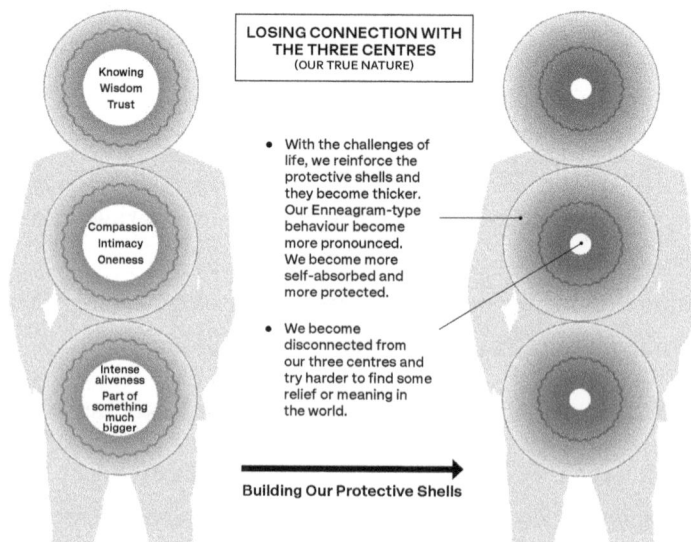

LOSING CONNECTION WITH
THE THREE CENTRES
(OUR TRUE NATURE)

Knowing
Wisdom
Trust

Compassion
Intimacy
Oneness

Intense
aliveness
Part of
something
much
bigger

- With the challenges of life, we reinforce the protective shells and they become thicker. Our Enneagram-type behaviour become more pronounced. We become more self-absorbed and more protected.

- We become disconnected from our three centres and try harder to find some relief or meaning in the world.

Building Our Protective Shells

strategies. The shells become thicker and more rigid. We become more entrenched in our Enneagram-type behavioural patterns. The protective shells, and our Enneagram-type behaviours, become our self-constructed prison; they keep us away from our true nature and from the joy of life. This gradual covering over of the three centres is shown in the diagram above. The joy and aliveness of the centres become increasingly difficult to access.

This sad progression towards disconnection was illustrated in a recent poster. Along the top of the poster were four joyful, giggling babies. Beneath the babies were four grumpy old men, the years of confusion and disappointment etched in their faces. The poster posed the simple question:

What happened?

As we become familiar with the Enneagram, we will begin to see our behaviour more clearly. We will see its limitations; it is keeping us away from something much bigger and more enriching. We will see our coping strategies in action, and realise that, in most situations, they are not necessary. They are keeping us away from everything we want. And once we see these unnecessary and limiting behaviours for what they are, we have the opportunity to explore them and let them go. This is the Way of the Enneagram. It is the slow, but deliberate dismantling of the protective shells.

*   *   *   *

The Enneagram – The Nine Different Ways We Protect Ourselves

'Ennea' is the Greek word for nine. The Enneagram identifies nine different patterns of habitual behaviour we use to protect ourselves. The nine behavioral patterns are recognisable and distinguishable from each other and each of us behaves, primarily, in a way that aligns with one of these patterns. These nine habitual patterns are the nine Enneagram personality types. They are usually just referred to as the nine Enneagram types.

The Enneagram describes the nine types with great clarity; it is usually easy to identify which of the types matches our own behaviour. Most people are surprised how accurately and comprehensively the Enneagram describes their behaviour. Hence the Enneagram is a very potent way of becoming aware of our coping strategies and the particular ways we protect ourselves.

As we get to know the nine Enneagram types - and our own type in particular — it will also become clear that our Enneagram-type behaviours have developed to cover over painful beliefs in the unconscious. The nine different personalities, or identities, have developed in response to nine different unconscious beliefs. As we come to know our type, we will also get insights into the unconscious belief it is trying to conceal. These insights are of great value; our Enneagram type gives us knowledge of what is in our unconscious. As we bring these unconscious beliefs into our awareness, we no longer need to sustain the protective shells that conceal them. The protective shells can be dismantled and we are freed from the habitual behavioural patterns of our Enneagram type.

*　　　*　　　*　　　*

Some Introductory Ideas about the Enneagram
Enneagram research suggests that we are born into our particular type and remain the same type throughout our lives. The behavioural patterns we exhibit when we are seven, are still there when we are seventy-seven. Most parents who have studied the Enneagram agree with this proposition. The behaviours they see in their children at an early age continue to be there throughout their adult lives.

Research also shows that our Enneagram type is not determined by our family of origin or by the way we were raised. This is readily apparent in most families where the Enneagram types of the siblings, who have the same genetic background and similar childhood experiences, are not related in any meaningful way, to each other or to their parents. Studies on twins have shown that there is no relationship in the Enneagram types of the twins. In the most recent and comprehensive study of 36 pairs of identical twins, only two were the same Enneagram type. (2) This finding is supported anecdotally by twins attending our workshops, who have usually wondered why, in spite of their biological similarities, they have felt and behaved very differently to their twin siblings. The research on twins challenges any theories that our Enneagram type is determined by genetic inheritance, by the time or day of birth or by the way we were raised.

Finding one's Enneagram type is the subject of many books and it can also be helped by online questionnaires. For some people it is easy; after reading the nine type descriptions, they can immediately identify which type they are. For others, it is not so obvious, but after deeper reading, research and guidance nearly everyone can confidently identify their Enneagram type.

*   *   *   *

The next chapter will explore the origins and history of the Enneagram. It will also give an overview of the nine Enneagram types and the psychological forces that lead to their formation. This is the beginning of the Enneagram exploration of what unconscious content underlies each of the nine types. It is with this knowledge that we can begin to recognise what needs to be revealed and freed. It is only then that we will gain unfettered and uninterrupted access to the energies of the three centres and the return to the Golden World.

CHAPTER 2

The Nine Enneagram Personality Types

Know Thyself. —The words inscribed above
the entrance to the Temple of Delphi.

The Origins and History of the Enneagram

The Enneagram has a long history that is sometimes vague and imprecise. It is now generally accepted that the Enneagram had its beginning with the writings of Evagrius around 320 AD. Evagrius had a promising career as a Church scholar in Constantinople (then known as Byzantine and now known as Istanbul). Difficult personal circumstances led him to leave Constantinople, choosing exile with the Desert Fathers in Egypt. There he devoted himself to a monastic life of prayer and contemplation. From the observation of himself and his fellow monks, Evagrius identified the nine Passions:

Anger, Pride, Vanity, Envy, Avarice, Fear,
Gluttony, Lust and Sloth

He believed the Passions were distorted human behaviours that kept the monks trapped in the limited realm of their own habitual behaviours. Despite the dedication of the monks, they all were limited by unconscious behaviours that kept them safe but prevented them from realising what they really wanted. Evagrius also observed that these blockages were not the same for all monks. Each monk was challenged by one particular Passion. One monk might struggle with Anger; his fellow monk might struggle with Pride, and so on. Evagrius could see that the Passions were the different ways the monks distracted themselves to protect against any pain or discomfort that was arising within them. In keeping the pain away, the Passions also kept the monks away from the full experience of God. In Evagrius's words, "they keep us away from true union with God." (1). The Passions — the behaviours used by the monks to protect themselves — kept them away from the very thing they most yearned for. The protection that keeps out pain also keeps out God. And so, the nine Passions were born, and they continue to be at the very centre of Enneagram teaching.

The writings of Evagrius were not supported by the Church until the arrival of Pope Gregory the Great in 540 AD. This pope recognised the wisdom in Evagrius's writings, particularly the Passions. However, he did dispense with two of the Passions — Vanity and Fear. These two Passions are unlikely to have been seen by him as obstacles. For someone who came to be known as Pope Gregory the Great, the limitations of vanity would be difficult for him to acknowledge. Likewise, fear is an accepted part of Church doctrine, particularly the fear of God. Hence fear was probably seen as an integral part of religious life, and certainly not an obstacle to divine union. (2) This reduced the Passions to seven, and they became known as the Seven Deadly Sins.

The Enneagram remained untouched by the omissions of Pope Gregory and continued with the nine Passions identified by Evagrius. From the seventh century onwards, there was significant blending in the teaching of the Christian mystics and the writers of the Sufi tradition. Consequently, in trying to identify the source of modern Enneagram teaching, there is no real clarity regarding the contributions to its development. However, it is generally recognised that the Sufi mystics made a significant contribution to its evolution.

An important development of the Enneagram occurred through the explorations of George Gurdjieff, a Greek-Armenian spiritual teacher, in the early twentieth century. He discovered the nine-pointed Enneagram symbol in a monastery in Afghanistan and incorporated it into his own teachings. However, he did not use the nine-pointed symbol as the basis for identifying personality types.

The pivotal development of the modern Enneagram came with Oscar Ichazo in Bolivia in the 1950s and 1960s. In a moment of profound insight, he combined the Passions of Evagrius with the Enneagram symbol of Gurdjieff, and the supporting teachings of the Sufis. He placed the nine Passions on the nine points of the symbol, and then identified them as the basis of nine personality types.

Claudio Naranjo, a Chilean psychiatrist based in the US, studied the Enneagram with Ichazo in the late 1960s. Naranjo took the Enneagram to the US, where it was quickly absorbed into spiritual, religious, and psychotherapeutic communities. Several early teachers and authors emerged including A. H. Almaas, Sandra Maitri, Don Riso (later with Russ Hudson) and Helen Palmer (later with David Daniels). One of the encouraging features of today's Enneagram community is the level of harmony, cooperation, and friendship between Enneagram teachers from the different schools.

(Much of this short history of the Enneagram is drawn from the workshop teachings of Russ Hudson.)

*   *   *   *

Some Confirmatory Research

The observations of Evagrius were validated in some interesting 1977 research[3] reported by David Daniels[4]. The researchers found that babies and very young children have nine different attention styles. From birth, babies pay attention to their world in nine different ways. Daniels showed that the nine different ways of paying attention observed in babies, related closely to the nine Enneagram personality types. The remarkable thing about the study is that the researchers had no knowledge of the Enneagram; the research being undertaken before the Enneagram had reached the United States. Two insights come from this research:

1. It supports the idea that there are, in fact, nine different and recognisable personality types. The researchers were seeing the same nine patterns of behaviour observed by Evagrius, seventeen centuries earlier.

2. The behavioural patterns of the nine types are observable in babies. This aligns with the proposition we are born into our type and exhibit our type-based behaviour at a very early age.

*　　*　　*　　*

An Overview of the Nine Enneagram Types

A version of the modern Enneagram is shown in the diagram below. It includes the commonly used descriptive labels for each of the nine personality types. For example, Type One has been called The Reformer and this captures some of the aspects of a Type One personality; they want to make themselves and the world better. The descriptive labels used for the nine types are drawn from the work of Don Riso, Russ Hudson, and The Enneagram Institute. They are described in greater detail in *The Wisdom of the Enneagram* (5). Other Enneagram schools have adopted slightly different descriptive names. The names proposed by Helen Palmer (6), a well-known Enneagram teacher, have also been included in the discussion. They have a different flavour but point to similar underlying psychological patterns. For example, her name for a Type One is The Perfectionist, which is like The Reformer, but has a slightly different nuance.

The diagram also includes the Passion of each type identified by Evagrius. For Type One the original Evagrius name was Anger. Contemporary usage has changed this to Resentment which gives a more specific feeling to the anger that might be experienced by a Type One. Likewise, the original Passion for a Type Six was Fear, but it is now accepted that Anxiety is a more accurate description.

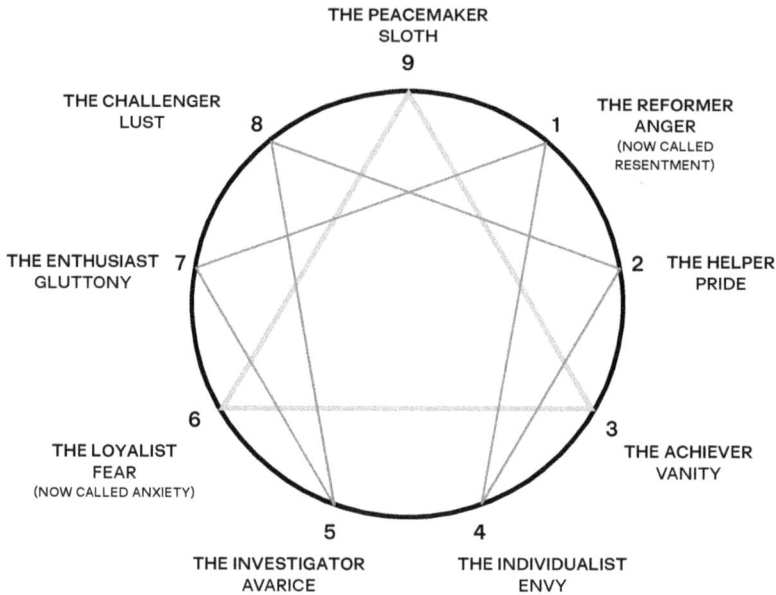

THE PEACEMAKER
SLOTH
9

THE CHALLENGER
LUST
8

THE REFORMER
ANGER
(NOW CALLED
RESENTMENT)
1

THE ENTHUSIAST 7
GLUTTONY

2 THE HELPER
PRIDE

6

THE LOYALIST
FEAR
(NOW CALLED ANXIETY)

3

THE ACHIEVER
VANITY

5

THE INVESTIGATOR
AVARICE

4

THE INDIVIDUALIST
ENVY

The nine Enneagram personality types are the nine different ways in which we try to protect ourselves. The patterns of behaviour associated with each type have developed to keep us safe; they are our coping strategies. They also become the nine different ways we lose connection with the three centres. The Enneagram provides very specific insights into the ways our coping strategies limit us, and points to practices to allow them to be dismantled. And in this way, we become reconnected to the deep life-force energies that support and guide us.

The three centres are useful in understanding the differences between the nine Enneagram types. The nine types can be divided into triads (groups of three). The three triads are:

The Gut (Instinctive) Triad	Type Eight, Type Nine, Type One
The Heart Triad	Type Two, Type Three, Type Four
The Thinking Triad	Type Five, Type Six, Type Seven

i) The Gut (Instinctive) Triad

The Instinctive Triad types (Type Eight, Type Nine and Type One) are at the top of the Enneagram circle. They are characterised by a disconnection from the Gut Centre (or Instinctive Centre) from which we derive our sense of aliveness, our connection to the ground of being, and our participation in something bigger than ourselves. As a result, these three types have strong questions and uncertainty about the nature of their own existence. Feeling they have lost this fundamental connection to life, they develop a false concept of themselves as separate, independent beings. But, at some level, they know that what they have created is not real. The existential struggle to maintain their own false sense of identity underlies the strong energy associated with these three types. The mantra for these types is:

"Don't mess with me!"

In other words, "I am doing my best to hold this identity together, and I don't want you messing with it." This determination to maintain and protect their identity is why this triad is also called 'the Rage Triad'.

An insight into the three Instinctive types is provided by the parable of the Garden of Eden. Imagine these three types have just been thrown out of the garden. They are on the wrong side of the wall, feeling shocked and confused. What do they do?

TYPE EIGHT

The Eight is feeling vulnerable and at risk. The Eight's response is to take control: "The only way out of this is to get tough and protect myself." Hence, one name for the Eight is the Challenger; an alternative name is the Boss. Eights seek reassurance that the false identity they have created is, in fact, real. They know they need to be as strong as possible, so they won't be challenged. They build protection around the heart, so they won't be harmed or hurt. This armour prevents them feeling their own vulnerability and can lead to an insensitivity for the feelings of others. They seek intensity as a confirmation that they are experiencing life fully. They want to 'amp up' everything they do, so they feel fully alive, perhaps because they can't fully feel their own feelings. They are not troubled by challenges or confrontation with others, as this adds to the full intensity of life.

The Passion of the Eight is Lust. This is not just about sexual desire, but a desire to intensify all experience. To live intensely provides a distraction from their feelings of being at risk, but it can degenerate into a need to constantly push against the world. The need to make experience bigger, louder, and stronger can lead to a sense of false aliveness. This feeds the urge for even more intensity; but this pursuit takes them further away from their own centres and the natural sense of being alive.

When Eights are healthy, they let go of the idea they are at risk, as well as their need for control. They are naturally strong, self-confident, and assertive without being controlling or demanding. They are committed to truth and can inspire others by their decisive and courageous action. They take care of others, becoming concerned about the wellbeing of the people around them. The armour around their hearts falls away and they become vulnerable, sensitive, and compassionate.

TYPE NINE

The Nine, having been removed from the Garden of Eden, is feeling disconnected from everything that is important and sets out to find connection by being pleasant and accommodating. They believe that conflict is threatening to connection and needs to be avoided at all costs. In their minds, they create a world which is harmonious and peaceful, even when it's not, and they can be reluctant to deal with the world as it is. Hence, one name for the Nine is the Peacemaker; an alternative name is the Mediator. Underneath the peaceful persona of the Nine, there is, like the Eight, the struggle to keeps things together. The mantra "Don't mess with me!" applies just as strongly to the Nine. There is a survival energy bubbling away in the Nine which wants to keep things, more or less, the way they are. If their status quo or comfort is disturbed, or they are provoked in other ways, it can manifest in strong and "unpeaceful" responses.

The Passion of the Nine is Sloth. This can sometimes be misunderstood as laziness, but this is not necessarily the case. Nines can be active and successful in the world, and, in recent decades, there have been a couple of US presidents who were probably Nines (Reagan and Obama). Sloth is more a spiritual laziness and an inclination to go along with whatever is happening at the time. They want to preserve the comfort of the status quo and become stubborn, doggedly hanging on to familiar behaviours, no matter how limited they are. This sometimes manifests as sleepiness and a reluctance to fully experience reality. Nines want to stay out of contact with their instinctual energies, particularly anger, so it does not disturb their peace.

When Nines are healthy, they let go of the idea they are disconnected, and they stop trying to avoid conflict. They become accepting, genuine, and present. They are good at listening, reconciling different points of view and bringing others together. They can bring a sense of harmony to others who will often feel at ease around them. Healthy Nines are patient but can still be clear and firm in achieving the outcomes and choices they want for themselves. They can be present with their own instinctual energies, without having to repress them or react to the world.

TYPE ONE

The One feels the remorse of being thrown out of paradise. They conclude that they must have done something wrong or that there is something wrong with them. They set about to recover paradise by improving themselves and improving the world. Hence, one name for the One is the Reformer; an alternative name is the Perfectionist. They bring a strong focus to getting things right and fixing whatever seems to be flawed. They become certain about what is wrong and critical about others and the world.

The Passion of the One is Resentment. It is a frustration that they and others are not perfect. Nothing ever quite attains the ideal;

nothing ever quite comes up to the standard. Ones feel that they must repress their unacceptable feelings of anger and resentment, and this makes them feel even more frustrated.

When Ones are healthy, they let it go of the idea that they are flawed and stop feeling responsible for making everything right. They become accepting of themselves and others. They are still principled and directed by a strong inner compass but manifest a quiet inner peace. They become wise and inspiring role-models that others will follow. Others have a sense that the Ones know what needs to happen and want to join them in their endeavours.

*   *   *   *

ii) The Heart Triad

The types in the Heart Triad (Type Two, Type Three and Type Four) have lost connection with their Heart Centre, from which they derive a sense of connection, value and compassion for themselves and the world. Consequently, the three types in this triad doubt their own intrinsic value and worth. They try to compensate for this by seeking validation and recognition from others or from the world. The mantra for this triad is:

"See me the way I want to be seen."

This search for external validation and recognition is why the Heart Triad is also known as "The Image Triad".

TYPE TWO

Twos doubt their own value and fear they are unloved and unwanted by others. They try to compensate for this belief and get the validation they desire by helping others. Hence, one name for the Two is the Helper; an alternative name is the Giver. Sometimes the strategy works but often it can end in frustration and disappointment. There is sometimes a detectable energy in the Two of "giving to get". When appreciation from others is not forthcoming, the resentment will be expressed in statements like, "After all I have done for you!"

The Passion of the Two is Pride. Twos want to be in service, but this leads to ideas about how worthy and selfless they are. They are not willing to feel their own hurt or to acknowledge that they have needs too. Instead, they manipulate their hearts to support a concept of themselves that they think is worthy. An important part of the Two's image is to be seen as selfless.

When Twos are healthy, they let go of the idea they are unloved and unwanted, and they stop looking for validation. They are empathetic, open-hearted, and warm. They are generous and do good works without expecting anything in return. They appreciate their own intrinsic worth and extend to themselves the same generosity and love that they extend to others.

TYPE THREE

Threes doubt their own value and fear they are worthless. They compensate for this by trying to excel in what they do and gain recognition and validation from others. They want to be seen by others as being "the best" so success and achievement are important to them. Hence, one name for the Three is the Achiever; an alternative name is the Performer. Of course, no matter how much success they achieve, or how much recognition they attain, it will never overcome the Three's feelings of being unworthy.

The Passion of the Three is Vanity. Threes need to present themselves to others as someone who has it all together and is the best at what they do. They want to stand out from the crowd, so they give a great deal of attention to their performance. They suppress personal feelings which they fear may interfere with how they are seen.

When Threes are healthy, they let go of the idea that they are unworthy, and they stop being concerned about their image and what others think of them. They are productive, motivated, and adaptable and their achievements help the world. They motivate and inspire others, rather than seeing others as potential competitors. They become authentic and allow themselves to pay attention to, and express, their feelings. With this, they gain a sense of their own intrinsic worth.

TYPE FOUR

Fours feel they have lost connection with the deeper meaning of life and therefore have no personal significance. They seek to recover this connection in aspects of life that offer depth, significance, and beauty. They want to be seen as being different and unique, and don't like to be associated with things that are superficial and mundane. Hence, one name for the Four is the Individualist; an alternative name is the Tragic Romantic. Fours seek to find meaning in the depths of their emotions. They will hang on to, and intensify emotions, particularly difficult ones, sometimes being seen by others as being overly dramatic.

The Passion of the Four is Envy. Fours believe they are missing something that other people seem to have. They think that something is wrong with them, and that they are failing to measure up to whom they want to be. Their tendency to intensify difficult emotions results in a sense that life is hard or unfair, and that they are suffering more than anyone else. They fantasise about the life they would like to lead and hope they will be rescued by someone who will make this fantasy possible.

When Fours are healthy, they let go of the idea that they have no significance, and they no longer need to be different or unique. They no longer need to hang on to, or intensify, their difficult emotions, allowing all their emotions to come and go. They become expressive, creative, and engaged, and their creativity can touch and inspire others. They find their own worth and meaning and can be present with, and express, any feelings that might be arising. Their true feelings can be the source of deep creativity.

iii) The Thinking Triad

The types in the Thinking Triad have lost connection with their own higher intelligence and inner guidance. They don't have an intuitive sense of what to do and don't feel they are being supported by a benevolent universe. Their response is to try to work out what to do through their own thinking and analysis. Even when they decide what to do, they don't trust their own thinking, which leads to further uncertainty and doubt. The mantra for the Thinking Triad is:

"I don't know what to trust."

The doubt and anxiety in this triad is why it is also called "The Fear Triad".

TYPE FIVE

Fives believe that if they gather enough information then they will know what to do. They also believe that the information they gather will help them find a place in the world. Hence, one name for the Five is the Investigator; an alternative name is the Observer. Not surprisingly, many of the great scientists and philosophers have been Fives. Fives have trouble in making sense of the world and finding where they fit. They are often withdrawn and reclusive, preferring to spend time in their own deliberations than with other people.

The Passion of the Five is Avarice. They feel they lack the ability and capacity to be open and generous with themselves and with others. They feel small and helpless and that there's not enough of them to go around. They sustain an image of intellectual competency, and at the same time, try to minimise their involvement and heart connection with others. They accumulate every potentially significant piece of information, believing that eventually they will know enough to feel confident.

When Fives are healthy, they can let go of the idea that they are helpless, and they can't find their place in the world. They no longer believe in their own scarcity. They can engage and share with others and become confident that they have an important contribution to make to the world. They can see the world with a clear mind and delight in sharing the things that fascinate them. They remain curious but are no longer attached to any particular beliefs about the world.

TYPE SIX

Sixes seek security and support in what they see as an unsafe world. They try to make the world safer, not only for themselves, but for everyone else. Their concern for safety is the basis of their dependability. Hence, one name for the Six is the Loyalist; an alternative name is the Devil's Advocate (someone who can see what might go wrong). Sixes have great difficulty in making decisions, often seeking the advice of others, and then still being uncertain as to what to do. This outside advice can never replace the loss of their own inner guidance.

The Passion of the Six is Anxiety. To a Six, the world looks scary, and they don't believe they have the inner strength to deal with it. It is how they might feel alone and frightened in the jungle at night. They have a sense that something terrible happened in the past (the loss of connection with the Centres) and that it will happen again in the future. They keep seeking ways to find security, but nothing seems to work, and their anxiety grows stronger.

When Sixes are healthy, they let go of the idea that they have lost their inner guidance and that they need to find security outside of themselves. They become secure within themselves and trust their own inner guidance. They become courageous and decisive while also being aware of the challenges to be addressed. They are appreciated for their stability, dependability, and their loyalty to others, which come as an intrinsic expression of the heart.

TYPE SEVEN

Sevens have a deep sense of emptiness, so they want to enjoy as many experiences as possible. They like having choices and fill their lives to the limit. This is often contagious for others, who enjoy being part of the Seven's zest for life. Hence one name for Type Seven is the Enthusiast; an alternative name is the Epicure. Sometimes the anticipation and planning of the next experience distracts Sevens from the enjoyment of what they are doing now. For Sevens, the grass often looks greener in the next paddock, particularly when the current paddock is the source of some discomfort. In wanting to move to the next experience, they deny themselves the opportunity to fully feel their feelings.

The Passion of the Seven is Gluttony. They have an insatiable desire to fill themselves up with experiences to overcome a deep sense of emptiness. They try to create a life of abundance and excitement that masks the underlying pain. They distract themselves by anticipating and planning what they are going to do next. With the mind being revved up with exciting options, the experience they are having now is unlikely to be satisfying.

When Sevens are healthy, they let go of the idea that they are trapped in pain, and they no longer need to reach for the next experience. They can be with whatever is in front of them and appreciate life as it is now. The grass in this paddock is just as green as the grass in the next paddock. They engage with life with a sense of joy, fun, and happiness without looking ahead and anticipating what might be next. Healthy Sevens are entertaining, prolific, and accomplished and their enthusiasm for life can inspire others.

Some Important Insights
These short profiles give some flavour of the nine Enneagram types and also provide some useful insights. The first is that each of the nine Enneagram-types is formed in response to a loss of connection with one of the Three Centres.

TYPES EIGHT, NINE AND ONE
Losing connection with the Gut (Instinctive) Centre and the sense of aliveness and of being part of something much bigger.

TYPES TWO, THREE AND FOUR
Losing connection with the Heart Centre and the sense of connection, value and compassion for themselves and the world.

TYPES FIVE, SIX AND SEVEN

Losing connection with the Head Centre and the sense of deep knowing, wisdom, and trust.

Each Enneagram type develops a specific way of compensating for the loss being felt. We want to convince ourselves and the world that with our coping strategies and identity in place (our Enneagram type), we can cover over the loss we are feeling. This gives an insight into the psychological underpinnings of each type; they are based on a very specific underlying, but unconscious, sense of loss. This is explored in detail in Chapter Four, What Each Enneagram Type Tries to Conceal.

The second insight is that each type can be healthy, unhealthy or somewhere in between. If each type can let go of an unconscious belief about themselves, the need to protect themselves is diminished. The protective shells begin to be fall away and we can all behave in ways that are not limited by our type. This is a crucial part of Enneagram teaching. It offers a way of being freed from the limitations of type and reconnecting with our centres. While it is valuable to know which Enneagram type we are, it is equally important to focus on becoming more healthy within our type. This path to freedom is explored in Chapter Five, Basic Fear and the Levels of Health.

Finally, as we become familiar with all the types, we see that everyone's behaviour is being limited by their coping strategies and the unconscious beliefs they are trying to conceal. With this realisation, we can begin to have compassion for ourselves and each other when conflicts and challenges arise. We are all responding from the need to protect ourselves and sometimes behave in ways that are unconscious, reactive, and destructive.

CHAPTER 3

Finding Your Enneagram Type

*If we do not observe ourselves, we cannot ever hope
to be our own masters. We will be like marionettes
yanked by every impulse tugging on our strings.*
—Don Riso, *Enneagram Transformations*

There are many online questionnaires that can be accessed to help
you identify your Enneagram type (1). It is worth trying a few of
them; many of them are free. They provide a useful starting point in
finding your type, but it is important not to take the results of any
questionnaire as being conclusive or definitive. Finding your type is
best done slowly, without wanting to reach a conclusion too quickly.
It is also important not to be influenced by the opinions of others.
It is much more valuable to do your own research and find your type
in your own way and in your own time. This way, you have a deeper
awareness of what lies behind your assessment of what type you are.
To accept someone else's opinion denies you the benefit of your own
enquiry. For similar reasons, it is not helpful for you to tell other
people what type you think they are.

Having done a few questionnaires, you may find some consistency in the results. Or you may not. From this starting point, here
are some other approaches you may like to try.

Behavioural Patterns in Everyday Life

One approach I have found to be more useful than questionnaires is based on the work of Roxanne Howe-Murphy and is drawn from her book *Deep Coaching Using the Enneagram* (2). It summarises the behaviours we are likely to see in each of the nine types. It is based on many decades of counselling and coaching work and has a practical, down to earth feeling about it. It has the advantage of being based on recognisable, everyday behaviours, rather than thoughts, beliefs, and aspirations that each of the types might hold about themselves. It avoids some of the problems of a questionnaire, where sometimes we feel we are being forced to give a score to a question to which any answer feels uncomfortable. Unlike a questionnaire, you can also see how each of your answers contributes to the assessment of your type.

To begin, read the eight questions for each type set out below:

- If a question strongly resonates for you, give it two ticks. This means it is a behaviour you are very familiar with.

- If there is a moderate feeling of familiarity about a behaviour, give it one tick. You feel there may be times when you behave like this.

- If a question has no familiarity for you at all, ignore it and move onto the next question.

- If you get to the third question for a type, and none of the behaviours have felt familiar to you in anyway, then you know that this is probably not your type. Put a cross through the questions for that type and move on to the next type.

The Questions

i) The Gut (Instinctive) Triad

Type Eight

1. In relationships, do you take the stand of being the strong, in-control person? Someone has to.

2. Do you want to take control so you can protect yourself and others from the injustices in life?

3. Do you have a hidden sense that others are against you and will treat you unfairly or take advantage of you in some way?

4. When you have a sense that you, or the territory you control, is being threatened, do you notice that you are quick to react?

5. Do you believe that showing your feelings and vulnerabilities would be a sign of weakness?

6. Is it important to you that things get done your way?

7. Do less confident people tend to keep a respectful distance from you?

8. Do you notice you feel more alive when your energy is expanded?

Type Nine

1. Are you inclined to go along with others rather than express your opinion or preferences? Do you discount your own priorities?

2. Do you find in conversations with others that they do most of the talking? Do you want to be asked a question before talking about yourself?

3. Do you avoid situations that might produce conflicting ideas, strong emotions, or even mild dissent?

4. Are you inclined to minimise problems even when it is clear there is an issue to be addressed?

5. When you feel yourself getting angry, do you try to suppress or control your anger at all costs? Do you tell yourself that you shouldn't get angry?

6. Are you inclined to 'make nice' on the outside but try to withdraw from the interaction at the same time?

7. Are you sometimes stubborn, digging in your toes with a smile on your face?

8. Do you sometimes feel apathetic, indifferent, and numb? That you are missing in action?

Type One

1. Do you feel obligated to do the right thing and to fix whatever you feel needs fixing?

2. Do you feel inclined to point out to others what needs to be done differently, and make sure it gets done correctly in accordance with what is right?

3. Do you like to spend time on issues and projects that have significance for the greater good?

4. Do you feel you have a strong inner compass of what is morally right or wrong?

5. Do you feel the weight of an inner critic, also known as 'the judge', that is constant in its negative commentary on others and oneself?

6. Do you assume responsibilities that are not really yours?

7. Do you get angry or resentful with yourself or others?

8. Do you hold a significant amount of tension in your body by attempting to restrict unacceptable emotions?

ii) The Heart Triad

Type Two

1. Do you feel you have an innate sense of what others need?

2. Do you think that others should be able to read your mind about what you want or need?

3. Do you find you attract people into your life who, from your perspective, need rescuing?

4. Do you feel that you must reach out and give, because the needs of others are more important?

5. Do you think you offer others an emotional warmth that allows others to feel cared for?

6. Do you feel that you must sacrifice yourself by forgetting about your own needs?

7. Do you feel inclined to flatter others as a way of winning them over?

8. Do you feel that your attention and energy is focused on being with others, and creating closeness and intimacy with them?

Type Three

1. Do you feel that you are very adaptable and can easily adjust to changing circumstances and different environments?

2. Do you feel that much of your life is focused on creating goals and striving to achieve them?

3. Do you feel that you are very efficient in the way you do things, minimising your energy for non-priorities?

4. Do you put a lot of energy into being the best at everything you do, including things that are meant to be fun?

5. Do you pay a lot of attention on presenting a successful image, while still knowing, inside, that something is missing?

6. Regardless of your level of success, do you feel the need to push yourself even harder, especially if someone else is being acknowledged in your area of expertise?

7. Is it important to you for people to know who you are and what you have achieved?

8. Do you tend to create exaggerated or embellished stories that will shine the best light on you?

Type Four

1. Do you like to be dramatic and overly expressive, even about events that others would see as mundane?

2. Do you generate intense feelings through your imagination and then hold on to the feelings tightly?

3. Do you think that other people have it easier than you or that your life pales in comparison to others?

4. Are you inclined to dump your miseries on your friends and expect them to rescue you from your unhappiness?

5. Do you spend time fantasising about your desired life, desired partner, and ideal situation?

6. Do you feel you are somehow exempt from the so-called rules that apply to other people's behaviour?

7. Do you tend to over-indulge in too much of something — whether that be food or sex or drugs — as a way of further reinforcing your moods?

8. Do you retell your story to others repeatedly and continually focus on re-experiencing the feelings?

iii) The Head Triad

Type Five

1. Do you find you withdraw into your mind for stimulation?

2. Does your inner world of ideas take more time and energy than engaging with the external world and living your life?

3. Do you have difficulty coming to the end of a project or task, as you're not sure that you've covered all the bases?

4. Do you find yourself wanting to practice, practice, practice, while being reluctant to give the final performance?

5. When engaged with exciting ideas, do you almost forget to eat? To sleep? To take care of daily living activities?

6. Do you like to be in the role of the expert? Do you want to know more than anyone else?

7. Do you like to minimise your physical and emotional needs, as they are a distraction from new ideas and projects?

8. Do you want to know as much as possible about a particular subject so you can master it?

Type Six

1. Do you ask others for their opinion on what to do and in some cases ask several people for advice about the same situation?

2. Do you see yourself as someone who is responsible and can be counted on by others?

3. Do you take your commitments seriously and consistently follow through?

4. Do you tend to change your mind frequently?

5. Do you often decide to do something and then, on reflection, decide you don't want to do it?

6. Do you experience a background level of anxiety in day-to-day living?

7. Do you get confused by the mental chatter and indecision in your head, which seems to have many views about what to do?

8. Do you focus on what could go wrong and spend energy trying to make it safe?

Type Seven

1. Do you wait until the last moment to make plans in case something better comes along?

2. Do you find your humour and sense of fun are a common source of enjoyment for others?

3. Do you notice your tendency to push your energy out into the world, which might show up as talking fast, sometimes forgetting to inhale, etc?

4. Do you find you are always on the go, often over-booking yourself and trying to be in a lot of different places at almost the same time?

5. Do you have a difficult time saying 'no' to all the wonderful opportunities that come your way?

6. Do you find yourself in the role of entertaining others and revving up the excitement?

7. Do you attempt to override any inner discomfort, sadness, or boredom by moving on to the next activity?

8. Do you spend a lot of your attention anticipating and planning what is next?

It is important to remain open and curious in the next phase of this exercise. It is not simply a matter of counting which type has the most ticks, although you can do this. It is more useful to identify the three types that received the highest number of "two tick" responses. Your type is likely to be one of these three types.

Review your answers for these three types, particularly the questions to which you responded with one tick. Are these behaviours more familiar than you first thought? When you combine all your responses to a type, is there a bigger picture emerging with which you can identify? In workshops many people will suddenly find their type in exercises like this; they almost fall into it. It may be just one sentence they read, and they know it to be true. This recognition seems to come from a deeper sense of knowing than any rational searching process.

It is also useful to discuss your responses to these three types with a friend who knows you well. Explain to them why you responded to the questions in the way you did. If possible, give recent examples of when you behaved in these ways. Their task is to listen to what you are saying. They may be able to contribute other examples where they have observed these behaviours in you. More often than not, a conversation like this will clarify your likely type. If you are still uncertain at the end of the conversation, repeat the conversation with another friend. It is important that your friends, if they are familiar with the Enneagram, do not tell you what type they think you are. The purpose of the exercise is to 'know thyself'. To be given someone else's opinion about your type is definitely not helpful and is often wrong.

After the review with friends, it is useful to re-score the three types with the highest number of "two ticks". This may result in a slightly different answer than the first time you did it. The type which now has the highest number of 'two ticks' is most likely your Enneagram type. Try it out for a while and see how it feels. Watch your own behaviour and notice how frequently these behaviours arise. Once we are made aware of them, it is often surprising how frequently we notice them. The types with the second and third highest scores may also have some significance for you. It is still possible that one of them may be your type. They may also be important in other ways, and these possibilities will be discussed in the next sections.

The Wings

Having identified your type, either with questionnaires or the exercise above, you may find you also get high scores for types that sit next to your type on the Enneagram circle. For instance, if you are a Type Two, you may find you have a reasonably high score for Type One or Type Three. You are still predominately a Type Two, but you are being influenced by one of the types next to you. This influence from a neighbouring type is known as a Wing. A Type Two might exhibit some of the behaviours of a Type One (slightly more disciplined, concerned for standards, etc., than a typical Type Two). They would be described as a Type Two with a One Wing.

Alternatively, a Type Two with a Three Wing would be slightly more outcome-driven, more focused on the job and not as concerned for the wellbeing of others.

You can only have a Wing with the types directly on either side of your type. (A Two can only have a One Wing or a Three Wing). Some people don't have a Wing at all; they are not influenced by the types on either side. Others feel they may have two Wings, one on either side, but this is less common.

There is no underlying theory about Wings; it is more something that has been observed in practice over time. It can sometimes make finding your type a little more difficult. Rather than having clearly defined patterns of behaviour that are unique to a type; the behaviours become blended, and they are a little less easy to identify. Some Enneagram books give comprehensive descriptions of the types combined with their Wings and these can be helpful when trying to understand the influence of Wings.

The Horney Groups – Withdrawn, Assertive or Compliant
Another useful framework for finding your type had its origins in the work of Karen Horney, a Freudian psychiatrist working in New York in the 1940s and 1950s. Her work pre-dated the modern Enneagram, but Enneagram scholars have used her classifications to help understand the behaviours of the types.

She proposed that, under stress, we react to people in one of three ways:

1. THE WITHDRAWN GROUP
(Described by Horney as: "Respond to stress by moving away from people".)
Identified by Enneagram scholars as Types Four, Five and Nine.

2. THE ASSERTIVE GROUP
(Described by Horney as: "Respond to stress by moving against people".)

Identified by Enneagram scholars as Types Three, Seven and Eight. The words "moving against people" is too narrow to describe the behaviour of Type Three and Type Seven. For Enneagram purposes, a more comprehensive description for this group, particularly for Types Three and Seven, is "moving to control the space".

3. THE COMPLIANT OR DUTIFUL GROUP
(Described by Horney as: "respond to stress by asking themselves
    what is the right thing to do?")
Identified by Enneagram scholars as Types One, Two and Six.

To help find the Horney Group to which you belong, spend a few minutes with the following questions. Try to recall a few recent situations with work, friends, or family where you didn't quite know what to do.
    In a difficult or confusing situation:

Do I want to withdraw? ... Types Four, Five and Nine
Do I want to assert myself? ... Types Three, Seven and Eight
Do I look for the right thing to do? ... Types One, Two and Six

When you think you have found your Horney Group, you can take the enquiry further, and look at the differences between the types in each group.

The Withdrawn Group (Fours, Fives and Nines)
While all three types are inclined to withdraw, they withdraw in different ways and towards different destinations.

- Fours withdraw into a world of fantasy where they can allow their emotions and fantasies to have free reign. They are usually less withdrawn than Fives and Nines, trying to involve others in their dramas. They like an audience to acknowledge the depth of their emotional stories.

- Fives withdraw into their heads where they are happy to pursue their own thoughts and concepts.

44

- Nines withdraw into an inner world that is peaceful and harmonious. They have a PR Department out the front that interacts with the world and keeps the peace.

The Assertive Group (Threes, Sevens and Eights)
While all three types are wanting to control the space, they do it in different ways and with different agendas.

- Threes have a more complicated agenda then Sevens or Eights. They want the positive regard of others so they feel like the centre of attention. Their request to others is: "Look at me and affirm my value."

- Sevens move into a space and want to lift everyone up. They tell themselves: "I must stay up all the time, pushing my energy into the world and keep others up."

- Eights move into a space and want to control it. Their challenge to others is: "Here I am. I am in charge. Deal with me!"

The Compliant or Dutiful Group (Ones, Twos and Sixes)
While all three types are wanting to do the right thing, they have different views about what the right thing is.

- Ones want to improve themselves and the world. They can see the possibility of a better world and are keen to fix the things that are wrong. The question to themselves is: "In this situation, how can I make things better?"

- Twos are very committed to helping others to prove their own value and selflessness. They can see others needs very clearly but have difficulty in recognising their own. The question to themselves is: "In this situation, how can I help this person?"

- Sixes want to make the world safe for everyone including themselves. They are constantly scanning the environment to see what can go wrong. The question to themselves is: "In this situation, how do I make things safer?"

Many people have found the Horney Groups to be a useful way to find their type. Usually, it is fairly easy to find the group to which you belong. It is more difficult to make the distinction between the types within each group. For example:

In the Withdrawn Group, it can be hard to tell the difference between a Five and a Nine. (Fives are concerned with ideas and concepts while Nines are looking to avoid disharmony and conflict).

In the Assertive Group, it can be hard to tell the difference between a Three and an Eight. (Threes are consistently seeking validation from others, while Eights are not that concerned with what others think).

In the Dutiful Group, it can be hard to tell the difference between a One and a Six and this is probably the most difficult distinction that arises in Enneagram typing. (Ones are trying to improve things and make them better while Sixes are trying to make things safer).

The Gifts to the World

There is one more exercise that might be helpful in finding your type. It is not usually used for typing purposes, but it is a good overarching test to confirm whether you have landed on the right type, or not. It is called the Gifts to the World.

Richard Rohr, a Franciscan priest, identified that each of the Enneagram types brings to the world qualities that are unique to their type (3). His work acknowledges and celebrates the contribution of each type and how the diversity of the Gifts enrich our world. The Gifts are natural expressions of the heart. They are the intrinsic qualities that manifest when we are in our natural state. No effort is required; the Gifts arise in innocence, without agenda and without any thought.

Type One:	Integrity, fairness
Type Two:	Caring, compassion

Type Three:	Inspiration to get things done
Type Four:	Creativity, beauty
Type Five:	Innovation, clarity
Type Six:	Warm-hearted dependability
Type Seven:	Joy, optimism
Type Eight:	Strength, truth
Type Nine:	Acceptance, calmness

In the exercise below, you are asked to reflect on the Gifts for your type. In your reflection, identify the times in your life when you have brought these particular Gifts to the people who are close to you. Ask yourself the question:

At what times have I brought ... (Insert the name of your Gift) ... to the world?

In workshops, we have found that when someone is working with their correct type, the answers to the question flow easily and quickly. When someone has mistyped themselves, they find the exercise quite difficult and struggle to find answers. When encouraged to work with a different Gift, they can usually find one that flows easily for them. Again, this is not a definitive indicator of type, but if the exercise is flowing easily for someone it suggests they are tapping into the intrinsic energies of their own type.

*   *   *   *

The awareness of the Gifts gives an insight into the beautiful natural qualities that exist within all of us. The Gifts are an external expression of what exists at the three centres. They are called the Essence Qualities (4). In the moments when we are connecting with our soul, we express those intrinsic natural qualities:

For a Type One, *integrity and fairness* is the expression of the underlying intrinsic qualities of *goodness, dignity and blessedness*.

For a Type Two, *compassion and caring* is the expression of the underlying intrinsic qualities of *love and sweetness*.

47

For a Type Three, *inspiring others to get things done* is the expression of the underlying intrinsic qualities of *radiance and glory*.

For a Type Four, *creativity and beauty* is the expression of the underlying intrinsic qualities of *intimacy and depth*.

For a Type Five, *discovery and innovation* is the expression of the underlying intrinsic qualities of *illumination and clarity*.

For a Type Six, *warm-hearted dependability* is the expression of the underlying intrinsic qualities of *awakeness and intelligent relatedness*.

For a Type Seven, *joy and optimism* is the expression of the underlying intrinsic qualities of *freedom, fulfilment, and joy*.

For a Type Eight, *strength and directness* is the expression of the underlying intrinsic qualities of *truth and realness*.

For a Type Nine, *acceptance and calmness* is the expression of the underlying intrinsic qualities of *connection and oneness with everything*.

*   *   *   *

A more practical side of the Gifts is demonstrated by exploring how each type might naturally contribute to the workings of a well-functioning village:

Type One:	Kindly magistrate
Type Two:	Nurse at the hospital
Type Three:	Business owner/major employer
Type Four:	Running the art school/dance studio
Type Five:	Living on the edge of town; villagers sneak out for advice
Type Six:	Manager at the council, ensuring services are maintained
Type Seven:	Running the pub
Type Eight:	Police inspector
Type Nine:	Counsellor/coach

If the roles were changed, the village would not work nearly as well (for example, if a One was running the pub or if a Four was the police inspector). On a bigger scale, we could wonder about the progress of civilisation without the unique contribution of Fives, a type that includes many of the world's pioneering scientists and philosophers.

*   *   *   *

Richard Rohr also notes that we can subvert the purity of the Gifts to construct a desirable self-image. The Gifts, as an innocent expression of the heart, will usually be met with appreciation and gratitude from others. We can be seduced by these moments of appreciation and try to make the Gifts part of our identity. Of course, then the innocence is gone, and everyone can feel the difference. They lose their beauty and their uncomplicated heart qualities.

- The natural *integrity and fairness* of the One becomes judgmental and critical.

- The natural *compassion and caring* of the Two becomes overly invasive and people pleasing.

- The natural *inspiration to get things done* of the Three becomes driven and competitive.

- The natural *creativity and depth* of the Four becomes self-absorbed and moody.

- The natural *discovery and innovation* of the Five becomes overly analytical and withdrawn.

- The natural *warm-hearted dependability* of the Six becomes anxious and suspicious.

- The natural *joy and optimism* of the Seven becomes scattered and focused on what is next.

- The natural *strength and directness* of the Eight starts to become controlling and confronting.

- The natural *acceptance and calmness* of the Nine becomes overly complacent and over-accommodating.

Other Approaches to Finding and Understanding Your Enneagram Type

There are many more pieces of Enneagram teaching that can be helpful in fully knowing and understanding your Enneagram type. They include teachings about the Stress Points/Security Points and the Instinctive Variants (the Subtypes). These are important and interesting topics and are well covered in other Enneagram books. The exploration of the Subtypes in Beatrice Chestnut's book *The Complete Enneagram* (5) is highly recommended.

The intention of this book is to provide enough material to identify your Enneagram type. Hopefully the last two chapters have allowed you to do this, or have at least directed you to further reading, which has made that possible. Now the focus is to delve deeper into understanding what keeps us so tenaciously limited to our type-behaviour, and how we might move beyond these limitations.

CHAPTER 4

What Each Enneagram Type Tries to Conceal

What is this discomfort about?

Our Psychological Inheritance

A central concept of the Enneagram is that at some deep level in the unconscious, there is an all-pervading sense of separation and grief. Many spiritual traditions and early civilisations also hold the belief that there was a moment in time when we became separated from connection with the divine. In Christianity and Judaism, it was the moment at the beginning of the Old Testament when we were thrown out of the Garden of Eden. These myths usually include the idea that we had done something wrong and that this was the cause of our separation. In Christianity, it is called Original Sin. That this myth is a recurring theme in so many traditions and civilisations suggests that it is an intrinsic and enduring aspect of the human psyche. It is part of our psychological inheritance.

In our own lives, we can only speculate as to when this experience of separation first occurred. It could have been at the moment of conception. Or it might have been in the womb, when we first sensed we were separate from our mothers. Or it could have occurred at birth when there was very clear evidence we were entering into the world as separate, physical beings. And it may have developed further when, as small babies, we began to encounter the challenges of the world. Or it may have been a combination of all these experiences.

Whatever the explanation, the core idea is that we have been forcibly separated from our connection with some omnipotent and supportive source. We have come into the world with an experience of separation. And with this experience, the Enneagram suggests that we adopt one of nine possible beliefs about ourselves as separate beings. Each of the nine beliefs are slightly different, all of them are fearful and all of them are about our incapacity to cope and survive as separate beings. In the Enneagram, these core existential beliefs are the nine Basic Fears.

Most Enneagram theorists agree that we carry our particular Basic Fear from birth, and it remains our core fear for the rest of our lives. Our Basic Fear is profoundly unacceptable for all of us; it challenges our wellbeing, safety and self-worth. It is certainly something we want to keep away from our awareness, and hence we do our best to keep it buried in the unconscious.

Basic Fears for the Gut (Instinctive) Triad
The Gut (Instinctive) types have lost connection with the Gut Centre. They have lost the sense that they are part of something bigger; they have lost connection with the source of creation. There is a sense of profound separation and fear — that they are here as separate beings. This gives rise to their Basic Fears, all coming from a sense of vulnerability and inadequacy to cope in a world where they are separate.

Type Eight	Fear of being harmed or controlled by others
Type Nine	Fear of being disconnected and cut off from everything including love
Type One	Fear of being flawed or defective

Basic Fears for the Heart Triad

The Heart types have lost connection with the Heart Centre, from which they derive a sense of connection, value and compassion for themselves and the world. They doubt their own value and their sense of worth. This gives rise to their Basic Fears, all coming from a sense of having no worth or value.

Type Two	Fear of being unloved and unwanted
Type Three	Fear of being worthless
Type Four	Fear of having no personal significance

Basic Fears for the Thinking Triad

The types in the Thinking Triad have lost connection with the Head Centre and their own higher intelligence and inner guidance. They have lost their intuitive sense of what to do and they don't believe they are being supported by a benevolent universe. This gives rise to their Basic Fears, all coming from a sense of feeling helpless, unsupported or deprived.

Type Five	Fear of being helpless and unable to find a place in the world
Type Six	Fear of having no support or guidance and unable to survive alone
Type Seven	Fear of being deprived or trapped in pain

How Our Basic Fear is Reinforced

The Basic Fear is a profound, existential fear, which is buried deep in the unconscious. We are usually not aware of its presence even though it is driving much of our behaviour. It is the ongoing root cause of our Enneagram type and all the behaviours that flow from it. It is there from the beginning, but it grows stronger when we experience personal trauma or challenges. For example, a Type Two child has the underlying belief, 'I am unloved and unwanted.' If the child experiences adversity with a parent, the pain they experience will reinforce the belief they are 'unloved and unwanted'. For a Type Seven child, the same adverse experience would reinforce their belief that they are 'deprived or trapped in pain'. For both children, the experience will reinforce their Basic Fear and strengthen the need to protect themselves.

The Compensating Self-concept

The concept we create to protect ourselves from our Basic Fear is the Compensating Self-concept. It is always the exact opposite of our Basic Fear. We are trying to convince ourselves, and the world, that our Basic Fear is not true. In the discussion that follows we use Type Eight as an example to demonstrate how the Compensating Self-concept is a response to the Basic Fear of each type. This shows the psychological underpinnings of the types and why we behave the way we do. It also demonstrates how the Basic Fear ultimately leads to the Passion for each type. The analysis for Types Eight is set out below; the analyses for all the types are included as an appendix at the end of this chapter. They have been repeated in full for each type because they are such a key part in understanding the behaviour of the types. It is recommended that you spend time becoming familiar with the analysis for your type.

TYPE EIGHT

For an Eight, the Basic Fear is "of being harmed or controlled by others". This is a painful belief and not one the Eight wants to experience. It is relegated to the unconscious where it can't be felt. To keep it concealed, Eights create a concept for themselves which is opposite to, and a denial of, their Basic Fear. The concept is:

"I am strong, assertive and in control."

Eights then dedicate themselves to a lifetime of being strong, assertive and in control. The need to be strong and in control becomes a core part of their identity and is central to their Enneagram type. Eights are sometimes so involved in being strong and in control, they miss the opportunity to engage in life as it is.

To sustain their self-concept, Eights want to intensify their experiences so that they feel they are living fully and are in control of their lives. They need to make experiences bigger, louder, and stronger to distract themselves from the Basic Fear of being at risk. This urge to 'amp up' their experience is the basis of the Passion of Lust.

For an Eight, Lust and the need to amplify experience to create a false sense of aliveness, covers over the grief of believing they are at risk of being harmed or controlled. Better to maintain a false sense of aliveness, than having to acknowledge and feel the pain of believing they are at risk of being harmed or controlled by others. Paradoxically, their pursuit of intensity cuts them off from the natural experience of aliveness. The ideas behind this material have been mostly drawn from *The Wisdom of the Enneagram*. (1)

This analysis gives some insight into why we hold on to our Compensating Self-concept so tenaciously. It is covering over something we want to keep out of our awareness. The Basic Fear is there, and we don't want to feel it. We become very committed to keeping the Compensating Self-concept alive and in place. For example, Eights feel compelled to be *strong, assertive and in control*. Similarly, Nines feel compelled to be *peaceful, easy-going, and kind*. And so on, for all the types. This becomes a core part of their identity and a central part of their Enneagram type. These behaviours are so important to each type, it is difficult for them not to behave in this way. This is true even when they suspect these behaviours do not serve them. For all the types, the psychological consequences of not maintaining the Compensating Self-concept are too threatening to let us behave in any other way.

My Own Experience as a Type Nine

As a Nine, I have come to realise how much energy I invest in trying to be 'peaceful, easy-going and kind'. When I am confronted by a difficult situation or the potential for conflict, my efforts automatically go into diffusing the conflict and maintaining the peace. This will be happening without me really being aware of what I am doing, or why I am doing it. It has become second nature to me. In some situations, it might be the appropriate response. However, over time the response becomes habitual and repetitive. I scan for conflict when it is not there and become overly concerned about maintaining harmony at all times. Sometimes, I avoid conflict by procrastinating instead of taking needed action. In the pursuit of harmony, I move away from aliveness and engagement with life and move towards the Passion of Sloth. All of this is being driven by my underlying need to keep away from my Basic Fear of 'being disconnected'. And my behaviour, as I withdraw from people, is perpetuating disconnection, the very thing I am trying not to experience.

*   *   *   *

What Are the Ways We Try to Conceal Basic Fear?
We can start being curious about how much of our behaviour is being driven by our Basic Fear and our need to keep our self-concept in place. We can reflect on these tendencies at any time and enquire how much of our behaviour is subtly influenced by trying to keep away from our Basic Fear. A useful question to begin the reflection is:

"What are the ways I try not to feel ... (Insert your Basic Fear)?"

To simplify the question, it is not necessary to include the Basic Fear's full description. It can be abbreviated down to one or two words from the following list:

Type Eight	At risk
Type Nine	Disconnected
Type One	Flawed
Type Two	Unloved
Type Three	Worthless
Type Four	Insignificant
Type Five	Helpless

Type Six	Unsafe or unsupported
Type Seven	Deprived or trapped in pain

For a Type Four the question becomes:

"What are the ways I try not to feel insignificant?"

Their exploration might reveal a tendency to create intensity and drama in their lives. This is their way of trying to create some sense of depth and uniqueness, so they don't feel ordinary and insignificant. These behaviours are part of their Compensating Self-Concept of 'being sensitive, different and unique'. They may find they are creating emotional drama, so they feel different and unique. There is some cost to this behaviour, but the payoff is that it protects them from the feeling of being insignificant. This reflection on Basic Fear can be done alone, but it is much more powerful when it is done with another person.

In workshops, this question about how we avoid feeling our Basic Fear has proven to be really important. It has given many people a glimpse of their own behaviour and how much energy goes into keeping away from their Basic Fear. Often, they will see a lifetime of behaviour flash before them, and they will see how pervasive and subtle it is. They will also see how pointless and limiting these behaviours are. These are valuable moments of insight. It is where they 'catch themselves in the act', seeing that their lives are being restricted by the limitations of their Enneagram type. The insight will often be followed by a question as to whether they want to continue to live like this, or do they want something more authentic and fulfilling. In the example above, the Type Four, might wonder whether they really want to create unnecessary drama and intensity in their lives, recognising that this does not really serve them. Perhaps instead, they could connect to the creativity and depth that is naturally available to them at their centres.

*   *   *   *

Precious Insights into Basic Fear

When we have moments of insight like this, we also have the opportunity to see if we can feel the underlying Basic Fear. It is there, but it is still largely unconscious. We often just feel uncomfortable, without knowing what's causing the discomfort. If we can catch just a glimmer of it, it is very valuable. Whenever we find ourselves following the dictates of our Compensating Self-concept, we can know that we are trying to get away from our Basic Fear. This is the time to stop and reflect and ask ourselves the question:

> **What is this discomfort about? Is there an unwanted fear**
> **I am trying to conceal?**

Over time, we begin to become familiar with our Basic Fear. We begin to recognise its familiar flavour, and we know when we are trying to cover it over. We don't want to brush it aside and push it back into the unconscious, where it will grow stronger. As it becomes more conscious, it begins to lose its power.

Quite a few people can identify times in their childhood when their Basic Fear was activated by difficult events in their lives. In response to the Basic Fear, they sought relief by resorting to behaviour to reinforce their Compensating Self-concept. A Type Eight friend remembers a time when he was about ten and his parents separated. His mother was trying to look after him and his younger sister, but she was distracted with the challenges of separation. He can remember feeling that she was not really coping, and he and his sister were at risk. He recalls deciding he had to step in and take charge. While this may have been an understandable response at the time, it reinforced a pattern of behaviour of trying to take charge whenever he felt at risk. He now uses this childhood memory as a way of getting in touch with his Basic Fear. With his knowledge of the Enneagram, he recognises that his habitual need to take charge is driven by his Basic Fear of feeling at risk. When he feels the tendency to jump in and take charge, he asks himself whether this is necessary. In most cases, it is not. This is a good, practical example of someone who is slowly liberating themselves from the limitations of their Enneagram type.

Many of us can probably recall similar incidents where, at an early age, we used our Compensating Self-concept as a coping strategy to keep safe. These can be useful memories to remind us of our tendency to revert to behaviours dictated by our Enneagram type.

*   *   *   *

Becoming aware of our Basic Fear, how we try to conceal it, and how we get to feel it, is the subject of the next chapter, Basic Fear and the Levels of Health.

Appendix to Chapter Four

The Basic Fear and the Compensating Self-concept For All of the Types

Type Eight

For an Eight, the Basic Fear is "of being harmed or controlled by others". This is a painful belief and not one the Eight wants to experience. It is relegated to the unconscious where it can't be felt. To keep it concealed, Eights create a concept for themselves which is opposite to, and a denial of, their Basic Fear. The concept is:

"I am strong, assertive and in control."

Eights then dedicate themselves to a lifetime of being strong, assertive and in control. The need to be strong and in control becomes a core part of their identity and is central to their Enneagram type. Eights are sometimes so involved in being strong and in control, they miss the opportunity to engage in life as it is.

To sustain their self-concept, Eights want to intensify their experiences so that they feel they are living fully and are in control of their lives. They need to make experiences bigger, louder, and stronger to distract themselves from the Basic Fear of being at risk. This urge to 'amp up' their experience is the basis of the Passion of Lust.

For an Eight, Lust and the need to amplify experience to create a false sense of aliveness, covers over the grief of believing they are at risk of being harmed or controlled. Better to maintain a false sense of aliveness, than having to acknowledge and feel the pain of believing they are at risk of being harmed or controlled by others. Paradoxically, their pursuit of intensity cuts them off from the natural experience of aliveness.

Type Nine

For a Nine, the Basic Fear is "of being disconnected and cut off from everything including love." This is a painful belief and not one the Nine wants to experience. It is relegated to the unconscious where it can't be felt. To keep it concealed, Nines create a concept for themselves which is opposite to, and a denial of, their Basic Fear. The concept is:

"I am peaceful, easy-going and kind."

Nines then dedicate themselves to a lifetime of being peaceful and easy-going. 'Peacefulness' becomes a core part of their identity and is central to their Enneagram type. Nines are sometimes so involved in being peaceful, easy-going and kind they miss the opportunity to engage in life as it is.

To sustain their self-concept, Nines want to maintain harmony in their lives above all else. They are uncomfortable with conflict or any disturbance to their peace and believe they must keep their own instinctual energies under control. The dedication to harmony stops them doing and saying what they really want. This reluctance to engage in life fully is the basis of the Passion of Sloth.

For a Nine, Sloth and the need to avoid conflict and disharmony in themselves and the world by disengaging, covers over the grief of believing they are disconnected and cut-off from everything including love. Better to maintain the pretence of a false but peaceful identity, than having to acknowledge and feel the pain of believing they are disconnected and cut-off. Paradoxically, their pursuit of harmony cuts them off from the natural experience of being connected.

Type One

For a One, the Basic Fear is "of being flawed or defective." This is a painful belief and not one the One wants to experience. It is relegated to the unconscious where it can't be felt. To keep it concealed, Ones create a concept of themselves which is opposite to, and a denial of, their Basic Fear. The concept is:

"I am good, have integrity and am beyond reproach."

Ones then dedicate themselves to a lifetime of being good and beyond reproach. 'Goodness' becomes a core part of their identity and is central to their Enneagram type. Ones are sometimes so involved in being good and encouraging others to be good, that they miss the opportunity to engage in life as it is.

For Ones, trying to sustain the self-concept of being good can lead to a sense of frustration. However hard they try, Ones can never be good enough and neither can the people around them. The disappointment and frustration of never realising their self-concept leads to the Passion of Resentment.

For a One, Resentment towards themselves and others covers over the grief of believing they are flawed. Better to be consumed in resentment than have to acknowledge and feel the grief and pain of believing they are flawed. Paradoxically, the pursuit of being good, cuts them off from their natural goodness and wholeness.

Type Two

For a Two, the Basic Fear is "of being unloved and unwanted". This is a painful belief and not one the Two wants to experience. It is relegated to the unconscious where it can't be felt. To keep it concealed, Twos creates a concept of themselves which is opposite to, and a denial of, their Basic Fear. The concept is:

"I am loving, thoughtful and selfless."

Twos then dedicate themselves to a lifetime of being loving and selfless. This 'selflessness' becomes a core part of their identity and is central to their Enneagram type. Twos are sometimes so involved in being selfless, they miss the opportunity to enjoy life as it is.

To sustain their self-concept, Twos start to believe that everybody needs their help: that they are God's helper, or even, that they are here to clean up God's mess. This inflated concept of themselves is the basis of the Passion of Pride.

For a Two, Pride, and the belief they are doing selfless work supporting others, covers over the grief of believing they are unwanted and unloved. Better to maintain the pretence of a false but selfless identity, than have to acknowledge and feel the pain of believing they are unloved. Paradoxically, the pursuit of being loving and selfless cuts them off from the natural experience of being selfless.

Type Three

For a Three, the Basic Fear is "of being worthless and without value." This is a painful belief and not one the Three wants to experience. It is relegated to the unconscious where it can't be felt. To keep it concealed, Threes create a concept of themselves which is opposite to, and a denial of, their Basic Fear. The concept is:

"I am outstanding, capable and well-adjusted."

Threes then dedicate themselves to a lifetime of being outstanding, capable, and well-adjusted. 'Being outstanding and capable' becomes a core part of their identity and is central to their Enneagram type. They are sometimes so involved in being outstanding and capable, they miss the opportunity to engage in life as it is.

To sustain their self-concept, they start to believe that they are better than everyone else. This inflated concept of themselves is the basis of the Passion of Vanity.

For a Three, Vanity, and their presentation to the world as someone who has it all together covers over the grief of believing they are worthless. Better to maintain the pretence of a false but impressive identity, than have to acknowledge and feel the pain of believing they are worthless. Paradoxically, the pretence of having it all together cuts them off from the experience of their natural worth and radiance.

Type Four

For a Four, the Basic Fear is "of having no identity, no personal significance." This is a painful belief and not one the Four wants to experience. It is relegated to the unconscious where it can't be felt. To keep it concealed, Fours create a concept of themselves that is opposite to, and a denial of, their Basic Fear. The concept is:

"I am sensitive, different and unique."

Fours then dedicate themselves to a lifetime of being sensitive, different, and unique. 'Sensitivity and uniqueness' become a core part of their identity and is central to their Enneagram type. Fours are sometimes so involved in being sensitive and unique, they miss the opportunity to engage in life as it is.

Trying to sustain their self-concept of 'being sensitive and unique' can ultimately lead them to feel they have been left out and that they don't have what everyone else has. This is the basis of the Passion of Envy.

For a Four, Envy, and melancholic fantasising that they should be or have more, covers over the grief of believing they are insignificant. Better to maintain the drama and anguish that there is something wrong with their lives, than have to acknowledge and feel the pain of believing they are insignificant, and their life has no meaning. Paradoxically, the pursuit of being sensitive and unique cuts them off from their natural depth and beauty.

Type Five

For a Five, the Basic Fear is "of being helpless, and unable to find a place in this world." This is a painful belief and not one the Five wants to experience. It is relegated to the unconscious where it can't be felt. To keep it concealed, Fives create a concept of themselves which is opposite to, and a denial of, their Basic Fear. The concept is:

"I am clever, competent and can find the answer for you."

Fives then dedicate themselves to a lifetime of being clever and being able to come up with answers. This 'cleverness' becomes a core part of their identity and is central to their Enneagram type. Fives are sometimes so involved in being clever and competent, they miss the opportunity to engage in life as it is.

Trying to sustain their self-concept can lead them to withdraw from the world to focus on their mental deliberations. This becomes their priority, and they begin to ration their emotional involvement with other people, believing that this would be a distraction. This rationing of their emotional resources is the basis of the Passion of Avarice.

For a Five, Avarice and the withdrawal from life and any heartfelt connection with others, covers over the grief of believing they are helpless and there is not enough of them to go around. Better to maintain the isolation and live in a world of self-created concepts, than have to acknowledge and feel the pain of believing they are helpless and have no place in the world. Paradoxically, the pursuit of being clever and competent, cuts them off from their natural profound knowing.

Type Six

For a Six, the Basic Fear is "of having no support or guidance." This is a painful belief and not one the Six wants to experience. It is relegated to the unconscious where it can't be felt. To keep it concealed, Sixes creates a concept of themselves which is opposite to, and a denial of, their Basic Fear. The concept is:

"I am solid, attentive and dependable."

Sixes then dedicate themselves to a lifetime of being solid and dependable. This 'dependability' becomes a core part of their identity and is central to their Enneagram type. Sixes are sometimes so involved in being solid and dependable, they miss the opportunity to engage in life as it is.

Trying to sustain their self-concept of being 'solid and dependable' is challenging for a Six. No matter how hard they try, they still find they are living in a risky world with no support or guidance about what to do. This makes them feel even more threatened and is the basis of the Passion of Anxiety.

For a Six, Anxiety and their fear that something terrible will happen, covers over the grief of believing they have no support or guidance and are unable to survive on their own. Better to maintain the fear that this is dangerous world in which they don't have the strength to survive, than have to acknowledge and feel the pain of believing they have no support or guidance. Paradoxically, the pursuit of being solid and dependable cuts them off from their natural guidance, knowing and trust.

Type Seven

For a Seven, the Basic Fear is "of being deprived or trapped in pain." This is a painful belief and not one the Seven wants to experience. It is relegated to the unconscious where it can't be felt. To keep it concealed, Sevens creates a concept of themselves which is opposite to, and a denial of, their Basic Fear. The concept is:

"I am happy, spontaneous and fulfilled."

The Sevens then dedicate themselves to a lifetime of being happy and fulfilled. 'Fulfilment' becomes a core part of their identity and is central to their Enneagram type. Sevens are sometimes so involved in being fulfilled that they miss the opportunity to engage in life as it is.

Trying to sustain their self-concept of being 'happy and fulfilled' is challenging for a Seven. They spend time anticipating and planning, jamming their life full of as many experiences as possible. No matter how hard they try, they don't feel satisfied. They search harder for another experience, still hoping to find fulfilment. This is the basis of the Passion of Gluttony.

For a Seven, Gluttony and the need to keep reaching for the next experience, covers over the grief of believing that they are deprived and trapped in pain. Better to maintain a false world of excitement and options, than having to acknowledge and feel the pain of believing they are deprived and trapped in pain. Paradoxically, the pursuit of happiness and excitement, cuts them off from their natural experience of joy and fulfilment.

CHAPTER 5

Basic Fear and the Levels of Health

One dark night, fired by Love's urgent longings, I went out by a secret ladder, unseen. — St. John of the Cross

Our Basic Fear resides in the unconscious and is a major influence on our lives. We try to repress it to keep it away from awareness. This is a futile struggle; the memory of it continues to be there, growing stronger as it is repressed. Despite our efforts to keep it away, it creeps into our awareness. It makes us feel uncomfortable and we start to think it is true. We seek relief in our Compensating Self-concept, trying to over-ride our Basic Fear. We reinforce our protective shells and our identity. In doing so, we become more isolated from our three centres. Our lives become limited, and we become more self-absorbed. The Basic Fear gets stronger, and it becomes more difficult to keep it repressed. If this process continues, our behaviour becomes irrational, unpredictable, and alienating to others.

The Levels of Health

This downward movement of self-absorption and alienation was explored by Don Riso, a renowned Enneagram scholar. It has become one of the most important parts of Enneagram teaching as it adds a new dimension to the Enneagram. It not only identifies the downward movement of self-absorption, but also provides a way of moving upwards. He called the work the Levels of Health or the Levels of Development. (1) The potential to move to higher Levels of Health makes the Enneagram a more dynamic, more hopeful, and more optimistic framework. Other typing models, like Myers-Briggs, are helpful in identifying type, but don't offer a defined path to freedom.

Riso observed that people could not only be identified by their Enneagram type, but also how healthy they were in their type. He identified nine Levels of Health:

- Levels One, Two and Three were defined as being "healthy,"

- Levels Four, Five and Six being "average" and

- Levels Seven, Eight and Nine being "unhealthy".

At Level One, the influence of Basic Fear is minimal. The difficult content of the unconscious has been largely emptied out or was never there. The need for protective strategies is low. There is no need to sustain an identity. Someone at this level has developed a strong trust in the benevolence of existence and feels little need for protection. They are fully open to the experiences of life and the energies of the three centres shine through to the world. They are inspiring people to be around. They are a demonstration of what happens as we move towards freedom.

At Level Nine, Basic Fear has been strengthened by a life of challenges and suffering and our efforts to conceal it. The protective shells have become thick and opaque. They have developed to a point where the person is completely cut off from world. They are so entrenched in their delusions and identity, it is difficult for others to connect with them. At this level, they have developed strong personality disorders and serious psychological challenges. It is the final stage of a descent into serious dysfunction.

The diagram illustrates how the protective shells grow thicker as we descend the Levels of Health. The thickness of the shells is represented by the width of the triangle at any point. The left-hand triangle (shaded and representing the thickness of the unconscious

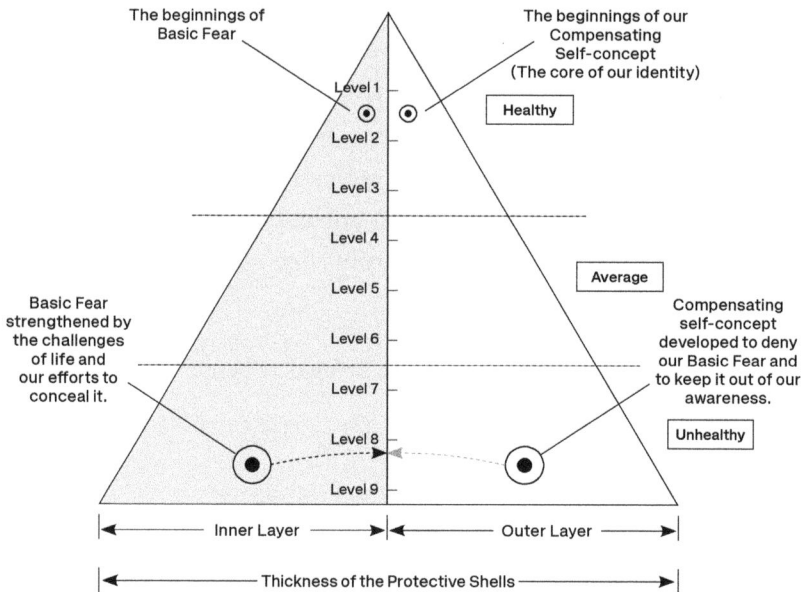

The beginnings of
Basic Fear

The beginnings of our
Compensating
Self-concept
(The core of our identity)

Level 1
Healthy

Level 2

Level 3

Level 4

Level 5
Average

Basic Fear
strengthened by
the challenges
of life and
our efforts to
conceal it.

Level 6

Compensating
self-concept
developed to deny
our Basic Fear and
to keep it out of our
awareness.

Level 7

Level 8
Unhealthy

Level 9

|← Inner Layer →|← Outer Layer →|

|← Thickness of the Protective Shells →|

inner layer) shows the increasing strength and influence of the Basic Fear as we move down the levels. As the Basic Fear gets stronger, so also does the Compensating Self-concept and our identity (the right-hand triangle representing the thickness of the *outer layer*). At each level, we try to match the strength of the Basic Fear by investing more energy into the Compensating Self-concept and strengthening our identity. As a result, the Compensating Self-concept gets stronger, and the *outer layer* gets thicker. It is like a never-ending dance: the Basic Fear gets a little stronger, and we feel the need to reinforce the Compensating Self-concept. The denial of the Basic Fear makes it stronger again, and so on, as we take ourselves down the Levels of Health.

Moving Down the Levels

To explore the movement down the levels from Level One to Level Nine, Type One will be used as the example. The same dynamic applies equally to all the other types, although the specific fears and motivations are different. Riso's descriptions of the Levels of

Health of all nine types are included as an appendix at the end of this chapter.

The exploration for a Type One commences with someone at Level Two. The unconscious content at this level is very mild. Anyone at this level has either undertaken significant work or has had a very fortunate and loving life. They are very healthy people. The Basic Fear for a Type One ("of being flawed or defective") first begins to creep in at this level. It is very subtle and probably arises as a slight inkling: "Maybe there is something not quite right about me." The usual response is to cover over the fear and, by denial, push it back into the unconscious. As we have seen, part of the denial is to develop a self-concept based on the image, "I am good, have integrity and am beyond reproach." The self-concept ("I am good") counters the Basic Fear ("I am flawed"). At this point, the Type One begins a lifetime journey of attempted self-improvement, trying to prove to themselves and the world that they are not flawed.

At Level Three, the One is living a life which is "highly ethical and self-disciplined" and with "a strong sense of purpose and conviction." They are inspiring and appealing people to be with. Despite their dedication to improving themselves, the One continues to experience lingering evidence of being "flawed." Perhaps their efforts are not enough, and they need to redouble their commitment to being good. They feel they must become more serious in improving themselves and the world and this shift takes them from Level Three to Level Four. In moving from Level Three to Level Four, they pass what Riso called the "Wake-Up Call". This is a little warning bell to remind us we are now moving from healthy to average Levels of Health. Ones are being asked to pause and consider whether they really "are obligated to fix everything themselves." Does the future wellbeing of the world really depend on them? It is an opportunity to catch themselves in their self-absorption and be wise enough not to be captured by the agenda of compulsive self-improvement.

Moving Past the Red Flag

If Ones persist in their efforts of proving their goodness, they become more entrenched in their self-righteousness and more convinced about the poor standards of the people around them. The coping strategy of "being good" is used to conceal the underlying fear "of being flawed". As the fear is denied and covered over, the fear grows stronger. By Level 6, self-absorption around correctness has become strong. They are reproaching and correcting others for not living up to their standards. They are becoming very self-righteous. As they move from Level 6 to Level 7 there is another opportunity to take stock of what is happening: the 'Red Flag'. The question to consider here is: "Are my ideals wrong and counterproductive?" Clearly, the answer is that their ideals have become very dysfunctional. However, in many cases, Ones at this level cannot see what is happening; they ignore the 'Red Flag'.

If they cross into the unhealthy levels at Level 7, Riso believed that outside support or intervention by a therapist would be required to move them back up the levels. Their thinking has become so distorted that they are unable to help themselves. This observation doesn't just apply to Ones; it applies to all the Enneagram types as they move to Level 7. If intervention doesn't happen, the fear becomes uncontrollable and manifests in the irrational and deeply disturbed behaviours of Levels 8 and 9. These behaviours can often be related to personality disorders. The definitions and description of these disorders are given in the Diagnostic and Statistical Manual of Mental Disorders (DSM) (3). A possible personality disorder for a One is Obsessive-Compulsive Personality Disorder. This would have its origins in the One trying to make things perfect and trying to enforce their standards on the world.

One of the more public demonstrations of a One's journey down the levels comes from the evangelistic teachers on American television, who, in many cases, are Ones. Their preaching is about their own worthiness and the work they do in correcting the "sinfulness" of others. On more than one occasion, their careers have finished in public disgrace. In one notorious case, the preacher was found in the back of a station wagon doing the very thing that he had condemned so publicly. Ironically, it is the good intentions and high principles of a One that take them down the Levels of Health. Hence the insight:

"The road to hell is paved with good intentions."

The sad insight from this movement down the levels is that at Levels 8 and 9 we behave in a way that is driven by the original Basic Fear. Ones were afraid of being flawed and finish up acting out all their irrational desires and impulses. Their behaviour is the very opposite of everything they aspired to. This, of course, is true for all the other types. It confirms the old piece of wisdom:

"What we resist, persists."

Fortunately, only a few descend all the way to the lower Levels of Health. The purpose of the Enneagram is to allow us to move upwards. Hopefully, with awareness, we can progress to Level One, where we are free from Basic Fear and the need to develop a protective self-concept. At that level, Ones become "wise, discerning, accepting, hopeful, and often noble."

The journey of the Ones down the Levels of Health is summarised below. Only brief descriptions for each of the nine levels have been included, but they give an overview of the progression down the levels. Similar summaries for all nine types are included as an appendix at the end of this chapter. More complete descriptions of each level are given in *The Wisdom of the Enneagram* by Don Riso and Russ Hudson, the source of this valuable material.

Type One
Basic Fear: *Of being flawed or defective*

HEALTHY LEVELS: Levels 1 to 3
Level 1: Liberated Ones are wise, discerning, accepting and often noble

Level 2: Ones feel the disturbance of their Basic Fear and comfort themselves with their self-concept: *I am good, have integrity and am beyond reproach.*

Level 3: Ones reinforce their self-concept, living their lives with high standards. They are highly ethical and possess a strong sense of purpose.

Wake-up Call: Ones feel obligated to fix everything themselves.

AVERAGE LEVELS: Levels 4 to 6

Level 4: Ones want to convince others of the correctness of the opinions. They become serious, driven, and critical, trying to remedy problems.

Level 5: Ones worry that others will condemn them for any deviation from their ideals, so they vigorously organise themselves and their world.

Level 6: Ones are frustrated others will mess up the order they have created. They reproach others for not living up to their standards.

Red Flag: My ideals may be wrong and counterproductive.

UNHEALTHY LEVELS: Levels 7 to 9

Level 7: Ones begin to fear their ideals may be causing problems. To defend against this thought, they silence criticism and become highly self-righteous.

Level 8: Ones begin to act out their repressed desires while publicly continuing to condemn them. They cannot stop themselves.

Level 9: Ones realise they have lost control of themselves and are doing the very things they can't tolerate in others. They can commit punitive acts against themselves and others.

DSM inclination: Obsessive-compulsive personality disorder

Most of us sit between Level Three and Level Six. We find our equilibrium level of health and remain, more or less, at that level for many years. We find a balance that gets us through life, although often without much joy. In periods of sustained stress, we might move down a level or two. When the stressful circumstances pass, we return to the level we were at before the onset of the stress. If we make these downward movements on an ongoing and regular basis, we eventually move to the lower level on a more permanent basis. This can be illustrated by the idea that at each level we are issued with a bungee-jumping cord that is guaranteed for ten thousand jumps. If we regularly jump downwards to the next level, eventually the cord loses its elasticity, and we remain at the lower level. We are then issued with a new cord, and the process starts again. This gives an insight into how people slowly move down to unhealthy levels. They experience their lives as being consistently stressful and continue to make downward movements. Over many years, the incremental downward movements take them to seriously unhealthy levels.

Moving Up the Levels of Health

Don Riso's work on the Levels of Health is a valuable description of the self-absorbed downward movement to the lower Levels of Health. But the most important aspect of Riso's work is that it provides an opportunity to move up the Levels of Health. The window for this occurs when something triggers us. It might be something as simple as someone saying or doing something we don't like. We feel upset and we react in a way that, for a moment, alleviates or distracts us from our experience of inner discomfort. We attack, we defend, we argue, we withdraw, we sulk, and so on. These reactive responses become an entrenched part of our coping strategies. They become an integral part of our identity. We get into the habit of automatically reacting in this way whenever a challenge occurs. Each time we respond in this way, the shells get thicker. We move further into our Enneagram-type behaviours and incrementally move down the Levels of Health.

What is really happening in this moment of upset is that something in our unconscious, primarily our Basic Fear, has been activated. Whatever was said or done to cause the upset activates the Basic

Fear and other difficult memories and trauma in the unconscious. When activated, this uncomfortable unconscious content begins to leak into our consciousness and makes us feel disturbed and unsafe. We are reminded of everything we have been trying to conceal, particularly our Basic Fear. For a Type One, the trigger reminds them 'of being flawed or defective'. It is not surprising that the response to this inner discomfort is so strong. The trigger also challenges their attempts to sustain their Compensating Self-Concept, 'to be good and beyond reproach.' Often the trigger will involve some direct challenge to the validity of the self-concept and the identity they are trying to sustain. In the Type One example, it may simply be a criticism of their behaviour, but it directly challenges the idea that they are 'beyond reproach'. The dynamics of the trigger are the same for all the types; it is just the content that is different.

Sitting on the Steps
The movement down from one level to the next comprises many thousands of reactive moments, and each moment can be envisaged as one small step. Our downward descent through the levels is a staircase of many small steps.

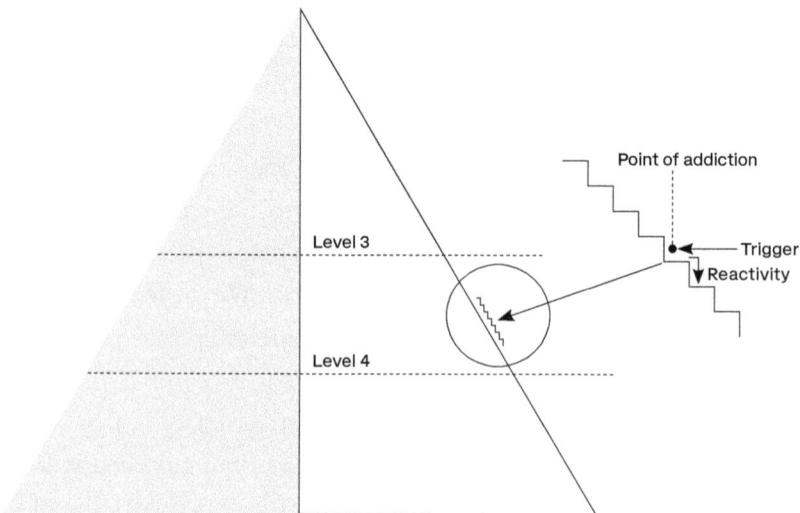

It is useful to envisage ourselves as 'sitting on the steps' between each reactive downward movement. The trigger occurs and we feel the urge to react. In this moment we have an important choice to make. We can respond in the habitual, reactive way that takes us down another step. The alternative is to sit on the step and 'catch ourselves in the act'. It requires courage and attention to override our strong inclination to react. It is something we must learn slowly and practice with less important triggers, like having to wait in a queue of traffic. It helps to move our focus to our breathing, as this can break the momentum of the reactive energy, or at least slow down the reactive process. As we sit on the step, we can remember Eckhart Tolle's advice:

"Watch it, feel it, allow it."

We can watch the reactions in the body as we feel the stomach contract, the jaw tightens, or the adrenalin begin to flow. We can feel what is happening in the body and move our focus into watching it with curiosity. Importantly, we can allow the energy to be there and just accept it as the experience that is happening right now. We don't make judgements about whether the energy is good or bad, but just allow it to be there.

At the time we are triggered, every sinew in our body is urging us to do something to find relief from discomfort. This is our 'point of addiction'. We may not be reaching for a substance (or we might be), but the urge to do something or say something has the same feeling as the addict's urge to use drugs. It has the same irrational, out-of-control compulsion that overpowers any good intention not to react. The 'point of addiction' is the important moment in which we can challenge our addiction to push the discomfort back into the unconscious.

Each time we can 'sit on the steps' and not react, we move up a step. The psychic energy around the Basic Fear is allowed to move in and touch the Compensating Self-concept. There is no attempt to push the discomfort back. When two fiercely opposing energies are allowed to sit side-by-side, they move into each and are united. A dismantling process begins to happen. We start to realise that we don't need our coping strategies, and, over time, they cease to be our habitual, default response. We also notice that discomfort is not intolerable, and if we can sit with it, it passes. Importantly, without reactivity, our lives and our relationships begin to improve. It is paradoxical, that the thing we try to avoid, namely discomfort, is the very thing that can lead us up the Levels of Health to growth and freedom. It is our ability to be with discomfort that allows us to move to the freedom of Level One, and to reconnect with ourselves and the three centres.

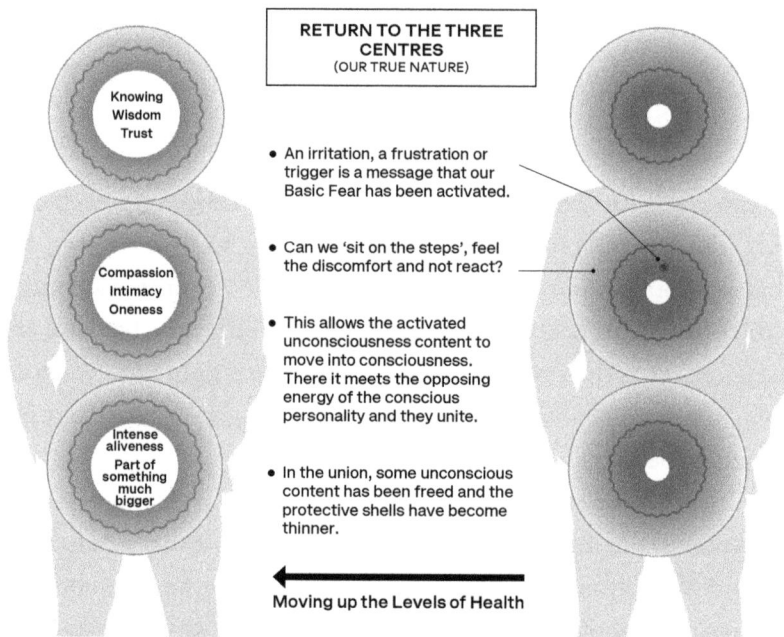

RETURN TO THE THREE CENTRES
(OUR TRUE NATURE)

Knowing
Wisdom
Trust

Compassion
Intimacy
Oneness

Intense
aliveness
Part of
something
much
bigger

- An irritation, a frustration or trigger is a message that our Basic Fear has been activated.

- Can we 'sit on the steps', feel the discomfort and not react?

- This allows the activated unconsciousness content to move into consciousness. There it meets the opposing energy of the conscious personality and they unite.

- In the union, some unconscious content has been freed and the protective shells have become thinner.

Moving up the Levels of Health

The Point of Choice

Our habitual reactions can be unpleasant and destructive to ourselves and to others. We need to remind ourselves that even though they are habitual, conditioned, and addictive, we still have a choice. Over time, we can work our way up the Levels of Health by simple practices at the times we are triggered. We can see each of these moments as 'a point of addiction'. It is better to see them as a 'point of choice'. In *Man's Search for Meaning*, Victor Frankl (2) made the important observation that:

> "Between impulse and response there is a space. In that
> space is our power to choose our response. In our
> response lies our growth and our freedom."

That realisation came to him in the most adverse of all circumstances imaginable — as a prisoner in a concentration camp. If he could find this perspective and wisdom in such adversity, it encourages us to find the same perspective in the day-to-day irritations of life. Our work is to recognise the space between impulse and response, and to do what we can to make that space bigger. We then have the possibility and the time to choose a response that serves our growth and our freedom.

St John of the Cross, a sixteenth century Christian mystic, is well known for his writings about "the dark night of the soul". He saw these deep moments of overwhelming emotion, the dark nights, as an opportunity for spiritual growth and redemption. His best-known quote speaks to the potential of the dark night:

> "One dark night, fired by Love's urgent longings,
> I went out by a secret ladder, unseen."

Don Riso's Levels of Health can be considered as the secret ladder. They are like a ladder that allows us to slowly climb back to Level One and out of the limitations of identity. Each time we are triggered we can see the experience as a "dark night" referred to by St. John. Perhaps more realistically they could be called the 'mini dark nights of the soul.' They do not involve the months or years of anguish endured by the early Christian mystics. For them, it was long periods of deprivation and suffering that brought them to their moments of surrender. Our moment of surrender can be much simpler. The trigger can be the reminder that we are believing in our Basic Fear, and it is causing our suffering. Even though the moments may look small and insignificant, they do offer the opportunity for redemption and our gradual return to the Golden World. In these 'mini dark nights', we can either protect ourselves in the habitual way or we can stay with the discomfort and surrender to 'Love's urgent longings'.

Appendix to Chapter Five

The Levels of Health for the Nine Enneagram Types

Type One
Basic Fear: Of being flawed or defective

HEALTHY LEVELS: Levels 1 to 3

Level 1: Liberated Ones are wise, discerning, accepting and often noble

Level 2: Ones feel the disturbance of their Basic Fear and comfort themselves with their self-concept: I am good, have integrity and am beyond reproach.

Level 3: Ones reinforce their self-concept, living their lives with high standards. They are highly ethical and possess a strong sense of purpose.

Wake-up Call: Ones feel obligated to fix everything themselves.

AVERAGE LEVELS: Levels 4 to 6

Level 4: Ones want to convince others of the rightness of the opinions. They become serious, driven, and critical, trying to remedy problems.

Level 5: Ones worry that others will condemn them for any deviation from their ideals, so they vigorously organise themselves and their world.

Level 6: Ones are frustrated others will mess up the order they have created. They reproach others for not living up to their standards.

Red Flag: My ideals may be wrong and counterproductive.

UNHEALTHY LEVELS: Levels 7 to 9

Level 7: Ones begin to fear their ideals may be causing problems. To defend against this thought, they silence criticism and become highly self-righteous.

Level 8: Ones begin to act out their repressed desires while publicly continuing to condemn them. They cannot stop themselves.

Level 9: Ones realise they have lost control of themselves and are doing the very things they can't tolerate in others. They can commit punitive acts against themselves and others.

DSM inclination: Obsessive-compulsive personality disorder

Sourced from *The Wisdom of the Enneagram* by Don Richard Riso and Russ Hudson, which includes more comprehensive descriptions of each of the levels.

Type Two
Basic Fear: Of being unloved and unwanted

HEALTHY LEVELS: Levels 1 to 3
Level 1: Liberated Twos are joyous, gracious, and humble

Level 2: Twos feel the disturbance of their Basic Fear and comfort themselves with their self-concept: I am loving, thoughtful and selfless.

Level 3: Twos reinforce their self-concept by doing good things for others. They are generous with their time and energy and are appreciative, encouraging, and supportive of others.

Wake-up Call: I must go out and win them over.

AVERAGE LEVELS: Levels 4 to 6
Level 4: Twos begin to fear that whatever they have been doing is not enough. They want to cultivate friendships and win people over by pleasing, flattering and supporting them.

Level 5: Twos worry that the people they love will love someone else more than them. They attempt to have a claim on people by putting the needs of others before their own.

Level 6: Twos are angry that others are taking them for granted but are unable to freely express their hurt. Instead, they complain about their health, draw attention to their good deeds, and remind others how much they owe them.

Red Flag: I am driving people away.

UNHEALTHY LEVELS: Levels 7 to 9

Level 7: Twos fear they are driving people away. They try to elicit pity as a substitute for love and keep others dependent on them to prevent them from leaving.

Level 8: Twos begin to become so desperate for love that they begin to pursue it obsessively. They may act out their need for affection recklessly and inappropriately.

Level 9: The realisation that they may have been "selfish" or even harmed others is too much for unhealthy Twos. They fall to pieces playing out the role of victim and martyr.

DSM inclination: Histrionic personality disorder

Type Three

Basic Fear: Of being worthless and without value apart from achievements

HEALTHY LEVELS: Levels 1 to 3

Level 1: Liberated Threes are self-accepting, genuine, and benevolent.

Level 2: Threes feel the disturbance of their Basic Fear and comfort themselves with their self-concept: I am outstanding, capable and well-adjusted.

Level 3: Threes reinforce their self-concept by developing themselves and their talents. They are competent, confident, and persistent, becoming exemplary in whatever they do.

Wake-up Call: I am beginning to drive myself for status and attention.

AVERAGE LEVELS: Levels 4 to 6

Level 4: Threes begin to fear that they will be overshadowed by the accomplishments of others. They need to distinguish themselves from others by over-achieving.

Level 5: Threes worry that they will lose the positive regard of others. Ambitious but self-doubting, they want to be admired and desired.

Level 6: Threes are afraid that others will not notice them unless they are hugely successful. They are self-promoting, competitive and arrogant as a defence against secret neediness.

Red Flag: That I may be failing, that my claims are empty and fraudulent.

UNHEALTHY LEVELS: Levels 7 to 9

Level 7: Threes fear that they are failing and that their claims may be empty and fraudulent. They begin to deceive themselves and others, saying whatever will impress people.

Level 8: Unhealthy Threes have become so desperate for attention that they will concoct any story to cover over their deterioration. They will go to great lengths to hide their misdeeds.

Level 9: Unhealthy Threes feel there is nothing they can do to win the positive attention they need. They may seek revenge on real or imagined tormentors.

DSM inclination: narcissistic personality disorder

Type Four

Basic Fear: Of having no identity, no personal significance

HEALTHY LEVELS: Levels 1 to 3

Level 1: Liberated Fours are self-renewing, redemptive and revelatory.

Level 2: Fours feel the disturbance of their Basic Fear and comfort themselves with their self-concept: I am sensitive, different, and unique.

Level 3: Fours reinforce their self-image by expressing their individuality through creative action. They explore their feelings and impressions and find ways of sharing them with others.

Wake-up Call: Holding on to and intensifying feelings through the imagination.

AVERAGE LEVELS: Levels 4 to 6

Level 4: Fours begin to fear that their changing feelings will not sustain them and their creativity, so they use their imagination to prolong and intensify their moods.

Level 5: Fours worry that others will not recognise their uniqueness. Aloof, self-conscious, and melancholy, they believe their fragility will attract a rescuer.

Level 6: Fours fear that life's demands will force them to give up their dreams. They feel they are missing out on life and envy the stability of others, so they exempt themselves from "the rules."

Red Flag: I am ruining my life and wasting my opportunities.

UNHEALTHY LEVELS: Levels 7 to 9

Level 7: Fours fear that they are wasting their lives. To save their self-image, they reject everyone and everything that doesn't support their view of themselves.

Level 8: Fours have become so desperate to be the individual of their fantasies, they hate everything about themselves that doesn't correspond to it.

Level 9: The realisation that they have wasted their lives is too much for unhealthy Fours. They may attempt to elicit rescue through self-destructive behaviour or simply end their lives.

DSM inclination: Depressive personality disorder

Type Five

Basic Fear: Of being helpless and unable to find a place in the world

HEALTHY LEVELS: Levels 1 to 3

Level 1: Liberated Fives are clear-minded, knowing, profound and compassionate.

Level 2: Fives feel the disturbance of their Basic Fear and comfort themselves with their self-concept: I am clever, competent and can find the answer for you.

Level 3: Fives reinforce their self-image by mastering a body of knowledge or skills that will make them competent and strong. They explore new ideas and forms that can result in profoundly original ideas, inventions, and art.

Wake-up Call: I withdraw from reality into concepts and mental worlds.

AVERAGE LEVELS: Levels 4 to 6

Level 4: Fives begin to fear that their skills are insufficient, and they need to prepare more. They feel unsure of themselves and prefer to inhabit the safety of their minds.

Level 5: Fives worry that the needs of others will distract them from their projects. They minimise their needs, becoming highly strung, cerebral, and secretive.

Level 6: Fives fear others will threaten the niche they have been creating. Their own ideas can be bizarre and they are scornful of those who cannot understand them.

Red Flag: I am never going to find a place in the world or with people.

UNHEALTHY LEVELS: Levels 7 to 9

Level 7: Unhealthy Fives fear that they are incapable of finding a place in the world. To gain some security, they cut off all connection with the world, retreating into an increasingly isolated and empty world.

Level 8: Fives feel so small and helpless that almost everything becomes ominous to them. They are filled with dark fantasies and strange perceptions. They cannot stop their overheated minds.

Level 9: Feeling they can no longer defend themselves from their pain and terror, unhealthy Fives want to escape from reality. They attempt this through psychotic breaks or schizoid withdrawal.

DSM inclination: Schizoid personality disorder.

Type Six

Basic Fear: Of having no support or guidance, of being unable to survive on their own.

HEALTHY LEVELS: Levels 1 to 3

Level 1: Liberated Sixes are secure with themselves, grounded, serene and valiant.

Level 2: Sixes feel the disturbance of their Basic Fear and comfort themselves with their self-concept: I am solid, attentive and dependable.

Level 3: Sixes reinforce their self-image by responsibly working to create mutually beneficial systems. They are well-disciplined and practical, often foreseeing potential problems before they arise.

Wake-up Call: Becoming dependent on something outside myself for guidance

AVERAGE LEVELS: Levels 4 to 6

Level 4: Sixes begin to fear that they will lose their independence but also believe they need more support. They invest themselves in people and organisations that they believe will help them but are uneasy about it.

Level 5: Sixes worry that they cannot meet the conflicting demands of their different commitments, so they try to resist having any more pressure put on them. They are anxious, pessimistic, and suspicious.

Level 6: Sixes fear that they are losing the support of their allies, and they are extremely unsure of themselves, so they look for the causes of their anxiety.

Red Flag: My actions have harmed my security.

UNHEALTHY LEVELS: Levels 7 to 9

Level 7: Sixes fear that their actions have harmed their own security. Their reactive behaviour may have caused crises in their lives, so they trust themselves even less.

Level 8: Sixes become so insecure and desperate that they begin to believe that others will destroy whatever safety they have left. They harbour paranoid ideas about the world.

Level 9: The realisation that they have committed acts for which they will likely be punished is too much for unhealthy Sixes. Guilt and self-hatred lead them to punish themselves.

DSM inclination: Paranoid personality disorder

Type Seven

Basic Fear: Of being deprived or trapped in pain.

HEALTHY LEVELS: Levels 1 to 3

Level 1: Liberated Sevens are appreciative, ecstatic and deeply grateful.

Level 2: Sevens feel the disturbance of their Basic Fear and comfort themselves with their self-concept: I am happy, spontaneous, and fulfilled.

Level 3: Sevens reinforce their self-image by fully engaging in life and by doing things that will ensure they will have what they need. Their passionate gusto for life is revealed in great versatility and prolific output.

Wake-up Call: Feeling something better is always available somewhere else.

AVERAGE LEVELS: Levels 4 to 6

Level 4: Sevens begin to fear that they are missing out on other more worthwhile experiences; thus, they become restless and interested in having more and more options.

Level 5: Sevens worry that they will be bored or frustrated and that painful feelings will arise, so they keep themselves excited and occupied. They pump up the energy around them.

Level 6: Sevens are afraid there will not be enough of whatever they believe they need, so they become impatient, seeking instant gratification.

Red Flag: My activities are bringing me pain and unhappiness

UNHEALTHY LEVELS: Levels 7 to 9

Level 7: Sevens fear that their actions are bringing them pain and unhappiness. They are highly impulsive and irresponsible and do whatever promises relief from anxiety.

Level 8: Sevens become so desperate to escape their anxiety that they fly out of control, recklessly acting out their pain rather than feeling it. Hysterical activity alternates with deep depression.

Level 9: The realisation that they may have ruined their health, their lives and their capacity for enjoyment is too much for unhealthy Sevens. They feel panic-stricken and trapped.

DSM inclination: Bipolar personality disorder (previously known as manic depressive).

Type Eight
Basic Fear: Of being harmed or controlled by others.

HEALTHY LEVELS: Levels 1 to 3

Level 1: Liberated Eights are magnanimous, courageous, forgiving and sometimes heroic.

Level 2: Eights feel the disturbance of their Basic Fear and comfort themselves with their self-concept: I am strong, assertive and in control.

Level 3: Eights reinforce their self-image by taking on challenges. They prove their strength through action and achievement and through protecting and providing for others.

Wake-up Call: I must push and struggle to make things happen.

AVERAGE LEVELS: Levels 4 to 6

Level 4: Eights begin to fear that they do not have enough resources to succeed with their projects. They become expedient about getting the resources they want.

Level 5: Eights worry that others will not respect them or give them their due. They boast, bluff, and make big promises to get people aligned with their plans.

Level 6: Eights are afraid that others are not backing them up and they may lose control of the situation. They put pressure on others to do what they want through threats and oppression

Red Flag: Others are turning against me to retaliate.

UNHEALTHY LEVELS: Levels 7 to 9

Level 7: Eights fear that others are turning against them. They feel betrayed and unable to trust anyone, so they become determined to protect themselves at any cost.

Level 8: Eights become so desperate to protect themselves and so fearful of retaliation they begin to threaten potential rivals before they can threaten them.

Level 9: The realisation that they have created powerful enemies who can defeat them is too much for unhealthy Eights. They try to destroy everything rather than let anyone triumph over them or control them.

DSM inclination: Antisocial personality disorder

Type Nine
Basic Fear: Of being disconnected and cut off from everything including love

HEALTHY LEVELS: Levels 1 to 3
Level 1: Liberated Nines are self-possessed, dynamic, serene and present.

Level 2: Nines feel the disturbance of their Basic Fear and comfort themselves with their self-concept: I am peaceful, easy-going and kind.

Level 3: Nines reinforce their self-image by creating and maintaining peace and harmony in their world. They use their level-headed approach to mediate conflicts and soothe others.

Wake-up Call: Outwardly accommodating myself to others.

AVERAGE LEVELS: Levels 4 to 6
Level 4: Nines begin to fear that conflicts will ruin their peace of mind, so they avoid conflicts by going along with others. They consider many matters not worth arguing about.

Level 5: Nines worry that any significant change in their world or any strong feelings will disrupt their fragile peace, so they set up their lives to prevent things getting to them.

Level 6: Nines are afraid that others will demand responses from them that may arouse anxiety or ruin their peace, so they downplay the importance of problems and deflect others.

Red Flag: I will be forced by reality to deal with my problems.

UNHEALTHY LEVELS: Levels 7 to 9

Level 7: Nines fear that reality will force them to deal with their problems. They may react by defending the illusion that everything is okay and stubbornly refusing to confront problems.

Level 8: Nines are so desperate to hang on to any shred of inner piece they have left that they fear acknowledging reality at all. They try to block out awareness through dissociation.

Level 9: Very unhealthy Nines feel unable to face reality at all. They withdraw into themselves and become completely unresponsive.

DSM inclination: Passive-aggressive and dependent personality disorders.

CHAPTER 6

Using Discomfort to Move Up the Levels of Health

Everything that irritates us about others can lead us
to an understanding of ourselves. — Carl Jung

Pema Chödrön is a Buddhist abbess at an abbey in Nova Scotia, Canada. She has written many practical books including *When Things Fall Apart*, *Taking the Leap* and *Living Beautifully*. A common theme in her teaching is her encouragement to look at the unusual ways we react when we have been triggered. She uses the Tibetan word *shenpa*, which can be translated as "the urge to react". It is the urge to do something to alleviate the discomfort when we have been triggered. She compares it to having scabies and the irresistible urge to scratch the itch. We feel the reactive energy moving in the body. We sometimes lose control of ourselves and can react in many irrational ways. We scramble to find ways of getting rid of the discomfort and to find relief. Chödrön describes shenpa in simple words:

> Someone says a mean word to you and then something in you tightens. Then it starts to spiral, and you start blaming them or getting angry at them or denigrating yourself. Then words and actions follow. And if you have strong addictions you go right to the addiction to cover over that bad feeling that arose when

someone said this mean word to you. This is a mean word that hooks you; it gets you. Another might not affect you. We are talking about a word that touches that sore place. That is shenpa. We experience it as tightening and the self-absorption gets very strong at this point.

Someone criticises you; they criticise your work; they criticise your child and there is shenpa, almost co-arising. It is there as soon as the words have landed. It's not thoughts, its closer to an emotion and then it breeds thoughts. It is almost pre-emotion. You can just feel it happening.

Somebody says something to you or to someone else and you feel this sort of closing down and you are hooked. Now if you can catch it at that level, it is very workable. You have the possibility of being very curious about this urge to do the habitual thing, to strengthen the habituation. You can feel it and it is never new. It always has a familiar taste in the mouth; it has a familiar smell. When you begin to get the hang of it, you feel like this has been happening forever. It causes you to feel the fundamental, underlying insecurity of the human experience. This insecurity is inherent in a changing, shifting impermanent illusory world as long as we are habituated to having ground under our feet. It is all part of a chain reaction that starts with the tightening, which happens involuntarily, then there is the urge to move away from it in some habitual way. This is usually in the mind initially and is something that you say to yourself about them. Or it is accompanied by this bad feeling. And in the West, it is common to turn it against yourself. "Something is wrong with me." Maybe it is still not verbal at this point. But it is already pregnant with a kind of little gestalt, a little drama.

— (Taken from the audio recording *Getting Unstuck Part 2* by Pema Chödrön)

Chödrön suggests that going home for Christmas can be like going to a shenpa party. With family, everyone knows each other's "buttons" so well. Each year we resolve not to behave like we did last year and not to be drawn into the same old family conflicts. Notwithstanding our good intentions, after a few hours, shenpa arises and we get sucked back into our habitual reactions.

What should we do with shenpa?

Chödrön's description of shenpa is so accurate. It is easy to recognise the bodily and emotional responses she is talking about; we have all come to know them very well. When we are triggered and shenpa is arising, our first response is to do something to get relief from the bad feeling. There are many ways we can do that. For some, the response is physical, and directed towards the person who has triggered us.

FOCUSED ON THE WORLD/OTHER	FOCUSED ON SELF
Finding relief through negative thinking and creating stories	
• Blame	• Self-blame
• Judge	• Self-justify
• "Build the Story"	• Agonise
BLAME • Nit Pick	• Self-doubt SELF-BLAME
• Condemn	• Shame
• Criticise	• "Not good enough"
• Collude	• Rationalise
Finding relief through intensifying negative emotions	
• Complain	• Self-pity
• Resent	• Self-victimise
• Whinge	• Sulk
WHINGE • Catastrophise	• Collapse WALLOW
• "How could you?"	• Dramatise
• Spurn	• Amplify anxiety
• Manipulate	• Self-absorption
Finding relief through reactive and defensive behaviour	
• Attack	• Withdraw
• React	• Distract
• Defend	• Dissociate
FIGHT • Get Even	• Sedate FLIGHT
• "Fix" FREEZE	• Transcend
• Snipe	• Repress
• Explode	• Accommodate

For others, it is to withdraw and shut down. How do we behave in the "moment" of irrationality when we have first been triggered? Some of the many shenpa reactions are listed in the table above.

The table is divided into two halves. The reactions on the left-hand side are directed at other people or the world in general. Something they have done has upset us and many of these reactions have a theme of finding relief through getting even. We can *blame* them for what they have done and construct stories about the injustice. Or we can *whinge* to other people and to ourselves and make our emotions even stronger. Or we can *fight* them in some way either physically, verbally or emotionally and try to regain control of the situation.

The reactions on the right-hand side of the table are directed at ourselves. This can include *self-blame* and increasing our feelings of regret and shame. It can also include *wallowing* in our self-absorption or finding other ways of indulging our emotions. It is strange that we think blaming ourselves or indulging our negative emotions is going to give us relief. However, as we intensify our negative feelings, even towards ourselves, it distracts us from the underlying unconscious pain that we are trying to avoid.

At the bottom of the table are the two well-known instinctive reactions of *fight* or *flight* that are driven by our survival instincts. They happen independently of our thoughts and emotions and without any input from the rational mind. Potentially, the most dangerous reaction is *fight*, where we try to take revenge or get even with the person we think is causing our discomfort. In some cases, it can be dangerous to the wellbeing of others, being driven by out-of-control, pent-up, instinctive survival energy. Similar instinctive survival energy also drives the reaction of *flight*, although it is less dangerous. We avoid the experience by withdrawing, dissociating or sedating ourselves so we can get away from the threat. There is a third instinctive strategy, *freeze*, which happens when we are caught between *fight* and *flight*. The instincts are overwhelmed and we are immobilised, frozen in fear. All three instinctive reactions are automatic. They are happening even before we realise that we are under threat.

To some extent, this is also true of all our shenpa reactions. We find ourselves blaming, whinging, and wallowing as an automatic response even before we realise what we are doing. We are hooked and have lost control of how we are behaving. The challenge is how quickly we can notice it and catch ourselves in the act.

It is common that we will try several reactions. For example, we might withdraw and sulk for a while. When that is not giving us relief, we might call a friend and collude with them about the terrible thing that has just happened. Then we might "build the story" about how unreasonable the other person has been. Or we might turn to alcohol or

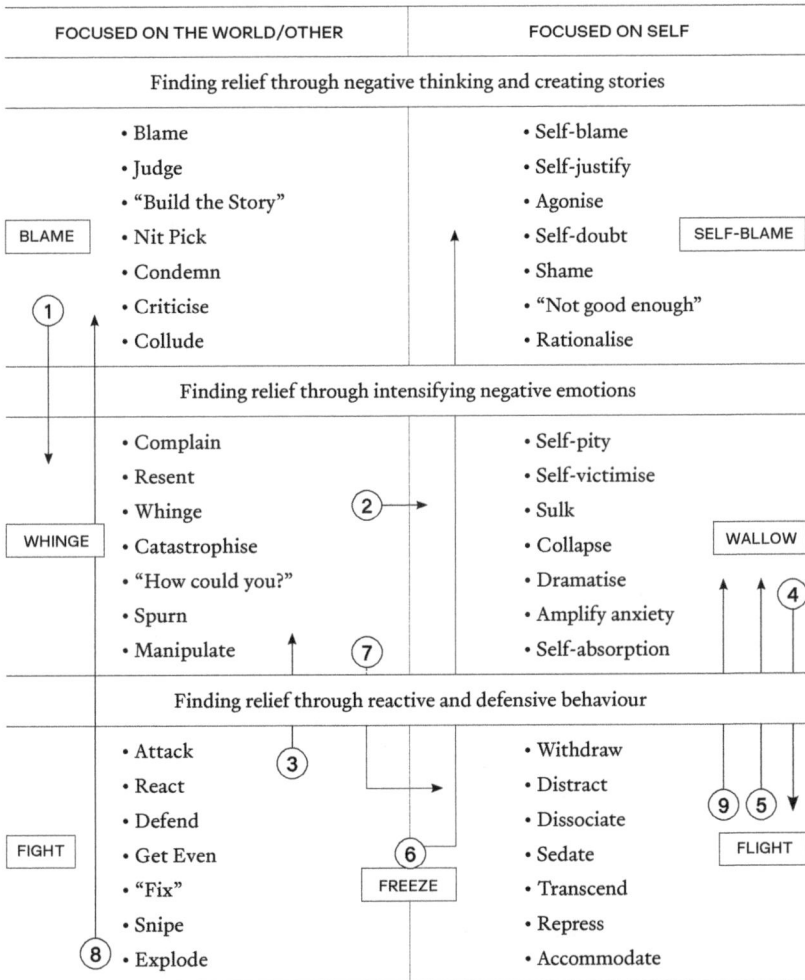

FOCUSED ON THE WORLD/OTHER	FOCUSED ON SELF
Finding relief through negative thinking and creating stories	
BLAME 1 • Blame • Judge • "Build the Story" • Nit Pick • Condemn • Criticise • Collude	• Self-blame • Self-justify • Agonise • Self-doubt SELF-BLAME • Shame • "Not good enough" • Rationalise
Finding relief through intensifying negative emotions	
WHINGE • Complain • Resent • Whinge 2 • Catastrophise • "How could you?" • Spurn • Manipulate 7	• Self-pity • Self-victimise • Sulk • Collapse WALLOW • Dramatise • Amplify anxiety 4 • Self-absorption
Finding relief through reactive and defensive behaviour	
FIGHT • Attack 3 • React • Defend • Get Even 6 • "Fix" FREEZE • Snipe 8 • Explode	• Withdraw • Distract • Dissociate 9 5 • Sedate FLIGHT • Transcend • Repress • Accommodate

drugs. We can continue moving from reaction to reaction and be caught in shenpa for a long time. It can last for a few minutes, or it can last for a lifetime. In extreme cases it can last forever, as we continue to build the story against the other person and how badly we have been wronged.

Most of us, at some time, have probably reacted in all of the ways mentioned in the chart. However, our primary and preferred way of reacting is likely to be related to our Enneagram type. The chart above summarises how people in our workshops believe they react. Their initial reaction is shown by the circle with their type within the circle; their secondary or follow-up reaction is shown by the arrow.

For example, the initial reaction of a Type Eight might be to *fight* (attack, get even, etc.). This is represented by the circle around the number '8' in the lower left-hand box. Their secondary reaction might be to find someone to *blame* (condemn, criticize, etc.). This is represented by the arrow in the top-left-hand box.

Of course, this study is not accurate or conclusive, but is included to show there is a likely connection between our Enneagram type and the way we react. The important opportunity for all of us in this exercise, is not to see how other types react, but to become very familiar with our own behaviour when we are triggered.

*   *   *   *

All the shenpa reactions in the table are attempts to get relief from discomfort. Each time we respond in these ways we are making the protective shells thicker and we move one small step further down the Levels of Health. None of the reactions are better than any other. The only useful response is to sit on the steps and allow the shenpa to be in our bodies. The important question is:

"Can we feel the shenpa, and not try to get relief?"

Shenpa becomes a useful reminder that something is happening: that our Basic Fear has been activated. When we feel the energy beginning to build, we can remind ourselves that this is shenpa. It is the signal to be on full alert and watch our reactions. We know that if we do react, it might give us some short-term relief, but the outcomes are not what we want. We know where our reactions will take us because we have been there a thousand times before. And we know we don't want to go there again.

Shenpa is a tangible reminder that we are at the point of choice. It is a gift. We can choose to react, reinforce the protective shells, and go down another step on the Levels of Health. Or we can 'sit on the step', feel the discomfort in the body and not try to get relief from it.

*   *   *   *

Nawab's Laundry

I was staying at an ashram in India where the laundry was operated by a rather difficult man called Nawab. He had been in the job for many years and was paid almost nothing. He was disempowered and unfriendly, and the absence of even a hint of customer service had become a popular subject of discussion in the ashram. Each morning at breakfast someone would add to the growing list of difficult laundry experiences endured at the hands of Nawab. One morning a woman at the table pointed out that Nawab was actually doing a pretty good job. The laundry always came back on time. It was always neatly folded, and nothing was ever lost. The table went silent. We all knew she was right: Nawab was doing a pretty good job.

The lack of any social niceties with Nawab had made us all feel uncomfortable and ill-at-ease. Nawab offered us absolutely nothing other than a good laundry service. We had all found this difficult and, at some subtle level, had been triggered by his unfriendly behaviour. He had the ability to trigger everyone's Basic Fear, regardless of their type.

We had sought relief from our subtle discomfort by having our morning session of collective whinging and blaming. We were colluding with each other, building stories against Nawab, and easing our own discomfort by blaming him. It was a little shenpa party, where we found relief from the accumulated, little moments of discomfort we had all experienced with Nawab.

What I was doing was the very opposite to what was required to move up the Levels of Health. Once I came to see this, the visit to the laundry became my opportunity to watch my Basic Fear in action and to see how quickly I moved to protect myself in unfriendly situations. My reactive energy towards Nawab dissipated almost immediately and I became grateful for the efficient service he provided.

I suspect Nawab is still at the laundry offering the same gift to everyone that passes through the ashram.

*　　*　　*　　*

Discomfort is the Doorway to Freedom

When we look at the crazy things we do when we get triggered, there must be something for us to learn. As Pema Chödrön says, we are scrambling to "get ground under our feet," and wanting to get away from, or eliminate, what we think is the cause of our discomfort. Our first false conclusion is that our discomfort is being caused by the other person. The fact is that the discomfort resides within us. It is never about the other. They are just reminding us of the painful unconscious content, particularly our Basic Fear, which has been in the unconscious since the beginning.

The Basic Fear and the challenges of our past have, over the years, been pushed into our unconscious. This unwanted content has been buried there because it was too unpleasant and painful to be accepted and allowed into awareness. We just didn't want to know about it. Usually, we have no direct awareness of this content, and we don't realise how it impacts our day-to-day behaviour. However, most of us can sense a low-level simmering discomfort that is in the background of our lives much of the time. It may be low-level background anxiety, frustration, or irritation about nothing in particular. Even when there is nothing going wrong, there is something in the background that is not quite right. This is the slow leakage of unconscious content into awareness. It is subtle, but we do have a sense of it; we assume it is a normal part of life.

Then something 'out there' triggers us. It activates the unconscious content, and our discomfort moves into awareness. The discomfort we feel is shenpa. We feel that the ground has been removed from under our feet. We will do anything that might give us short-term relief. Our effort goes into keeping our coping strategies in place to avoid feeling the discomfort. We create stories about others, we blame them, we collude with others in the story, we withdraw, we attack, and so on. We start forming fixated ideas about the world and others. We are reinforcing our coping strategies and moving down the Levels of Health. We think the disturbance is coming from the outside. In fact, it is coming from the unacknowledged, activated contents in the unconscious.

The Red Cape

In these moments of discomfort, when we have been triggered, there is an alternative to our habitual reactivity. The story of the bull and the red cape is instructive. At the bullfight, the bullfighter waves the red cape at the bull. The bull sees the red cape and charges. They put daggers in his back. He sees the cape again, and charges again. Eventually the bull is killed. You might think, "Silly bull, he keeps charging the red cape, and eventually it results in his death." However, it is not only the bull that is silly. We all have things that continue to trigger us — our red capes. We continue to react to the same things, year after year. Each time we react, it makes the protective shells a little stronger and we move down the Levels of Health.

The story of Ferdinand the Bull is much more encouraging. Ferdinand was a peaceful bull, wrongly recruited by the bullfight promoters. On the day he came into the ring, the matador was ready with his red cape waving. Ferdinand wasn't that interested in the red cape and went off to enjoy some grass on the other side of the arena. The matador was left confused and embarrassed in his very tight pants. Ferdinand is a good role model for all of us. Do we have to respond to the red cape every time we see it waved? Can we develop the discipline and the insight to see what is happening and choose not to react in the habitual way? Can we allow the reactive energies to be in the body, without having to react? Can we imagine the person is waving a red cape only to help us? It is happening so we can understand what is driving our behaviour.

Ferdinand's Question

Ferdinand was clearly a very healthy bull, probably at Level One or Two. When we see someone who is very healthy, we often decide we want to be like them. The person is clearly enjoying life, and the people around them are enjoying being with them. Sadly, we can't just decide we are going to move up several levels. When we are immersed in the challenges of Level Five, we can't decide we would now like to move to Level Two. The Basic Fear, and other unconscious content, are still there and we want to keep our coping strategies in place to remain safe. The movement up the levels needs to be a gradual one, requiring a slow recognition of unconscious content. If Ferdinand could talk, he would probably suggest that, when we feel the first signs of shenpa, we ask ourselves the question:

> **"What is it within me, which is causing me to react in this way?"**

This is Ferdinand's question; calling it by this name makes it easier to remember. It has proved to be a powerful question for people to ask themselves in a workshop. It is even more powerful when asked at the time we are being triggered.

More often than not, people will find that, behind the shenpa, they are being reminded of their Basic Fear. For example, for a Type Four, the triggering circumstances reminds them of their perceived insignificance or the lack of meaning they see in their lives. It is also likely that they will be struggling to keep their Compensating Self-concept in place. The triggering circumstances makes it difficult for them to sustain their self-concept, that they are different and unique.

Shenpa arises because the structures we have put in place to keep us safe are being challenged. And Ferdinand's question helps us to see what is happening: that the discomfort is within us and was waiting to be activated. As we develop insights into what is happening, we have the opportunity of learning not to react. Pema Chödrön refers to this discipline as "learning to stay". We can say to ourselves:

"Stay … stay … stay …"

It is like training a dog. The training is best commenced with little incidents that are not overwhelming. They may be mild irritations or frustrations, like someone taking our parking spot. These are moments of "mini shenpa". The dynamic is the same, but the energy is more manageable.

Our Triggers Have Something to Teach Us

Why is it that some situations or people trigger us? Other situations don't trigger us, but they may trigger other people. Jung made the observation:

"Everything that irritates us about others can lead us
to an understanding of ourselves."

He was suggesting that there are things in our unconscious that are triggered by particular circumstances in the world. Hence, the irritations become a way of exploring what might be in the unconscious. Basic Fear is an important part of our unconscious and is likely to be a significant source of our shenpa. These moments of shenpa are opportunities for our own development and liberation. We can truly begin to know ourselves, particularly the parts of ourselves that we don't want to know. Each time we can feel shenpa and catch ourselves in the act, we begin to dismantle the protective shells.

The discomfort we feel becomes the doorway to redemption and freedom. The irritation and frustration we experience points to the contents of our unconscious. We are desperately trying to keep these unconscious and disowned aspects away. Some of the time we succeed, but often we don't. It is in these moments of being triggered that we can see what is hidden.

It is useful to recall Eckhart Tolle's very practical mantra to guide us in the moments when we have been triggered:

"Watch it, feel it, allow it."

Can we simply observe the feelings in the body and notice what is happening? If our focus is directed on observing the body, it helps to take us away from our crazy thoughts and our urge to react. It brings our attention back to what is happening in us.

The last part of the mantra — "allow it" — is about allowing the reactions to be in the body. Sometimes we feel we need to get them under control, or even worse, to get rid of them. The words "allow it" can mistakenly be taken to mean that we must allow the behaviour that is triggering us. This takes us back into our minds and a debate with ourselves as to whether we can condone the other person's behaviour. This is not a useful place to go; we can get lost in these internal evaluations forever. We miss the wonderful opportunity to see what is happening in us. It takes us away from our feelings and away from the body. If this happens, bring the focus back to ourselves. The most important question is whether we can be with these uncomfortable energies that are manifesting in the body.

Accept – Then Act

There is sometimes a concern that just feeling and allowing the shenpa can lead to passivity and dissociation. If we are in a situation where the circumstances are not acceptable, it is not suggested that we just feel the shenpa and never act. Rather we need to first allow the difficult, uncomfortable, and reactive energy to pass before we take any action. If we act from a reactive place, it is likely to breed more reactivity in the people we react against. They will react to our reactivity and the situation can quickly spiral downwards. Likewise, if we need to make a decision, then it is wiser to make it when we are not caught up in the reactive energy of the moment.

There is a second part in Tolle's advice to, "Watch it, feel it, allow it." Once the reactive energies have dissipated then we can act. In his words,

"Accept — then act. Whatever the present moment contains, accept it as if you had chosen it. Always work with it, not against it; this will miraculously transform your whole life."

There is a temptation for us to fight the world, and this is particularly strong when we are triggered. We want to show that "we are right," or "they are wrong." or that the world shouldn't be like it is. This resistance inflates our sense of identity and makes our protective shells stronger. There is a moment of satisfaction in this reactive behaviour; we have a stronger sense of "who we think we are." We momentarily enjoy a false sense of empowerment. However, the feeling of satisfaction or exhilaration is short lived. As we come to our senses, the satisfaction is replaced with a sense of regret or guilt in the way we have behaved and the hurt we have caused to the people we love. Fighting the world is futile. While there are many areas where change is needed, we will never achieve change from a position of reactivity. "Accept — then act". It is only then that we can achieve the change we desire. This wisdom applies particularly to the moments when we are triggered. It also applies more generally; accepting life to be "as it is" is captured by another suggestion by Tolle to "say 'yes' to life."

Shenpa as a Gift

Shenpa plays an important part in the movement down the Levels of Health. It gives some insight into the reactivity that takes us down the steps. The triggering event is touching our Basic Fear. It activates our thoughts of inadequacy, unworthiness, fear, and disconnection. Our urge is to react to alleviate this activated discomfort. The reaction will be to reinforce our coping strategies and take us further into the limitations of our Enneagram type. With that, we will move further down the Levels of Health. This is shenpa in action. But it doesn't have to be like that and shenpa can be used in a positive way.

An understanding of shenpa can help us interrupt our journey down the levels and help us see clearly what is really happening. There is some inner discomfort that has been triggered, but we have a choice whether we want to respond in the habitual reactive way, or learn to stay. We don't need to bite the hook! We can remember that this is only a red cape, and we don't have to cause ourselves and other people suffering by reacting to it. We can be inspired by Ferdinand the Bull and enjoy the grass on the other side of the arena. Most of all, we can stay with the energies in the body and watch them do their work.

We can see what a wonderful gift we have been given.

Shenpa is the signal that something unconscious in us has been disturbed.

Because it is unconscious, it is difficult to recognise what it is. It can stay there forever and continue to cause us pain and suffering for the rest of our lives. It can take us down the Levels of Health. Shenpa is the bell that calls us to attention. If we listen to it, it can be the beginning of our liberation. Discomfort is the doorway to freedom, and shenpa is the voice that reminds us of this possibility. These insights are affirmed by further words from Pema Chodron:

"The way to be happy is to avoid pain and discomfort ... bad choice!"

The more we try to avoid pain, the more we will strengthen the protective shells and the more disconnected, alienated, and unhappy we become. In the appendix at the end of the chapter, there is an exercise called "My life would be better if ..." This explores how our life preferences and attitudes are often formed to help us keep away from discomfort.

Appendix to Chapter 6

'My Life Would Be Better If ...'
An Exercise to See How We Try to Keep Away from Discomfort.

As we become familiar with our reactive behaviours, we can gain some perspective on what disturbs us and how frequently this happens. We might be surprised how often we experience little moments of frustration and irritation. There might be periods in our life when we live in a state of continuous irritation. There is a low-level simmering discontent with our lives and ourselves. And of course, from this background level of irritation, it doesn't take much 'to go wrong' to move us into a full-blown shenpa reaction. We are scanning to see what is wrong, and when we find it, we go into our reactive behaviours. In Pema Chodron's words, we live with a strong "propensity to be disturbed". We believe that our lives should be different to the way they are. Life would be much better if things — or even if *we* — were different.

Here is a short exercise that helps us identify the areas of our lives that we think are not quite what they should be. This exercise can be done by yourself, but it is very beneficial to share the results with another person. Ask yourself the question:

My life would be better if ...?

In the table below are some of the areas in my life where I would like to see improvements. You are asked to compile a similar list but only include improvements that are specifically relevant to you. If you can't think of enough present-day examples, include some items from the past. The table is divided into three columns; the first relates to personal aspects about yourself; the second to the people in your life, and the third to more general conditions of the world.

Self	Other People	The World
I had more time	They appreciated me more	We had a better Prime Minister
I had more money	They did the washing up	Taxes weren't so high
I had a better house	My family was more supportive	The weather was warmer
I could travel more	My partner was more available	The service wasn't so bad
I was more enlightened	My children did more work	The shops were closer
I had more friends	My mother-in-law didn't interfere	The dogs didn't have to be fed

When you have completed your list, identify the three improvements that you think would be most beneficial to you. Draw items from any of the three columns and circle them as shown in the example. As you reflect on these three items, is there any low-level simmering energy around them? This might manifest as irritation, dissatisfaction, anxiety, or frustration. We might also wonder why we have selected these particular items. Other people, in similar circumstances, would probably have come up with a very different list. There is a reason, of course, as to why we chose what we did. And so, with curiosity, we can explore the underlying motivations behind our choices.

The exercise is exploring the extent to which our preferences and life choices are being influenced by the need to keep our protective shells and our identity in place. In particular, the improvements we have selected may have unconsciously been chosen to do two things:

i) to alleviate any discomfort arising from our Basic Fear, and,
ii) to support and sustain our Compensating Self-concept and our identity.

My own exercise as a Type Nine demonstrates this. The strongest item on my list is "We had a better Prime Minister". At the time I completed this exercise, we had a very aggressive and provocative

Prime Minister. He liked to attack anyone who didn't agree with him and did so in a very personalised and denigrating way. I was always disturbed by the conflict and disharmony he created. It reminded me of the Basic Fear within me, of being disconnected and cut off from everything including love. As a Type Nine, who aspired to peace and harmony, I found his behaviour quite troubling, and this went far deeper than any political differences. I felt disconnected from him and could also sense the disconnection and division he was creating in the community. When I was triggered by him, it was also challenging to sustain my Compensating Self-concept of being peaceful, easy-going, and kind.

The two other important items on my list, "My partner was more available" and "I had more friends" are more obvious examples of me, as a Type Nine, wanting more connection to alleviate the Basic Fear of being disconnected. There are many other items on my list that also have the same underlying theme of wanting more connection.

Review the improvements you have selected and explore their possible connection to your Basic Fear and Compensating Self-concept. Sometimes the connections are subtle, but usually, they will be found in at least two of the choices you have made. We want the world to behave in a way that supports our coping strategies and keeps the underlying Basic Fear undisturbed. If this is not happening, we become anxious and reactive. We feel threatened and vulnerable, and we want changes to ensure our protection stays in place.

This exercise confirms the insights from the discussion of the Levels of Health in the previous chapter. Many of our behaviours, desires and reactions are motivated by our determination to keep the shells of protection in place and to ensure the painful content of the unconscious remains undisturbed.

Another insight from "My life would be better ..." is that, even if we were granted all the wishes on our list, it would make very little difference to our level of happiness. There may be a moment of excitement or relief, but it wouldn't last very long. We soon revert to our usual way of being and develop a new list of improvements. In my own case, when the confrontational Prime Minister was removed, the relief and happiness lasted for about a week. It is part of our protective behaviour that we will always have a list of dissatisfactions. When we focus on our "improvements list" we don't have to pay attention to the real source of our discomfort. We mislead ourselves to believing the discomfort is coming from external circumstances, whilst all the while it is coming from within.

The exercise also highlights the dysfunctional thinking that keeps us in a state of ongoing dissatisfaction and discontent:

**I want the things I don't have,
I don't want the things I have.**

CHAPTER 7

Allowing the Protective Shells to Be Dismantled

"What you bring forth will save you. What you do not bring forth will destroy you." — Gospel of St Thomas

The three centres are a fundamental and central part of Enneagram teaching, as are the protective shells that we develop to protect them. The value of the Enneagram is the precision it offers in allowing us to become aware of the habitual behaviours of our Enneagram type. And as that happens, we can see the limitations of our protective shells of which they are a part. This possibility is described in some inspiring words about the Enneagram from Don Riso and Russ Hudson (1):

"As much as it (the Enneagram) reveals the spiritual heights that we are capable of attaining, it also sheds light clearly and non-judgementally on the aspects of our lives that are dark and unfree."

Ultimately, the Enneagram leads to connection with the centres, 'the spiritual heights', but not before we have explored 'the aspects of our lives that are dark and unfree'. And to begin this exploration, we need a deeper understanding of the protective shells and how they work.

Understanding the Protective Shells

The protective shells have two layers: the inner layer, which is unconscious, and the outer layer, which is mostly conscious. The fundamental purpose of the protective shells is to create distance from painful experiences, memories and beliefs and to keep them away from awareness. As difficult experiences or thoughts occur, they are relegated to the unconscious where they don't have to be felt. The memories of these experiences are locked out of awareness, so for the most part, we don't even know they are there.

The outer layer is made up of our coping strategies; it consists of the repetitive thoughts and ideas about ourselves that we hope will keep the contents of the unconscious concealed. If we can sustain these thoughts about ourselves, we hope they will counter the painful memories stored in the unconscious. We reinforce our coping strategies with habitual patterns of thinking and behaviour which we think will keep us distracted, protected and safe. These thoughts and beliefs, and the resulting patterns of behaviour, become a false self, the false part of our identity. We begin to live our lives as though this is 'who we are'. We want to keep this false self in place and defend it fiercely; partly because we erroneously think it is 'who we are', but also because it covers over the painful contents of the unconscious.

The outer layer is tailored specifically to conceal the underlying content in the unconscious; different painful memories require different coping strategies and different behaviours to keep them concealed. The way 'I think and behave' in any moment is largely determined by what I am trying to conceal. This idea is at the centre of the teaching on the Levels of Health. Our behaviour as we move up and down the Levels of Health is a response to our underlying Basic Fear, how strongly we are feeling it, and to what extent it is being triggered. Our behaviour, and our ongoing identity, is largely an expression of the unconscious content we are trying to conceal.

As we become more aware of our behaviour, we will get insights into the underlying content in the unconscious. This is particularly true when our behaviour is impulsive and reactive; it has a desperate or strident quality to it. We then know there is something very un-comfortable we want to cover over or avoid. By watching our own behaviour carefully, and becoming familiar with our habitual be-havioural patterns, we can sense what the underlying pain might be.

There is an ongoing struggle between the false self and the un-conscious, with the false self trying to keep the pain of the uncon-scious concealed. Most of the time we are not even aware that this inner struggle is occurring. But occasionally, as we become curious about our behaviour, we get glimpses of how much energy we are in-vesting in it. We are committed to defending our false self; we strug-gle to keep it in place, even when we know it is a futile endeavour. We "strut and fret our hour upon the stage" knowing how meaningless the outcomes will be. And all the while we could return to the under-lying richness of the three centres and an authentic connection with our true nature.

The two layers of the protective shells, the inner layer, the uncon-scious, and the outer layer, our identity and our false self, are illus-trated in the diagram below.

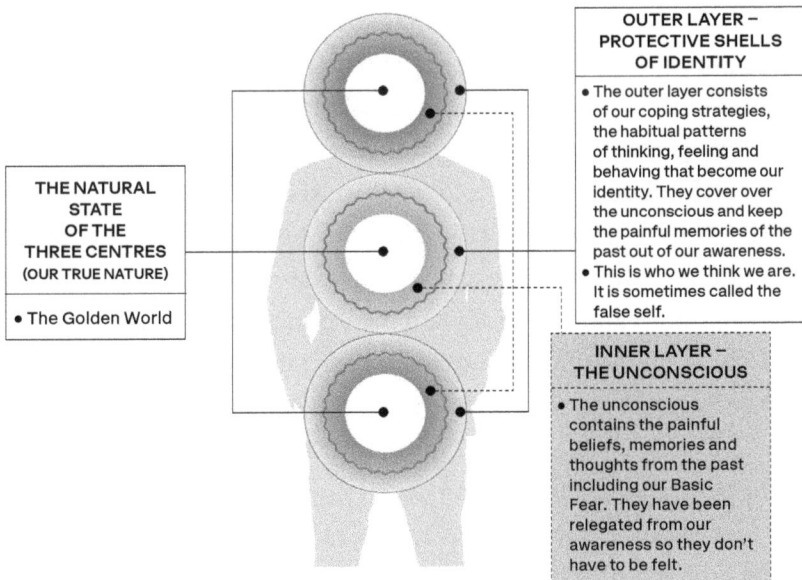

**OUTER LAYER –
PROTECTIVE SHELLS
OF IDENTITY**

- The outer layer consists of our coping strategies, the habitual patterns of thinking, feeling and behaving that become our identity. They cover over the unconscious and keep the painful memories of the past out of our awareness.
- This is who we think we are. It is sometimes called the false self.

**THE NATURAL
STATE
OF THE
THREE CENTRES
(OUR TRUE NATURE)**

- The Golden World

**INNER LAYER –
THE UNCONSCIOUS**

- The unconscious contains the painful beliefs, memories and thoughts from the past including our Basic Fear. They have been relegated from our awareness so they don't have to be felt.

Our Identity and Our False Self

Our identity begins to develop at an early age. As a baby, we see parts of our body and recognise that they are connected to us. We see ourselves in a mirror and start to identify with the image we see. "We learn our names. After that we become our names, we identify with the sounds of them. Then I am my name; I am the son of my father and mother; the brother of my sister." (2). We now have a name, a birth date, personal memories and a history. This is how we describe ourselves; we identify with this history.

The process of building identity continues beyond these historical facts. We start adding ideas and beliefs about 'who we are'. They are hopes and illusions and do not have a factual or historical basis. They give us some psychological comfort; they make us feel better, stronger or have some aspect that we think enhances our identity. They are built around a central concept, our Compensating Self-concept. We chose stories and beliefs about ourselves that help support this central concept; that 'I am good', that 'I am selfless', that 'I am capable' and so on. It also includes all the political, religious, social, and personal beliefs we adopt as we move through life, all of them being adopted because, in some subtle way, they support the identity we are trying to sustain. And of course, all our Enneagram-type behaviours are there to support our identity, and shore up our Compensating Self-concept.

Our identity also includes the messages and directions we receive from our parents, our teachers and other authority figures, particularly in childhood. We are told what we should believe and how we should behave. Our natural inclinations and inherent wisdom are often over-ridden by these external opinions. We adapt ourselves to these opinions and directions and incorporate them into our identity. Often the adaptions are based on fear; if we don't comply there will be negative consequences. Hence, our identity has been conditioned by our environment and by the views and directions of the more 'powerful' people around us.

Our identity is therefore made up of two parts. The first part is based on facts, history and biological characteristics; the second part is the 'false self'; the thoughts and beliefs we make up to keep ourselves comfortable and safe. It also incorporates the opinions and directives, both positive and negative, we have incorporated from others. All these ideas about 'who we are', and 'what we need to be', are our coping strategies. They are the core of our identity. We hope they will be an antidote to the fear and trauma that resides in the unconscious. So, our identity consists of a small factual, historical core, which we don't have to defend. And the bigger, non-factual part is just a collection of ideas we have adopted about ourselves; they are the false self.

When the false self is challenged, we find more stories and arguments to reinforce the beliefs about ourselves. We become even more personally invested in the stories and don't want to give them up. And as part of this, we become more entrenched in our Enneagram-type behaviours. We become more self-absorbed and go further down the Levels of Health. We then relate to the world from this self-constructed identity that cuts us off from the world and from our true nature. We are believing in a false self; a collection of thoughts and ideas, that have no basis in reality. And even when we are confronted by evidence that this false self has no substance, or is the cause of our suffering, we deny the evidence and persist with our illusion.

*   *   *   *

Terminology – Ego, Identity, Personality and Persona

'Identity', including the false self, is sometimes called the ego, the Latin word for 'I'. The word 'ego' has been used, and misused, in so many ways, it is less confusing to use the term 'identity'. It is our sense of who we are, both factual and false. It includes all the behavioural patterns that result from our beliefs about 'who we are' and 'who we want to be'.

Likewise, there are strong similarities between the words 'identity' and 'personality'. 'Personality' is often focused more on external behavioral characteristics. For instance, it might be said that 'she has a good personality', meaning she is extraverted and entertaining to be with. 'Personality' is also used in Enneagram teaching with terms such as 'Enneagram personality types' and frequent references to personality. Again, this has a slightly stronger emphasis on the external behavioral patterns associated with each of the Enneagram types. 'Identity' has a broader focus, which includes the external behaviours, but also the underlying beliefs about ourselves that result in those behaviours.

The terms ego, ego-identity, identity and personality are more or less interchangeable, but most of the time we will use the term 'identity'.

An important part of identity is the persona; it is the exterior expression of our identity. It is the facade that we want the world to see. Persona is the Latin word for mask and is another concept developed by Jung. The persona is the mask we present to the world. Many studies have shown that, as children, we learnt what behaviours pleased our parents. We also found the behaviours that resulted in disapproval and punishment. We then adapted our behaviour to meet the preferences of our environment. We continued this learning as we grew older and had similar experiences with our teachers, with our friends, at work and so on. The parts of ourselves that didn't seem acceptable to the world were relegated to the unconscious and they became part of our shadow. There is a great cost to us in this process of adaption. We become stereotypes of the person we think the world wants us to be.

When we are relating to someone with a well-developed persona it can feel like we are relating to a thin veneer of charming inauthentic behaviours. The interaction can feel fragile and limited, and that it wouldn't take much for this thin veneer to be disturbed.

Trapped in Our Identity
We have created a false identity for ourselves and we are committed to keeping it in place. With this narrow focus, and a limited understanding of our true nature, we become overly invested in

worldly outcomes. These outcomes are inevitably disappointing, and we begin to suspect there must be something missing. We are stuck in this false identity, sensing its fragility and trying to keep it together.

We are trapped in the outer layer and the narrow interactions of our identity with the world. We can't move our focus inwards because we encounter the disturbing contents of the unconscious. And we are reluctant to move our focus too openly into the world in case we find something 'out there' that will disturb our unconscious content or challenge our identity. We become restricted to the limited realm of the outer layer, cut off from the energies of the three centres and cut off from any authentic connection with the world. We live our lives believing this is who we are, imprisoned in this limited space, thinking that this is all there is.

We are disconnected from the energies of the three centres; they are a long way from our awareness. They are hidden behind the inner layer, the unconscious. They are difficult to access there because we must move through the unconscious to get there, and most of us are reluctant to travel through that uninviting terrain. The inner layer becomes the veil that prevents our connection with the three centres and our access to the Golden World. It is only in moments of grace, when we see through the hole in the veil, that we glimpse the beauty of what is available. And often, as the years pass, these glimpses becomes less frequent. As we move through life, we relegate more unwanted and difficult experiences into the unconscious. The inner layer become thicker and opaque; we get further away from the redemptive energies of the three centres.

Our Identity and Our True Nature

Much has been written about the confusion between our identity and a deeper sense of 'who we are'. We have glimpses of 'who we might be' behind the veil of the protective shells; we occasionally touch into the three centres and the Golden World. This experience has a completely different quality to it. It is where we feel the essence of who we are. Eckhart Tolle refers to it as the Deeper I, Jung called it the Self (with a capital s) and in Christianity it is called the Christ Mind. It has also been referred to as the Ground of Being. For us, it is the three centres and the Golden World.

As we move from our identity, to this very different experience, the question arises as to whether there are actually two selves. And which one is real. The confusion as to which self is real is captured in the expression 'I feel separated from myself'. The first self is our identity, the 'I' that is feeling separated. It is located in the outer layer of the protective shells. Over time we have come to believe this is 'who we are'. This is where we spend most of our time, and we try to make our experience there as comfortable as possible. But we know, that at a deeper level, there is another self; the one we 'feel separated from'. This 'other self' seems to sit underneath our identity, just a little bit beyond our reach. In spite of our tenuous and fleeting connection with it, it has an unchanging and familiar quality to it. When we move closer to it, there is a sense of connection with something real. And when we feel that, even for a moment, all the self-constructed ideas about ourselves fall away. We know that this is who we truly are. We have been freed, even for a short while, from the prison of our identity. This is a small step in our movement towards freedom.

The movement towards freedom has been described as the movement from being 'self-centred' to being 'centred in self'. When we are 'self-centred', we are pre-occupied with keeping our identity in place. Another expression for this is being 'self-absorbed'. We struggle to keep our false self together and unrealistically think the world should help us in this endeavour. At some level we know that the false self is inherently fragile; it is not sufficiently robust to withstand the difficulties and challenges of life. We become anxious about its survival and expect others to help in keeping it together. We then become disappointed and frustrated when the support and consideration we want is not forthcoming. And of course, we get even more reactive, when we think that others are threatening the survival of the false self. When we move to being 'centred in self' there is nothing fragile to sustain. We feel supported in each moment and trust in whatever is unfolding.

The Movement Back to Self - Two Inspiring Stories

These questions about self and identity arose for Eckhart Tolle in his late twenties. It was a time of crisis in his life; he had reached a point where he was contemplating suicide. He had the thought: "I can't live with myself any longer." (3) When he explored this idea further, he surmised there must be two of 'him'. There was the one he couldn't live with anymore, and there was the one who was aware of this other annoying 'him'. The one he couldn't live with anymore was his self-constructed identity, the false self, with its ceaseless chattering monkey-mind that was so relentlessly negative and dissatisfied. Tolle had become caught in the limitations of his identity and it was causing him a lot of suffering. He recognised that he could connect with something quite different, an underlying and authentic true self, the Deeper I. In our terms, he had connected to the three centres and to the Golden World. He could see the things he was pursuing in the world were not that important, in fact they were making him unhappy. They were distracting him from something much more fulfilling. He had found the wisdom and the joy of his being; an experience he has since been able to share with millions of people around the world.

There are many accounts, similar to Tolle's, where people have seen through the limitations of identity. In some cases, it has happened dramatically with a spontaneous recognition of something more authentic than the false self. Ramana Maharshi was a famous Indian sage who lived in the first part of the 20th century. His life of innocent simplicity and joy continues to inspire millions of people to the present day. Until the age of sixteen, Ramana lived a normal life of an ordinary Indian boy. He had no particular interest in religion or spirituality. Just prior to his sixteenth birthday, he started to explore, on his own accord, the nature of death and what would happen to him when we died. As part of this enquiry, he found there was something within him, beyond the body, that would be untouched by death; something eternal. He had found connection to his true nature. The connection was so powerful and all-encompassing it was all he desired from that moment forward. His sense of identity fell away and he lost all interest in worldly things, even food. At sixteen, he walked out of the comfort of his home in absolute awe of the union he had found with the divine. He wanted nothing more and remained that way for the rest of his life.

Edging Our Way Towards Freedom

Eckhart Tolle and Ramana Maharshi are but two examples of the many people who have moved beyond identity and connected to their true nature. It is a possibility that is open to all of us. But we cannot expect that what happened to them spontaneously will also happen to us.

For Eckhart, like most of us, there were difficult beliefs and memories of the past concealed in his unconscious. To counter this, he had engaged in the world, building a false self to cover over the pain. In his case, it was his life as an academic. But he found that regardless of his successes and the progress he made in the academic world, it didn't really help. The pain was still there. In fact, often when we succeed in our endeavours, the pain gets stronger. We realise that whatever we do, and whatever we achieve, it is not going to give us relieff. Often it is from this realisation of hopelessness and surrender, that we open to the possibility of something different. We give up the struggle to keep the false self in place. But as we let go of the false self, there is a challenge. The difficult contents of the unconscious have the opportunity to return to our awareness. They are no longer concealed by our identity and our striving in the world. The painful content begins to move into our awareness and we feel the discomfort as it arrives. As that happens, we are tempted to protect ourselves again. We want to reach for the distractions of the false self and the comfort of the protective shells.

But we have a choice. We can 'sit on the steps' and feel the discomfort in the body as it arises. It can be a moment when we feel despair and disillusionment with our lives. But eventually the discomfort passes. Each time we do this, we empty out a little of our unconscious content. There is then less unconscious pain to be concealed, and the need to keep the false self in place has been diminished, even by a little. And as part of this, the false self is being undone. With this, we slowly move up the Levels of Health. We are slowly edging our way towards freedom and the Golden World.

For most of us this will happen slowly, but as Eckhart showed, it is not always gradual. In his case it was dramatic and spontaneous. He saw through the futility of what he was doing, and that was the end of the false self. Likewise for Ramana, although it was for slightly different reasons. His transformation was not motivated by the pain of futile endeavour, but by a profound connection with what he wanted, his true nature.

The speed of the transformation is not really of our choosing; our only choice is to consistently allow the unconscious pain to be revealed and exposed. And when we don't, it becomes stronger. As we repress it, and refuse to acknowledge it, it becomes more active and more painful. Then we try to protect ourselves, and in doing so, we move down the Levels of Health. The three centres get pushed back further behind the unconscious. They become very difficult to access there and eventually they drop out of our awareness altogether.

* * * *

"What You Bring Forth Will Save You"

Bringing the difficult contents of the unconscious into awareness is the purview of modern psychology, particularly the field of depth psychology developed by Sigmund Freud and Carl Jung. This will be explored in depth in later chapters. But even before Freud and Jung, there was an awareness of the profound impact the contents of the unconscious could have on our mental wellbeing. Nearly two thousand years before Jung, Jesus anticipated the core of Jung's ideas with the insight:

> "What you bring forth will save you. What you do not
> bring forth will destroy you." (4)

Finding the aspects of ourselves that we have been trying to conceal for a lifetime is a difficult and uncomfortable task. It is the last thing we would want to do. But if we don't, we will spend our lives in a meaningless endeavour to keep the unconscious content concealed. Not only does that go on forever, we disconnect more and more from what we love and want. Whilst this is the most important task of a lifetime, it is one we respond to with some reluctance. This reluctance to explore the contents of the unconscious was identified by Marianne Williamson:

> "It takes courage ... to endure the sharp pains of self-
> discovery rather than choose to take the dull pain of
> unconsciousness that would last the rest of our lives." (5)

The dull pain is there in all of us. The only question is whether we have the courage and curiosity to endure the sharp pains of self-discovery and free ourselves from a lifetime of suffering.

The Enneagram helps us do that, pointing to where we need to look. It provides a way to identify and free the unresolved content in the unconscious. It can help us bring forth what needs to be brought forth. As the words at the beginning of the chapter remind us:

> "It (the Enneagram) sheds light clearly and non-
> judgementally on the aspects of our lives that are dark
> and unfree."

*   *   *   *

The Return to the Garden

One of the enduring myths of our world, which is shared across many traditions and religions, is the belief that we were thrown out of paradise by a punitive god because we had done something wrong. It maintains we are being punished for some indiscretion of our distant forebears. It offers no prospect for our return to paradise. We must endure what we have been given and try to appease an unhappy god.

This has always been an unlikely and unreasonable story. It perpetuates our disconnection from the joy of life. The reality is that paradise, the garden of Eden, is our connection to the three centres. That is where we experience the divine energies that emanate from the centres. The truth is that we have removed ourselves from the garden and cut ourselves off from the energies of our centres. They are still there but they have been covered over by the protective shells and are no longer in our awareness. And like our forebears, we are tempted to conclude that we must have been thrown out of the garden by an all-powerful god. This, of course, is not the case: we have done it to ourselves. However, what we have done, can — with attention to our purpose — be undone.

Our challenge is to bring the difficult content of the unconscious into our awareness, to bring forth what needs to be brought forth. And with this, the protective shells will be dismantled. In biblical terms, it is the return to the Garden. In our terms, it is the return to the Golden World. In that experience, the activities and challenges of the world are not important. Awareness expands beyond the realm of the protective shells. We surrender our concerns about what is wrong and right. We are simply being present with what is arising within us right now. There is no agenda and nothing to fix. We are sitting at the centre of our being and being touched by the experiences that arise.

The return to the centres is made easier by the realisation that we never really left. We have always been connected to the three centres and those energies are always within us. Our attention had simply been pulled away to the challenges of the world. We had forgotten, for a moment, our true nature and left it concealed behind our protective shells. We had been sucked into a drama of our own making.

*   *   *   *

THE WAY OF THE ENNEAGRAM

A Personal Reflection - My Own Sense of the Three Centres

Becoming aware of the three centres has significantly changed the way I experience life. This awareness is a source of gentle relief and reassurance. I feel less alone, and I am less troubled by the challenges I encounter. There is more space around what is happening. Some words from Chapter One help remind me of the existence of the centres and their fundamental importance to my life:

> **"They are where we feel the essence of our being and the spark of creation that keeps us alive."**

These words have given me a stronger sense of the three centres. I can occasionally feel the warmth and joy of the energy moving around my heart. It doesn't feel personal. And sometimes, when my thinking stops, I have a sense that everything is perfect, exactly as it is. I can trust I am living in a benevolent world. Again, it is not personal, it is universal. The sense of a personal 'I' falls away.

It has given me an ongoing sense that there is something divine within me. It is subtle and quiet; it is my connection with the divine; it is where God and I meet. And this is very important because, until now, I have only had an inkling of this connection. Strangely it is not something I can say much about. It is just there, and I don't even know exactly what it is. I was reassured by something written by Carl Jung. It feels like he is writing about the same thing:

> "The decisive question for us is: Are we related to something infinite or not? That is the telling question of our life. If we understand and feel that here in this life, we already have a link with the infinite, desires and attitudes change."

Having a sense of the centres is the 'link with the infinite' to which Jung was referring. And it feels that I can cultivate this sense and make it a more consistent part of my awareness. To do so, I need to remind myself that the centres are always there. The following practice helps me do this, particularly when I am feeling distressed or distracted:

Stop ... and breathe ... and try to find the centres in the body.

I can usually find at least one, often the Heart Centre. Initially the connection can be tenuous, but if I can stay with this tenuous connection, the awareness of the centre grows. And as this happens, my focus sometimes expands to the other two centres. With this, the mind stops. I can feel my heart soften and my body relaxes. My perspective on what is in front of me changes. It is the beginning of my return to the Golden World.

*   *   *   *

These reflections remind me that the energies of the centres are always there. These little reminders are invaluable, but they are still just a glimpse of what is possible. To access the centres on a more lasting basis requires the uncovering of our unconscious content and the resulting dismantling of the protective shells.

*   *   *   *

We can do many things to explore and reveal the contents of the unconscious. Some of these will be covered in later chapters. However, one of the most immediate and fruitful ways to access the unconscious is to explore the ways we behave in relationships. For many of us, relationships are the most challenging part of our lives. When we are triggered and irritated by other people, we can be sure that something in our unconscious is being stirred. The next two chapters focus on the opportunities to explore and uncover our unconscious content through our relationships. Chapter Eight focuses on all of our relationships; work, family and friends and even people we don't know very well. Chapter Nine explores the way we behave in close and intimate relationships and how this reveals the difficult contents of the unconscious.

CHAPTER 8

Using Relationships to Uncover Unconscious Content

Relationships are not there to make us happy; they are here to wake us up. —Eckhart Tolle

When we see the conflict and disharmony that is so prevalent in the world, it is easy to be discouraged and disappointed. The conflicts between countries, regions, tribes, and communities are never-ending, with no sign the level of conflict is abating. In the twentieth century over two hundred million people were killed in wars and internal country conflicts; it feels that this number could be easily exceeded in the twenty-first century. And the same level of conflict is reflected locally in our communities, at work, in our neighbour-hoods, in our families and in many of our relationships. It is likely that even more people are killed in local conflicts, family feuds and particularly domestic violence than are killed in military conflicts. People everywhere are struggling to co-exist and relate to each other in peaceful and harmonious ways. While we all aspire to loving and supportive relationships, this aspiration is difficult to realise in practice. Why are relationships so difficult and fraught with poten-tial for conflict? Why do so many marriages end in divorce and acri-monious dispute?

The answer might well lie in the structures and dynamics of the psyche explored in the last chapter. Most of us have moved away from our natural state and our connection with the three centres. As we struggle with the challenges of the world, we do what we can do protect ourselves and to sustain our false self. We have built the protective shells and hope they will protect us from the painful contents of the unconscious. But they don't. The unconscious content is still there, and it gets stronger as we try to conceal it. We defend the false self, and the more we defend it, the more fragile it becomes. We become self-centred and self-absorbed, and it doesn't take very much to upset us. We are primed to be triggered. When someone says something that stirs our unconscious pain, or challenges our fragile identity, we react. We are wanting the world to behave in a way that supports our coping strategies, and doesn't challenge our false self. And particularly, we don't want anyone to do anything that stirs our unconscious pain. And when the world doesn't behave the way we expect, we feel threatened and vulnerable. We react to the person who has triggered us. We blame the person who we think is the cause of our discomfort and pain. We get irritated with them, then frustrated and sometimes angry. In our reaction, we go further down the Levels of Health. As we do, our behaviour becomes more irrational and even vengeful. We do and say things that would normally be completely unacceptable to us. We have been sucked into a downward spiral of reactivity.

And of course, a similar dynamic is happening for the person with whom we are interacting. Our reactive behaviour is triggering them. They are also feeling threatened and vulnerable, and react to us, trying to keep their false self in place. As the interaction continues, the behaviour on both sides becomes more reactive and provocative. The level of conflict intensifies and both parties move further down the Levels of Health.

This dynamic, and the sad progression down the Levels of Health, explains much of the conflict in the world. It begins with all of us trying to cover over our own painful unconscious content, and then being triggered when other people do or say things that stir our unconscious pain. Identities are bumping into each other and triggering each other's unconscious pain. Then we react and blame each other for the pain we are feeling. We project things we don't like about ourselves on to the other person and then we judge them and make them the enemy. And this is why the conflict in the world continues, whether between national leaders, in our communities and families and with the people we love.

The most important work we can all do is to catch ourselves each and every time we are triggered. We must begin to know that the pain we are feeling is coming from within. It is our opportunity to find our past trauma and grief and bring them into our awareness. And above all, we must recognise that to blame the other is compounding our own pain and the pain and conflict in the world.

Some real-life examples of how these conflictual interactions develop, are described in the sections that follow.

A School at War

Several years ago, my partner and I were invited to a school to run an introductory Enneagram workshop for the teachers. An acting principal was standing in for the principal who was on extended leave. She soon realised that the school was suffering from serious management and morale problems, with two teachers in hospital and several other teachers on extended leave for health reasons. She could see that the teachers were effectively at war with the principal. There were many complaints about his harsh and uncompromising behaviour. The principal believed that there were procedures that had to be followed in running the school and it was necessary for the teachers to comply with these requirements. He had felt unsupported by the teachers and felt they were challenging his authority. A particularly contentious issue was the many forms to be completed by the teachers, which they saw as distractions from their work.

The Enneagram provided some perspective on the conflict between the headmaster and the teachers. The headmaster was a Type Eight. His Basic Fear "of being harmed or controlled by others" had been activated by the unwillingness of the teachers to meet his requests. He had then tried to enforce his authority, but this had antagonised the teachers even further. The teachers included all the Enneagram types, but Type Twos were by far the largest group. While Type Twos are used in this analysis, similar conclusions would apply for the other types.

The Basic Fear of the Type Two teachers is "of being unloved and unwanted." This had been activated repeatedly by the harsh approach of the headmaster. They had received no validation from him for their hard work, so they directed their efforts towards the students. They either ignored the headmaster, or they became resentful and rebellious towards him. As the level of personal animosity increased, the original issue of 'filling in the forms' faded into insignificance. Both sides now viewed each other as the enemy and did what they could to maintain their entrenched positions and negative feelings towards each other.

The Impact of Basic Fear in Relationships – The Worksheet
It is useful to analyse the teacher-headmaster interactions using the worksheet below. The worksheet demonstrates how the underlying Basic Fear of both types was driving the interaction. Each side was feeling threatened as their Basic Fears were triggered. The teachers were feeling 'unloved and unwanted' by the headmaster's harshness. The headmaster was feeling at risk 'of being harmed or controlled' by the rebellious attitude of the teachers. Both sides were trying to get relief by trying to reassure themselves that their Compensating Self-concepts were, in fact, true.

Both sides also moved to a perspective about the conflict that confirmed that what they were doing was 'right', and what the other side was doing was definitely 'wrong'. These are the Activated Positions shown in the diagram. The teachers felt unacknowledged by the headmaster and were focusing all their attention on the students, ignoring the headmaster. The headmaster was determined to enforce his authority, no matter what.

Activated Position		Activated Position
"The headmaster is never going to acknowledge the selfless work I do as a teacher. I will keep focusing on the students. I don't care about him and his forms."	**Amplified Issue** Ping pong 'Sword Talk'	"My authority is at stake here. I am going to bring some discipline in here and make them complete the forms, no matter what."

Basic Fear	Compensating Self Concept		Issue		Compensating Self Concept	Basic Fear
Of being unloved and unwanted	I am loving, thoughtful and selfless		"Filling in the forms"		I am strong, assertive and in control	Of being harmed and controlled by others

Type 2 **Teacher**	Type 8 **Headmaster**

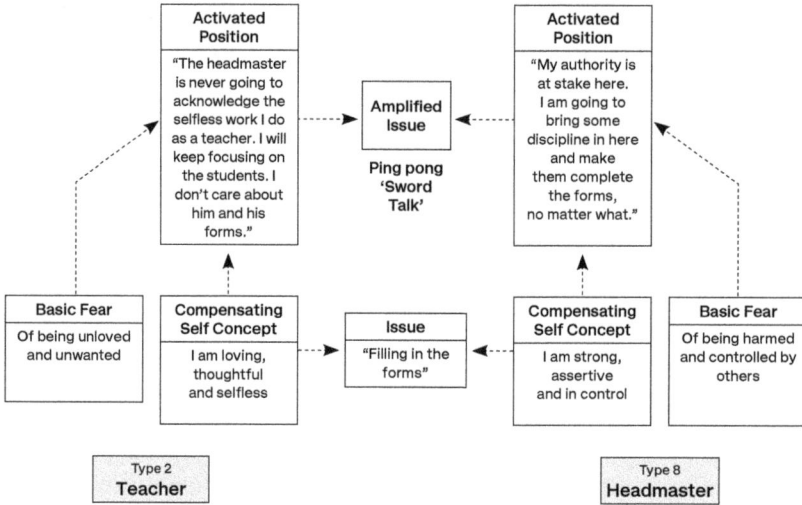

The interaction spiralled down with each reaction, each side becoming more convinced of the rightness of its position. This involved trying to demonstrate that the other side was wrong and deluded, while they were right. It is like a game of ping-pong in which each player hopes their next shot will be so convincing it will win the game. It never does. The game can go on forever; the rivals just keep hitting the ball back. All it would take is for one player to see the futility of what was happening and not hit the ball back. The game would be over.

The language in these interactions is also combative and can be characterised as "sword talk". It is threatening and unproductive, always escalating the tension between the two sides. It is like the language politicians use with every statement being a threat to the other side. It escalates into a tit-for-tat competition and the stakes keep getting bigger.

Basic Fear and Painful Unconscious Content

The difficult interactions between the teachers and the headmaster can, as we have seen, be understood by seeing how they were activating each other's Basic Fears. But a more comprehensive picture recognises that it was not only their Basic Fears that were being activated, but other unconscious pain and trauma. Their painful unconscious content sits beside their Basic Fear in the unconscious and there is a strong link and symbiotic relationship between the two.

The Type Eight headmaster will be triggered by anything that threatens "to harm and control him" (his Basic Fear). However, the intensity of the trigger will be much greater if there is a lot of other unacknowledged pain and trauma in his unconscious. His Basic Fear and his past trauma reinforce each other and make the intensity of the pain much stronger. Likewise, for the Type Two teachers, and the other teachers as well. Some of the teachers were not greatly troubled by the headmaster, or at worst, were slightly irritated by him. Others found him to be extremely harsh and impossible to work with. The extent to which the teachers were being triggered depended, not only on their Basic Fear, but also on their past unacknowledged pain and trauma. This past pain combines with, and amplifies their Basic Fear, and produces feelings that are threatening and overwhelming.

In any challenging interaction, *the cause and reasons for the triggering* can usually be traced back to the Basic Fears of the people involved. There is a mutual interactive triggering of each other's Basic Fear. The *intensity of the triggering* can usually be explained by the amount of unacknowledged pain in each person's unconscious. If one person is psychologically healthy (i.e. they have very little unconscious content), then they won't be triggered too much by what's happening. With no reactive response from them, the mutual interactive triggering and downward reactive spiral cannot get started.

The intensity of anyone's reaction to any challenging situation is an indication of our "propensity to be disturbed". It is our own unconscious pain that is being triggered. And this propensity to be disturbed probably manifests in most parts of our lives. The triggering is the opportunity to "catch ourselves in the act", and to look at the unacknowledged unconscious content that is causing us to react so strongly.

There is a reassuring insight that comes from what was happening at the school:

"It only takes one person not to react!"

*   *   *   *

Unfortunately, the situation at the school is not unique and is repeated in countless workplaces, families and relationships every day. The first useful response to any conflict is to give the situation some space. In the situation at the school, the acting principal realised it was pointless for her to try to impose a solution. What she hoped to do was to get everyone to step back from what was happening. The Enneagram workshop was part of this approach. It helped give the teachers a different and broader perspective and to see their part in the conflict. They could see they were being triggered and, at times, were responding from their Basic Fear. One of the questions they could ask themselves was: "What would happen if I didn't hit the ball back?" This question provides some space around the interaction and a less charged perspective.

As a footnote, in the days following the workshop, the animosity of the teachers towards the principal did begin to abate and there was some informal contact between the teachers and the headmaster. Two weeks later, the headmaster resigned and did not return to the school. The important outcome was not the resignation of the headmaster, but the recognition that in every difficult interaction we all need to examine what is driving our reactive behaviour. Hopefully the teachers could see their part in the conflict and why they were being triggered. In this discovery, they might also find that some of their other relationships were being affected by the same unconscious forces. This is where the possibility for growth and freedom lies.

How Does This Dynamic Play Out in Long-term Relationships?
The dynamics observed at the school apply equally strongly to long-term, one-on-one relationships. That recognition of the underlying triggers in ongoing challenges can be very helpful in resolving difficulties and supporting a movement up the Levels of Health for both partners.

The example below is based on a husband and wife who had been together for twenty-five years. The worksheet was completed by the husband. A similar worksheet was completed by his partner at a later date, but with almost the same conclusions. The husband is a Seven and in his early fifties. His partner is a Nine and is a few years younger. The husband loves classical music and enjoys going to concerts and impromptu gatherings with his classical music friends. Often the arrangements are made at the last minute without giving his partner much notice. As a Nine, his partner finds this difficult.

Her position is: "Your spontaneous commitment to others makes me feel disconnected, abandoned and not loved."

His position is: "Your desire to control me is making me feel imprisoned and I need to keep fighting for space and freedom."

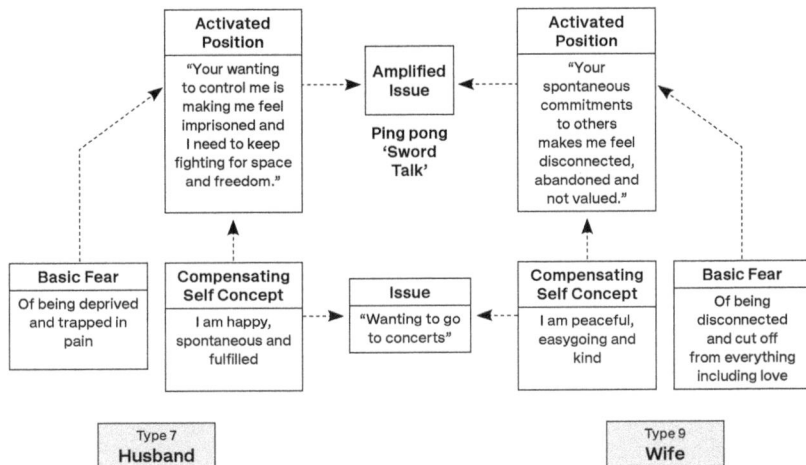

Activated Position					Activated Position
"Your wanting to control me is making me feel imprisoned and I need to keep fighting for space and freedom."	Amplified Issue				"Your spontaneous commitments to others makes me feel disconnected, abandoned and not valued."
	Ping pong 'Sword Talk'				

Basic Fear	Compensating Self Concept	Issue		Compensating Self Concept	Basic Fear
Of being deprived and trapped in pain	I am happy, spontaneous and fulfilled	"Wanting to go to concerts"		I am peaceful, easygoing and kind	Of being disconnected and cut off from everything including love

Type 7 Husband				Type 9 Wife

There are clearly some practical changes that both partners could make in the way they relate to each other. However, the worksheet gave a bigger perspective on how Basic Fear was playing out in the relationship. In recognising the unconscious influences, they both saw their partner's behaviour as less intentional and not directed at them personally. It provided the opportunity for both partners to look at their part in what was happening and to see how their behaviour was being influenced by their Basic Fears. The Seven husband might see how he busily fills his life with many activities as a way of getting away from his underlying fear of being trapped in pain. His Nine partner might see how she seeks a cosy and predictable domestic relationship as a way of covering over the fear of being disconnected.

Fortunately, in this relationship, the partners were both psychologically healthy. They had already done work to release much of the difficult unconscious content of the past. While they were still unsettled by their partners' behavioural patterns, they could understand what was happening in the dynamic between. They could recognise the reasons for their own discomfort, and also for their partner's discomfort. With compassion for themselves and for their partner, they could avoid being sucked into the downward spiral of reactivity.

A blank version of the worksheet is included as an appendix at the end of this chapter. It provides a simple way of exploring the dynamics in any challenging relationship. It provides a bigger and less personal perspective on the discomfort that may be arising. This bigger perspective is also supported by the following meditation that is recommended to anyone who is using the worksheet.

*   *   *   *

A Meditation
Behind the Challenging Interaction

1. Sit quietly and recall someone who has triggered you recently.
2. You may know their type; this helps. Or you might not. Either way, can you imagine that their "challenging" behaviour might reflect their own difficult circumstances or that they might be down the Levels of Health?
3. In either case, can you see that their behaviour is being driven largely by their Basic Fear? In which case, could you expect them to behave in any other way? Although they do not know it, this is

their way of keeping their coping strategies in place.

4. Can you have compassion for them that they are not behaving in a way they would like, but as an unconscious manifestation of their Basic Fear? They want to keep away from their own discomfort.

5. Given that you were triggered in the interaction, can you see that your behaviour was also being driven by your Basic Fear? That you were trying to keep your coping strategies in place?

6. Can you have compassion for yourself that you are not behaving in a way you would like, but as an unconscious manifestation of your Basic Fear? That you want to keep away from your own discomfort?

7. Can you have compassion for a world in which we all behave in ways we would not choose? Can you have compassion for a world in which we create suffering for ourselves and others, simply because we are trying to keep away from our own discomfort?

8. In meeting with others, are you willing to open your heart and reach out to see their pain? Can you see that in reaching out, you also become intimate with your own heart and your own pain? Their pain is touching your pain. The need to protect your heart disappears and the protective shells get thinner. With this, you reconnect with your own aliveness and the richness of being.

This meditation will help to soften our hearts and kindle some compassion for both ourselves and the other person. This process of defusing the conflict can be continued with the four-stage enquiry described in the next section that is recommended as a follow-up exercise for anyone using the worksheet.

Defusing Conflict in Relationships

This process is drawn from the work of Thomas Hubl and William Ury, who offer a program of workshops called *Meditate and Mediate*. Ury developed this model in his work as an international mediator in high-level humanitarian conflicts. There are four stages in the process.

The first stage, "Go to the balcony," is the invitation to stand back and observe what is happening, and to put some distance between

① **Go to the balcony (calm, bigger picture)**
- watching the interaction
- zooming in, feeling our body
- zoom out, look at the stage as a whole

② **What is the prize?**
What do I want in this situation?
What would be a good outcome?

③ **How do I get into their shoes?**
Listen. What are they saying?
Willingness to feel the other person. Allow their feelings in.

④ **Build the Golden Bridge for the other person?**
What is the person right about?
Say one thing that recognises the truth for them?

ourselves and the conflict. This is helped by the idea of zooming in and zooming out. As we zoom in, we get reacquainted with the energy of the conflict and can feel its disturbing energy in our body. As we zoom out, we recover the bigger perspective and can look at both sides of the conflict. We are encouraged to see the conflict as a *third-sider*, namely a person who is not emotionally involved in the dispute and can see what is happening more objectively. As we zoom out, we can revisit the worksheet and see the influence of Basic Fear in the interaction. In the example of the Seven and Nine's relationship, both partners might see the unconscious content they are trying to conceal and how this could be allowed to become conscious.

The second stage, "What is the prize?", can provide a sobering insight into what are our best interests in this situation. If the head-master and the teachers at the school had asked themselves this question, the headmaster might have seen that he really wanted a healthy school with motivated teachers. The teachers may have seen that they wanted an inspiring place to work and going to war with the headmaster was not going to achieve this.

Again, there is an even bigger prize on offer for both the teachers and the headmaster. The teachers might begin to see the underlying cause of their distress, their Basic Fear, and how it shows up in other parts of their life. Likewise, the headmaster might see that, underneath his attempts to be strong and in control, there is a fear of being harmed. He might also see how the need to be in control shows up in other parts of his life. Both sides could use the conflict to become more aware of their unconscious pain and to move up the Levels of Health.

The third stage, "How do I get into their shoes?", requires us to stop and listen to what the other person is saying. It asks us to get behind the words we are hearing and feel what might be going on for the other person. We can begin to understand what might be triggering the other person. If we have completed the worksheet, this stage of the process won't require much further work. If we can see the other's behaviour is being driven by Basic Fear, just like ours, we are well on the way to being able to get into their shoes. If the teachers at the school had some insight into the fact that the headmaster was feeling at risk, then it would have changed their behaviour significantly. Likewise, if the headmaster had seen the need in the teachers for some reassurance and validation, he too would have behaved differently.

The fourth and final stage, "Building the Golden Bridge for the other person", requires us to acknowledge one thing the other person is right about. We have to say something that recognises the truth for them. This is only possible if we have genuinely completed the first three stages and, to some extent, are familiar with the shoes of the other person. It doesn't have to be a complete endorsement of what the other person has been saying or doing, but simply an acknowledgment that we see some truth in it. For the headmaster talking to a teacher, it might be: "I see you have been working very hard and completing these forms is a distraction from your work." For a teacher speaking to the headmaster, it might be: "You have a lot on your plate, and you are required to submit these forms as part of your job." Building the bridge begins to dissipate the energy of "I am right, and you are wrong." The other person can feel the energy change and will usually reciprocate. It may be something as simple as: "Perhaps we can talk about this." Once the bridge is in place, communication can begin, and the escalated conflict can start to settle. Importantly, a space has been created, and in the space, we can begin to see our part in the conflict. We can see our own unconscious pain that is underlying our own behaviour. That is what we want more than anything. That the relationship might improve is just a secondary benefit to the important work of uncovering our unconscious pain.

The Real Purpose of Relationships

The exploration of conflict at the school and the challenges in the Seven-Nine relationship have provided the opportunity to explore three useful models to help defuse a challenging interaction and to reveal our own unconscious content:

- the worksheet and the recognition of the importance of the underlying Basic Fear in the interaction,

- the Meditation for Challenging Interactions, and,

- the four-stage Meditate and Mediate practice.

All three will be helpful in dissipating the energy of conflict and moving us out of our entrenched positions. The overriding goal, though, is more important than resolving a conflict with another person. When this difficult energy is arising in us, it is telling us something about the contents of our unconscious. If we can 'sit on the steps' and feel the energy move through our body, then we have the opportunity for the unconscious content to be revealed and for the protective shells to be dismantled. The real purpose of relationships is to explore and find the unwanted and disowned content in our unconscious. It is difficult, if not impossible, to do this by ourselves.

Harnessing the Healing Power of Relationships

Any discomfort we are experiencing with another person originates in us. It comes from our Basic Fear and the discomfort around past trauma or challenging experiences. It is the *pain inside* that is being activated by current circumstances. Everything we have tried to create to give us security is being challenged. Our usual response is to react to get relief from it. We are scrambling to do anything that might take away the bad feeling; to get "short-term symptom relief." It momentarily feels better, but then when the "symptom relief" fades the discomfort is still there. When the same circumstances arise again, we will behave in much the same way. The hope is that we can move to some more lasting resolution and don't have to spend our lives being triggered by other people. Pema Chödrön's concept of "the propensity to be disturbed" is a good measure of the unresolved pain within us. It is an indicator of the progress we are making in uncovering our unconscious content. Over time, we hopefully find that the people and situations that were once difficult for us, no longer trigger us. We might also find that other people notice that we have become less reactive and more enjoyable to be with.

The gift of relationships is that they supply an almost endless source of triggers. Our work is to be with the challenging energies that arise when we are triggered. And with that, we begin to empty out the contents of the unconscious. The meditation below helps us to be with the reactive energies and, at the same time, allows unconscious content to be revealed.

Gratitude Meditation

There are many times in each day in which we are triggered in minor ways. There are the little disappointments and irritations when things don't turn out quite the way we would have liked. Often the reactions and contractions in the body are very subtle but if we pay attention and check into the body, they are there. These moments of "micro-irritation" are wonderful opportunities to apply a simple practice to move towards wholeness. We probably have a hundred opportunities each day, so it doesn't matter if initially we only catch a few of them. The practice will, over time, become automatic.

1. Find the contraction in the body. Breathe and pay attention to the sensations in the body. Where are they? How strong are they?

2. Move your attention to the physical space around the heart. Stay focused on that area. Are there any sensations in that area? It doesn't matter if there are not. Stay focused in that area for a while.

3. Ask the question: "What am I grateful for in this moment?" Don't rush or force the answer. Give it time to let it come by itself. It doesn't matter if it doesn't. Just creating the space around the heart is enough.

4. Stay with the space you have created and let it to grow. You will notice the body begins to relax and there is nothing more to do.

The meditation is powerful because it focuses on what is being experienced in the body and around the heart. It hopefully keeps the mind out of the process, with all its ideas about what should or shouldn't be happening. This is difficult work as it is so easy to slip back into the comfort of our coping strategies.

Using Relationships to Access the Golden World
Relationships provide a constant stream of practical and day-to-day opportunities to uncover unconscious content. Can we remain still and unreactive in these moments of discomfort with other people? In this way we can explore and uncover the hidden pain in the unconscious. We have the choice of whether we want to harness the healing potential of relationships or persist with the safety of our habitual reactive behaviour. The choice can be expressed in the well-known expression:

"I can be right, or I can be happy."

More accurately, the choice can be expressed as:

> "I can be right, or I can use this challenging interaction
> to reveal the difficult content in my unconscious."

In getting some perspective on the underlying reason for the conflict, and feeling our unconscious pain, we can begin to let go of all the stories we have made up about the other person. Often, we can go for years, or sometimes a lifetime, building stories about why the other person is wrong or to blame. We are choosing to stay stuck in our own unhappiness and upset; we want to keep our grievance alive. We even choose to hang on to these stories long after the other person has passed. When we stay in this activity, it takes away any possibility of entering the Golden World. Some beautiful words from A Course in Miracles emphasise how important it is to release ourselves from this unhappy activity.

> **"The blood of hatred fades to let the grass grow green again,
> and let the flowers be all white and sparkling in the summer
> sun. What was once a place of death has now become a living
> temple in a world of light ... The holiest of all spots on earth
> is where an ancient hatred has become a present love."** (2)

These words leave no doubt about the power of letting go the grievances and negative stories we hold about other people, both alive and those who have passed. We need to do this primarily for ourselves; our grievances are blocking our entry to the Golden World. The fundamental importance of letting go our unhappy stories is confirmed by further words from A Course in Miracles.

> **"Forgiveness is the key to happiness"** (3)

Appendix to Chapter 8

Basic Fear in Relationships — The Worksheet
The worksheet can be used in any relationship where there is a recurring issue that continues to arise over a period of time.

1. Begin by filling in your type and the type of the other person. If you don't know their type, have a guess at what you think it might be. Then write in the Basic Fear and the Compensating Self-concept for yourself and for the other person. These words can be taken directly from Chapter Four.

2. Identify what you see as a recurring issue in the relationship and write it in the "Issue" box. It needs to be specific and practical. In the school example it was the forms; for the husband and wife it was his slipping away to go to concerts at the last minute. Issues like "we don't communicate very well" are not specific enough to work with.

3. Define what you see is causing you to be upset in the relationship and why your upset is justified. Write this in the "Activated Position" box. For the teachers at the school it was the lack of acknowledgement from the headmaster and his harsh way of exerting his authority. Try to do the same for the other person. You may have to speculate about what is upsetting them, but most likely the other person has told you what it is. Come to some conclusion as to what their activated position is? For the headmaster it was the challenge to his authority in the teachers not filling out the forms.

4. The important part of the exercise is to see the connection between the Activated Position and the Basic Fear and Compensating Self-concept for both parties. For the teachers, their Basic Fear of being "unloved and unwanted" was being triggered by the harsh behaviour of the headmaster. The lack of recognition from the

headmaster for their selfless work with the students challenged their Compensating Self-concept. For the headmaster, his Basic Fear "of being harmed by others" was being triggered by the uncooperative behaviour of the teachers. This behaviour also challenged the idea that he was "strong and in control".

5. The worksheet is intended to give a bigger perspective on the recurring issue and why both parties continue to be triggered. Hopefully the use of the worksheet introduces some understanding and compassion into what is happening. Just seeing it laid out on paper is often helpful.

6. As an adjunct to the worksheet, it is also helpful to complete the meditation, *Behind the Challenging Interaction,* included in this chapter.

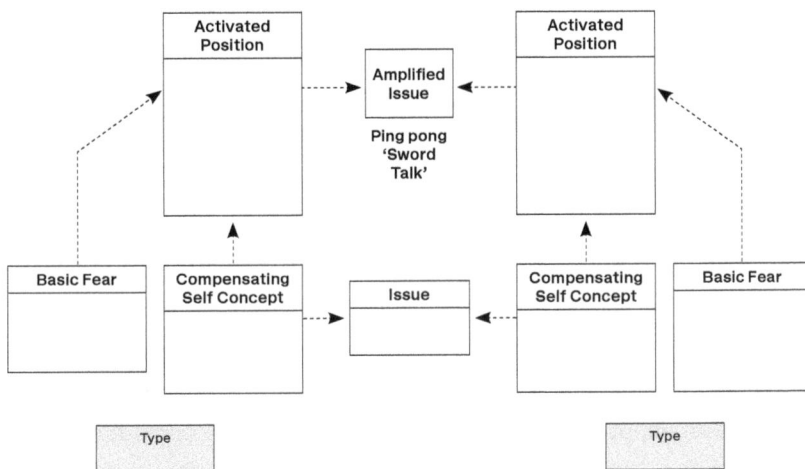

CHAPTER 9

The Challenges and Opportunities in Close Relationships

And stand together yet not too near together:
For the pillars of the temple stand apart,
And the oak tree and the cypress grow not in
each other's shadow. — Kahlil Gibran

Some years ago, a client, Marie, was describing the early years of her marriage. She had met her husband in her early twenties and was married soon after. The first two years of the marriage had been reasonably happy, but then the usual challenges began to arise. The relationship slowly got worse and reached a point where she had decided to leave. But then she decided to try an experiment. She wondered what would happen if, for three months, she was considerate and kind to her partner, regardless of what was arising. Not surprisingly, the relationship began to improve. Her partner responded to her kindness, and they began to enjoy being together. Twenty-five years later, they were still together.

I found her account quite surprising. It was so different to the many relationship stories I had heard. Surely there was more to saving a marriage than one of the partners deciding to be "considerate and kind". But, over time, I began to appreciate the wisdom of her little experiment. In close relationships, we are provided with an extraordinary opportunity to see how we respond when we are triggered by our partners. We have the choice of reacting in the habitual way and trying to get relief from the discomfort. Or we can 'sit on the steps' and feel the discomfort in our bodies. If we react in the habitual way, our reaction will almost certainly provoke a similar reaction from our partner. And we will then react to our partner's reaction, and so on. We get caught in the same game of ping-pong that happened with the teachers and the headmaster at the school. Each time we react and hit the ball back, we move down the Levels of Health, and so do our partners. We are locked into a sad dance, and we move down the Levels of Health together.

Both partners are blaming each other for the discomfort and pain they are feeling. Of course, the discomfort they are feeling is coming from within themselves; they would be having similar feelings of angst and dissatisfaction regardless of whom they were with. As part of the denial, they convince themselves that they would be better off with another partner. They leave the relationship and go looking for another partner. More often than not, the same thing happens again. The pity is that they continue to miss the opportunity to explore the underlying discomfort in themselves and bring it into awareness.

Whether through good luck, or her own inner wisdom, the little three-month experiment undertaken by Marie proved to be an effective way of not blaming her partner for her unhappiness and discomfort. Regardless of what was arising for her, she responded with consideration and kindness. This interrupted the downward spiral of reactivity, and both partners began to appreciate the things that had bought them together in the first place. Marie's three-month experiment serves a similar purpose to The Basic Fear Worksheet in the previous chapter. It breaks the cycle of reactivity and gives both partners a bigger perspective on the relationship. The worksheet has the added benefit of showing the pervasive and negative impact of Basic Fear on the way we relate. It reminds us that when we are triggered, our Basic Fear, or some other unconscious pain, has been activated. We think the discomfort we are feeling is being caused by our partners, and we blame it on them. In fact, the discomfort is coming from within us. All they are doing is reminding us of our Basic Fear and the difficult experiences of the past. And the same thing is occurring for our partners. Their Basic Fear is interacting with our Basic Fear. As Eckhart Tolle pointed out:

> **"Relationships don't cause us pain. They remind us of the pain that is already there."**

The unique opportunity being provided in our close relationships is that we are repeating the same dynamic with our partners on a regular basis. If we don't catch the lesson the first time, there may be another ten chances in the same day to see what's happening. And fortunately, in most cases, there are reasons why we can't easily leave the relationship. Effectively, we are locked in the classroom until we learn the lesson. It is our best chance to see that the discomfort we are feeling is coming from within. And if we stay with the discomfort, the difficult contents in our unconscious will, in time, be revealed and freed.

The Ways We Relate in Close Relationships

It is possible to take the exploration of relationships further with a short questionnaire, *The Ways We Relate in Close Relationships*. The questionnaire is based partly on the work of Collins (1) who developed the Adult Attachment Scale. It also incorporates insights from the Enneagram and the importance of Basic Fear in relationships. The questionnaire is included as an appendix at the end of this chapter. It is recommended that you take ten minutes to complete the questionnaire and calculate your scores. Alternatively, you can go online to the Enneagram Academy website and complete the questionnaire there (www.enneagramacademy.com). Your scores will be calculated and sent to you.

The questionnaire will give you two scores about the way you relate. The two dimensions being measured are:

1. *Wanting Less* This is a measure of the extent to which you:

- avoid being emotionally close and intimate with others, and,

- avoid depending on others and having them depend on you.

2. *Wanting More* This is a measure of the extent to which you feel you want more in relationships evidenced by a need for reciprocity, reassurance and security.

Your scores can be plotted on the chart below. The scores will be between one and five with the midpoint of the scale being three. The horizontal axis shows an increasing tendency towards avoiding closeness and dependence and valuing independence. It has been labelled *Wanting Less*. The vertical axis shows an increasing tendency towards wanting reassurance, reciprocity and security in relationships. It is labelled *Wanting More*. These two dimensions are the basis of the Four Quadrants of Relating.

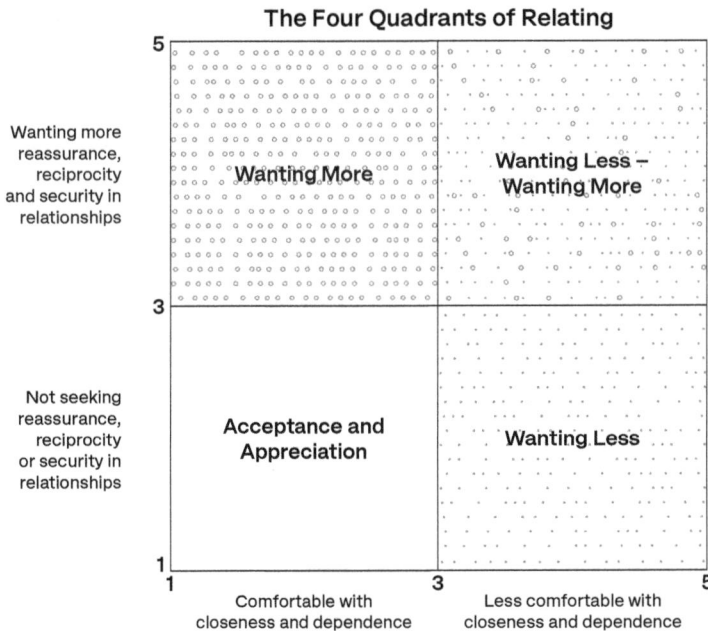

The Four Quadrants of Relating

Wanting more reassurance, reciprocity and security in relationships	**Wanting More** / **Wanting Less – Wanting More**
Not seeking reassurance, reciprocity or security in relationships	**Acceptance and Appreciation** / **Wanting Less**

5 — 3

1

1 — 3 — 5

Comfortable with closeness and dependence — Less comfortable with closeness and dependence

Some Observations about Your Scores

You will probably find that your scores change over time, depending on what is happening in your relationships and in your life. If you have recently experienced relationship difficulties or breakdown, your scores are likely to be higher, possibly on both dimensions. You might also find that your scores will be influenced by the relationship that is most important to you at the time of taking the questionnaire. However, the questionnaire is also designed to measure your general way of relating over time, as well as how you relate in a particular relationship or circumstance.

It might be expected that your Enneagram type will also influence your scores. So far there is not enough data to support any clear correlations between scores and Enneagram type. However, I have seen plenty of examples where scores are being strongly influenced by type. The Type Seven-Type Nine relationship discussed in the previous chapter is a good example. The Type Seven husband was involved with his classical music friends, often wanting to attend musical events, sometimes at the last minute. He sits clearly in the 'Wanting Less' quadrant, valuing his independence and wanting the freedom to spontaneously seek new experiences. It is likely that many other Sevens might be familiar with this quadrant, trying to escape from the fear of being trapped in pain. His Type Nine partner often felt disconnected and abandoned, particularly when he went off to these events at short notice. She sits in the 'Wanting More' quadrant, wanting reassurance and more connection with her partner. It is likely that many Nines are familiar with this quadrant; they want more connection as they seek to get away from the fear of being disconnected.

What is clear is that people at higher Levels of Health, score lower on both 'Wanting Less' and 'Wanting More'. They are accepting the relationship as it is. This observation, while consistently confirmed in practice, is hard to substantiate as there is no reliable measure of anyone's position on the Levels of Health.

Exploring the 'Wanting Less' Quadrant

Even though we might desire relationships that are close and mutually dependent, often we will find ways to subvert the intimacy we desire. We have built-up our protective shells, so we feel less vulnerable with other people. To get close to people, we need to let our protective barriers down. But this comes with significant risks. If we allow others to get too close, the risks are they might:

- do or say something that is threatening to us and trigger our Basic Fear or other unconscious content, or

- see through the protection we have in place and witness our fears, our inadequacies and the parts of ourselves we don't want them to see.

The prospect of both possibilities is threatening so we seek the safety of keeping others at a distance. We have a built-in sensor which tells us when the relationship is becoming too close. We then automatically begin to pull back. This feels good for a moment because we feel safer. But this pulling back is an escape; it takes us away from the opportunity for intimacy. It also removes the opportunity to explore what is concealed in the unconscious. In our pulling back, the protective shells have been strengthened and we move further into the 'Wanting Less' quadrant.

Moving Out of the 'Wanting Less' Quadrant

As we move up the Levels of Health, we will automatically, as a consequence move out of the 'Wanting Less' quadrant. Moving up the Levels of Health involves emptying out the difficult contents of the unconscious and we are left with less to conceal. We are less triggered by others, we have less to hide, and we are able to move closer to other people without feeling at risk. In fact, our willingness to move closer to others is a good measure of our progress up the Levels of Health.

There are two practices that will help us move out of the 'Wanting Less" quadrant towards greater levels of intimacy. They will also help us move up the Levels of Health. The first is a simple enquiry that you can do by yourself or with another person. Sit quietly and ask the question:

What do I do to create distance in my relationships?

You may find there are many patterns of behaviour that you use to keep distance from others. They are often quite subtle like steering the conversation away from topics that might be uncomfortable or not fully answering the other's questions. There will also be the more obvious things like working too hard or slipping into social media when you are with others. It is useful to have an inventory of your habits so you can get to know them. After a while you begin to see what you are doing and catch yourself in the act.

The second exercise is a little more challenging, but very powerful. Arrange with your partner to have a sharing session each month, preferably on the same day of each month, so it doesn't slip by. Each partner has ten minutes to share what's happening in their life and in the relationship. It's an opportunity to be really honest and reveal the things that may be difficult to share. The partner who is listening remains silent, particularly when the content is challenging for them. At the end of the ten minutes, both partners thank each other and then the roles are reversed. This is a wonderful exercise to provide a safe place for honest expression. It important not to have any follow-up discussions about what was said in the sharing, as this can quickly destroy the safety of the space being created.

Exploring the 'Wanting More' Quadrant

As small children we found objects that we incorporated into our identity. At the age of three, a young boy or girl might have strong identification with a truck or a doll. It is very clear in their minds that the truck or doll belongs to them. If another child tries to take it away, there is strong pushback: "This is my truck!" or "This is my doll!" The truck or the doll has become part of their world and part of their identity. The word 'my' expresses an extension of identity beyond the limits of the immediate self. As we progress through childhood, we continue to find objects and people to incorporate into our identity. Usually, they are things that will enhance or strengthen our identity. This is all part of healthy childhood development and the beginning of connections with outside objects and people.

As we grow older, our identification extends to things like cars, jobs, houses, family members, our children, and our partners. The strength of identification is revealed by the emotions and excitement when we add another object to our identity. It might be as simple as buying a much-fancied car. Our identity is enhanced by the purchase, and it feels good, at least for a day or two. Then the excitement subsides. We might still be grateful for the car, but the euphoria has faded; it is just a car. The excitement arises because our identity momentarily feels stronger by the addition of a shiny new car. It reassures us our identity is strong and secure.

When our identification extends to, and incorporates, other people, it can become challenging. There is a subtle line we cross when we move past friendship and incorporate others into our identity. We can become possessive. We create rules and expectations about how they should behave. We become quite indignant when *my* best friend or *my* child doesn't behave in a way that aligns with our expectations. It is one of the reasons why close relationships are often challenging. We have expectations that we would not hold for other people. We think we are entitled to hold these expectations because they are *my* family or *my* best friend. This is also true of partners, of course, where expectations can destroy an otherwise good relationship. One partner, or the other, decides that a new set of expectations and rules apply because now they are *my* partner. This comes as a surprise to their partner, who wonders what happened to the innocence and joy of their earlier relationship.

Our identity, and all the things that are part of it, build on our Compensating Self-concept. They all become part of 'who we think we are'. As we add things to our identity, it gets stronger, and we feel safer. We are strengthening the outer layer of the protective shells.

We no longer think of ourselves as just the limited idea of a person: the concept of ourselves has expanded to include all these other parts. And the more things we add, the safer we feel.

Our Basic Fear, and the other contents of the unconscious, get tucked away behind the outer shell, which is getting thicker as our identity develops. It feels safer, but we are becoming increasingly isolated from the three centres and from our true nature. We are trying to build an impenetrable fortress with the bricks of identity. We get anxious when the bricks aren't providing us with the reassurance and security we want. This underlines the urge to want more in our relationships. We want reassurance from our partners that the relationship is strong and is an indestructible part of our identity. Of course, it never can. We are trying to find reassurance in the relationship to relieve our own discomfort .... but regardless of how committed our partners are, we will never be completely reassured.

Cathexis

There is a psychological term, cathexis, which describes the investment of mental or emotional energy into one particular person, idea, or object. It comes from the Greek words, "I occupy," which points to its possessive quality. M. Scott Peck in *A Road Less Travelled* (2) discusses cathexis and how we cathect objects:

> Cathecting is the process by which an object becomes important
> to us. Once cathected, the object, commonly referred to as
> a 'love object', is invested with our energy as if it was part of
> ourselves, and this relationship between us and the invested
> object is called a cathexis.

Cathexis can apply to any object: a car, a pet, a child, a partner or a lover. Its defining aspect is that the object becomes "important to us" and we invest "our energy in it as if it was part of ourselves." It becomes part of our identity. It is a common part of everyday life and how we connect and relate to the world. We do it all the time in small ways. It can become more of a concern in our close relationships with friends, family, and partners. When we relate to others "as if they were part of ourselves" it can be confusing and possessive. In more serious cases, we can reach a point where we don't know 'where we end and the other begins'.

Cathexis and the 'Wanting More' Quadrant

Cathexis in our close relationships will lead to unrealistic expectations, attempts to control our partners, anxiety, disappointment, and frustration. It takes us further into the 'Wanting More' quadrant. The other person has become part of our identity and we become anxious about whether they are really committed to us. If our partner were to leave, not only would we lose a partner, we would also be losing part of ourselves. Hence, we feel threatened when the other person doesn't behave in a way that aligns with our expectations. Questions about their commitment begin to arise. These include questions like: "Do they really love me?", "Are they about to leave me?" or, "Do they feel the same way about me as I feel about them?" And so on. If these questions are arising, there is a high chance that cathexis has occurred. And of course, this leads to anxiety and insecurity. In some cases, the other partner will grow tired of the possessiveness and leave the relationship. Our insecurity and our anxiety have become a self-fulfilling reality.

Mild forms of cathexis probably exist in many close relationships. Peck said it can be confused with genuine love. The critical distinction between the two is whether our behaviour is motivated by our own interests, sometimes unconscious, or by a genuine concern for the interests of the other person. With genuine love we see our partners as they are, as independent, sovereign human beings, and not as an extension of our own identity. This is why the words from Kahlil Gibran are so relevant:

> And stand together yet not too near together:
> For the pillars of the temple stand apart,
> And the oak tree and the cypress grow not in each other's
> shadow.

Moving Out of the 'Wanting More' Quadrant

Moving out of the 'Wanting More' quadrant will also happen as we move up the Levels of Health. As we become healthier, we don't need to incorporate our partners into our extended identity, and we don't cathect our partners to make ourselves feel stronger. As a result, we will be less possessive and less anxious in our relationships.

A simple enquiry will help us move out of the 'Wanting More' quadrant. You can do it by yourself of with another person. Sit quietly and ask the question:

What are the ways I try to possess, control, or manipulate my partner?

Focus on the times when you feel anxious about the relationship. What do you do when questions about your partner's commitment arise? Are there attempts to control your partner's behaviour or to start asking them questions to get the reassurance you want? Do you go hunting for clues in their behaviour, seeking re-assurance that everything is okay? And when the re-assurance can't be found, do you jump to the worst possible conclusions? When you are anxious about the relationship, do you try to win their affection and commitment by doing things for them, being overly attentive or buying them gifts? The enquiry will give you a useful inventory of behaviours so you can get to know them. After a while, you will begin to see what you are doing and realise the limitations of relating in this way.

The 'Wanting Less - Wanting More' Quadrant

It might seem contradictory to be in the 'Wanting Less-Wanting More' quadrant. On one hand, we are wanting to create distance in our relationship, and at the same time, wanting more from the relationship. This is a confusing place to be, but it is probably more common than might be expected. In this quadrant, we feel we need more space in the relationship, because the intimacy is challenging our safety. But as we move away from the relationship, we become anxious about losing a reassuring part of our identity. So, we are tempted to move back to intimacy. It is a movement, backwards and forwards, between the threat of intimacy and the threat of solitude. When we have intimacy, we feel threatened and want solitude. When we have solitude, we feel threatened and want intimacy. And so, the dance of intimacy and solitude continues. And this is a dance that is familiar to many of us at some time in our lives.

The first step away from the 'Wanting Less-Wanting More' quadrant is to focus on the dimension with the highest score (either 'Wanting Less' or 'Wanting More'). To focus on both at the same time will perpetuate the confusion. Use the enquiry that has already been suggested for that dimension. Once you have worked with that dimension a few times, shift your focus to the other dimension.

Finding Your Partner in One of the Quadrants

If your partner is agreeable, it is very helpful if they complete *The Ways We Relate* questionnaire. Just seeing where both partners are located on the chart will be revealing; the underlying issues in the relationship will often become obvious. All the quadrant combinations are possible and so far, there is no research to show which are the most prevalent combinations. It is recommended that when both partners have located themselves on the chart, that you complete the Basic Fear in Relationships Worksheet from the previous chapter. This will give a good understanding of the impact of the Enneagram types on the relationship and the scores on the questionnaire.

One of the more challenging combinations is when one partner is in the 'Wanting Less' quadrant and the other partner is in the 'Wanting More' quadrant. This is a difficult combination for both partners and seems to be fairly common. As one partner tries to 'avoid closeness', the other partner responds by 'wanting more'. It has a self-perpetuating character to it. The more one partner 'wants more', the more the other partner will avoid closeness. And vice-versa.

It helps to understand this dynamic by locating both partners on the chart, because it makes it less personal. It also helps to remember that both partners are attempting to get away from the discomfort of their Basic Fear. The partner 'wanting more' is trying escape from their Basic Fear by bolstering their identity and covering over their Basic Fear with a more 'fulfilling' relationship. The partner 'wanting less' is trying to get space in the relationship so their Basic Fear won't be activated, and their inadequacies won't be exposed. If both partners can see the dynamic that is operating, they may choose to stay with their own discomfort and not blame it on their partner.

Mutual Cathexis and Romantic Love
A very interesting dynamic occurs when both partners are in the 'Wanting More' quadrant. On the surface, it would seem like the basis for a perfect partnership, and for a while it might feel like it is. Each partner is investing energy in the other "as if they were part of themselves." A mutual cathexis has occurred. The identity of each partner is being enhanced and strengthened by their connection with the other. And because both partners are 'wanting more', the cathexis gets stronger and stronger. The partners can lose themselves in the relationship; it gets to the point where they don't know where one partner ends and the other begins. There is an urge to get closer and closer and each movement closer feels exquisitely satisfying. The underlying Basic Fear is completely buried under the excitement of the union. The Basic Fear is still there of course, it just can't be felt for the moment. This psychological merging of identities can be amplified by sexual attraction and sexual connection, but this is not always part of it. The combination of merging with an idealised identity, the escape from Basic Fear and the pleasure of sexual connection is a potent cocktail. It is sometimes called the "love potion".

Mutual cathexis is more commonly known as romantic love or 'falling in love'. Inevitably, as most of us know, the fantasy cannot last. For a while, the idealised image of the other person drives the urge for "wanting more". Then something happens: one of the partners sees through the idealisation. They see the imperfections of their partner and realise they are in a relationship with an ordinary human being. The relationship is no longer covering over the pain of their Basic Fear, and they now blame this on the partner. When this happens, they will normally move quickly to the 'Wanting Less' quadrant. The relationship will often end dramatically, sometimes with enduring bitterness. It is not the loss of the partner that drives the bitterness; it is more the loss of an important part of their identity. Their anger at this loss is expressed in blame towards each other. Cathexis rarely ends gracefully.

In some cases, the relationship might continue but without the cathexis-based romance and excitement. The partners stay together, initially with regret and disappointment, mourning the passing of romantic love. But, with time, they might accept the realities of the relationship, and each other, and move towards compassionate, grounded human relating. Joseph Campbell (3) describes this possibility:

> Two people meet and fall in love. Then they marry, and the real
> Sam or Suzy begins to show through the fantasy, and, boy is it
> a shock. So a lot of little boys and girls just get a divorce and
> wait for another receptive person, pitch the woo again, and,
> uh-oh, another shock. And so on and so forth ... So what are you
> going to do when that happens? There's only one attitude that
> will solve the situation: compassion. This poor, poor fact that
> I married does not correspond to my ideal; it's only a human
> being. Well, I'm a human being too. So, I'll meet a human being
> for a change; I'll live with it and be nice to it...

These insights from Campbell confirm the experience of the woman, Marie, who decided to be kind and considerate to her partner for three months. It is a movement away from fantasy and thinking we will find comfort and relief in the relationship. The agenda falls away; we don't avoid closeness and we don't 'want more'. It is simple, innocent relating with another human being. This takes us to the final quadrant of relating, 'Acceptance and Appreciation'.

The 'Acceptance and Appreciation' Quadrant

As discomfort and frustration arise in a relationship, we are tempted to do one of two things to get relief:

- we can move away from the relationship to get away from what we think is causing the discomfort. In doing this, we move further into the 'Wanting Less' quadrant, or,

- we can decide that the relationship is not providing the comfort that we want or deserve; our partner should be doing more to support us. Again, we think that our discomfort is caused by our partner; they should be doing something that they're not doing, or they should stop doing something they are doing. We are shifting the blame for our discomfort on to them. In doing this, we move further into the 'Wanting More' quadrant.

Neither of these responses is helpful. They might provide some momentary relief, but they quickly take us into the downward spiral of reactivity. The only alternative is to own our own discomfort. And to do this we need to:

- own each fear, disappointment and grief as they arise,

- feel the discomfort in the body,

- avoid trying to escape, diminish, ignore or reframe the discomfort, and,

- be curious about the discomfort and know it offers the potential for freedom.

With this, we move into the 'Acceptance and Appreciation' quadrant. This is where we can experience undefended love where neither partner is making the other responsible for their frustration and discomfort. There is no agenda for the relationship or how it should look. There is a gentle appreciation and enjoyment of each other. And as we move into this quadrant, we also move up the Levels of Health.

Joseph Campbell (2) described this simple kind of human related-ness as "stirring-the-oatmeal love":

> Stirring oatmeal is a humble act - not exciting or thrilling. But it symbolises a relatedness that brings love down to earth. It represents a willingness to share ordinary human life, to find meaning in the simple, unromantic tasks: earning a living, living within a budget, putting out the garbage, feeding the baby in the middle of the night. To "stir the oatmeal" means to find the relatedness, the value, even the beauty, in simple and ordinary things, not to eternally demand a cosmic drama, and entertainment, or an extraordinary intensity in everything. It is the discovery of the sacred in the midst of the humble and the ordinary.

The beauty in these quiet moments of human relatedness is the same beauty described at the beginning of Chapter One. We are experienc-ing the divine energies of our own true nature. We are reminded of their existence by the simple beauty we experience in our partners. They resonate together and remind us of the exquisite beauty within. There is a simplicity and innocence in these moments.

This possibility is described by Jett Psaris and Marlena S. Lyons in their book *Undefended Love* (4):

> Slowly the hardened layers of our defence systems are peeled away and dissolved, and the walls between us become even thinner. As we become more exposed, we become more illuminated in the glow of our essential self and revel in the glow of our partner's beauty.

These words remind us that we can use relationships to allow our pro-tective shells to be dismantled. And as we do, we return to the experi-ence of the three centres. "We become illuminated in the glow of our essential self", a good description of our return to the Golden World.

Four Quadrants of Relating – Questionnaire

Please read each of the following statements and rate the extent to which it describes your feelings about close relationships. Please think about all your relationships (past and present) and respond in terms of how you generally feel in these relationships.

Please use the scale below by placing a number between 1 and 5 to the right of each statement in the column headed 'Raw Score'.

1 ——————— 2 ——————— 3 ——————— 4 ——————— 5
Not at all characteristic of me   Very characteristic of me

		RAW SCORE	ADJUSTED SCORE
1.	I find it relatively easy to get close to people.	_____	® □
2.	I find it difficult to allow myself to depend on others.	_____	□
3.	I often worry that partners don't really love me.	_____	◯
4.	I find that others are reluctant to get as close as I would like.	_____	◯
5.	I am comfortable having partners depend on me.	_____	® □
6.	I don't worry about people getting too close to me.	_____	® □
7.	I often feel my partners could be more emotionally available.	_____	◯
8.	I am somewhat uncomfortable being close to others.	_____	□
9.	I often worry that partners won't want to stay with me.	_____	◯
10.	When I show my feelings for others, I'm afraid they will not feel the same about me.	_____	◯
11.	I often wonder whether partners really care about me.	_____	◯
12.	I am comfortable developing close relationships with others.	_____	® □
13.	I am uncomfortable when anyone gets too emotionally close to me.	_____	□
14.	I often feel my partners could be more committed.	_____	◯
15.	I want to get close to people, but I worry about being hurt.	_____	◯
16.	I find it difficult to trust others completely.	_____	□
17.	Partners often want me to be emotionally closer than I feel comfortable being.	_____	□
18.	I often feel fulfilled in my relationships.	_____	® ◯

Calculation of Scores   □ WL   ◯ WM

Totals _____   _____

÷ 9 □   □

5	1
4 ® →	2
3	3
2	4
1	5

Adapted from the *Revised Adult Attachment Scale (Collins, 1996)*

Four Quadrants of Relating
Notes on Calculating Your Scores

1. Enter your Raw Scores in the column immediately
    to the right of the questions.

2. Transfer your scores to the column on the right-hand side
    of the page headed 'Adjusted Score'. For some questions
    (Questions 1, 5, 6, 12 and 18) you will notice a small ® beside the
    scoring box. For these questions you need to adjust your scores.
    A Raw Score of '5' becomes an Adjusted Score of '1',
    a '4' becomes a '2', a '3' remains as a '3',
    a '2' becomes a '4' and a '1' becomes a '5'.

3. Add up the Adjusted Scores in the rectangles (▭) and divide
    the total by 9. (There are 9 questions.). This is your score for
    Wanting Less (WL).

4. Add up the Adjusted Scores in the ovals (◯), divide the total by 9.
    This is your score for Wanting More (WM).

5. Plot your scores on The Four Quadrants of Relating chart.

PART II

OUR RETURN TO THE GOLDEN WORLD

Jason sailed through the Clashing Rocks into the sea of marvels, circumvented the dragon that guarded the Golden Fleece and returned with the fleece and the power to wrest his rightful throne from a usurper. — Joseph Campbell

For us, the Golden Fleece that Jason sought, is our reconnection with the three centres and our return to the Golden World. Before we embark on our journey, we need a map of the difficult terrain through which we will pass. In Chapters Ten and Eleven we explore the unconscious, and the challenging aspects of ourselves we might meet there. In Chapter Twelve we discover the healing qualities of the psyche and the inherent urge within all of us to move towards wholeness and freedom. In Chapter Thirteen the journey begins.

CHAPTER 10

Exploring the Unconscious

Until you make the unconscious conscious, it will direct
your life, and you will call it fate. — Carl Jung

Psyche is the Greek word for soul. Hence, psychology is the study of
the soul. This is an exciting and expansive vision of what psychology
could be. In recent decades, however, psychology seems to have for-
feited this grand vision. It has narrowed its focus to more pragmatic
goals such as improving ways of thinking or finding ways to amelio-
rate the challenges of life. While these goals are not without value,
let's return to the original mandate for psychology, the study of the
soul. We commence with some of the discoveries of the pioneering
psychologists of the past.

Freud and Jung
In the early days of their collaboration at the beginning of the last
century, Freud and Jung, separately and together, recognised the importance of the unconscious. They both believed that the contents of
the unconscious were the cause of neurosis or derangement in their
patients. They believed that the unconscious contained the difficult
experiences, traumas, and unwanted aspects of earlier life. They had
been placed in the unconscious because they had been too difficult
or overwhelming to deal with at the time they occurred. They had

strong associations with grief so there was a natural avoidance to bring them into awareness. In most cases, they remained in the unconscious, with no willingness or capacity to bring them into consciousness.

Freud and Jung found that by establishing a container of trust, their patients could begin to talk, and in time, express their difficult feelings. As the patients became more aware of their unconscious fears and traumas, the need to repress them lessened. There was less need to depend on their neurotic coping strategies and the patients began to recover. Their approach to treating patients became known as "the talking cure". Their goal was to reduce the severity of the patient's neuroses, at least to the extent that the patient could lead a reasonably normal, functioning life. It was a partial cure, but it worked. It also confirmed their suspicions that the neuroses they observed in their patients were caused by 'the wilful suppression' of unconscious content.

There was a famous case of a woman being treated by Jung who had been institutionalised for many years. It was assumed that she was beyond help and any attempts at treatment had ceased many years before. She roamed the wards of the hospital repeating statements like, "Naples and I together will supply the world with spaghetti." [1] The constant and repetitive babbling was the woman's way of keeping the painful content of the past concealed.

Jung became curious and began treating her simply by being with her and listening with empathy and compassion to what she was saying. Jung was greatly encouraged by her words because he felt behind the derangement there was 'another woman' longing to participate in the activities of life. She began to improve, and an authentic connection developed between them. While the woman didn't recover completely, Jung continued to treat her for many years and recognised her as one of the important cases in his career.

This case demonstrated to Jung that, even in extreme cases, the encouragement to release suppressed unconscious content could be the basis for healing the psyche. And this could be achieved by establishing a container of trust for the patient to speak freely. As the patient was able to bring their unconscious and disowned content into their conscious awareness, they, of their own accord, would slowly move to wholeness. There was nothing left to suppress.

Moving Towards Wholeness

We try to move towards wholeness and peace by removing the memories of painful experiences, or by eliminating the parts of ourselves we see as unworthy or undesirable. We do this by placing these memories and unwanted aspects in the unconscious and then trying to ensure they never come into consciousness. However, the attempts to find wholeness actually create separation. We pick out the parts of ourselves we are comfortable with, or approve of, and hope that this is 'who we are'. We want to get rid of the rest. How could we feel whole or at peace when we are only accepting part of ourselves? The parts of us that we don't accept become a seething cauldron of disowned pain and discomfort concealed in the unconscious, but which will inevitably leak into consciousness.

We need to reverse this process and bring back into consciousness all our disowned aspects. This is the last thing we really want to do. We have spent a lifetime trying to rid ourselves of this unwelcome content, but we now need to recover it. The task is made harder by the unconscious nature of the material. We don't know what is in the unconscious. It is mysterious and unknown, and it can only be explored indirectly. It requires constant and persistent curiosity. Our behaviour, particularly when we are out-of-control and irrational, is an outer manifestation of the unconscious content within. Irritation and frustration are valuable windows to the unconscious. It can also be accessed through dreams, therapies, meditations, and other activities when the rational part of the mind is no longer in charge. And from the work of Freud and Jung, and the many depth psychologists that followed, there is a much greater understanding of what is contained in the unconscious and how it got there.

The Four Levels of Unconscious Content

There are many ways difficult content finds its way into the unconscious. At the deepest level, Basic Fear is the all-pervading sense of separation and inadequacy that has been there since birth. The other levels of content are then laid down on this foundation. The different levels of unconscious content are shown in the diagram below.

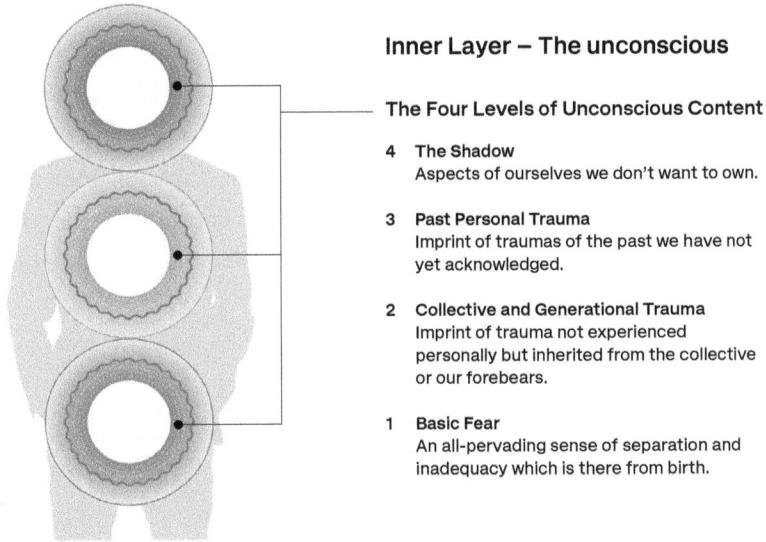

Inner Layer – The unconscious

The Four Levels of Unconscious Content

4   The Shadow
    Aspects of ourselves we don't want to own.

3   Past Personal Trauma
    Imprint of traumas of the past we have not yet acknowledged.

2   Collective and Generational Trauma
    Imprint of trauma not experienced personally but inherited from the collective or our forebears.

1   Basic Fear
    An all-pervading sense of separation and inadequacy which is there from birth.

Basic Fear

Our Basic Fear is profoundly troubling as it challenges the worth of who we are. As it is such a central part of the unconscious, it is worth revisiting the nine Basic Fears:

Type One	Fear of being flawed or defective
Type Two	Fear of being unloved and unwanted
Type Three	Fear of being worthless
Type Four	Fear of having no personal significance
Type Five	Fear of being helpless and unable to find a place in the world
Type Six	Fear of having no support or guidance and being unable to survive alone
Type Seven	Fear of being deprived or trapped in pain

| Type Eight | Fear of being harmed or controlled by others |
| Type Nine | Fear of being disconnected and cut off from everything including love |

Basic Fear is the core belief through which we experience life; we believe in some inadequacy about ourselves. When we experience life's challenges, it reinforces our feelings of inadequacy and makes our Basic Fear stronger. For example, a Type Two child has the underlying belief, 'I am unloved and unwanted'. If the child experiences adversity with a parent, the pain they experience will reinforce the belief that they are unloved and unwanted. Not only will the experience be painful in its own right, it will also compound the grief around the Basic Fear. Basic Fear is the foundational grief to which the other pain is added.

Collective and Generational Trauma

The next deepest level of unconscious content is challenging to understand and to recognise. Collective and generational trauma is something we have not experienced personally. It includes the trauma experienced by the collective but is present in us. In countries that have been ravaged by many decades or centuries of war, we can feel that deep sadness and grief in the people, even when the wars have been over for many years. The trauma might not have been experienced by the current generation, but they still manifest the wounds. It is embedded in the national psyche. Likewise, in our own families, the grief experienced by our forebears will be passed on through generations. We can have strong experiences of this grief while knowing that it hasn't happened to us. If each generation responds to inherited grief in unhealthy ways, it will be passed on to their children and to the generations to come. This passing forward of inherited grief is sometimes referred to as "the chain of pain". This is sometimes evident with things like alcohol where, in some families, the dysfunctional behaviour of addiction is passed down from each generation to the next.

Past Personal Trauma

The content in the next level of the unconscious results from diffi-cult personal experiences. It starts with our experiences as a baby, which can be confusing and traumatic. The trauma can be small and accidental. For example, we want sustenance or connection from our mother, but she is not available, so we feel disconnected. If the non-availability is constant or there is actual abuse, then the trauma will be significant. As we move into childhood and beyond, we continue to experience the traumas of life. Some seem small and others large and overwhelming (for example, physical, sexual, and emotional abuse, the death of a sibling or parent, a divorce, the end of a rela-tionship, and so on).

> As these things occur, we are often unable to be with
> the grief as it is arising.

The psyche reverts to the inbuilt protection mechanisms that allow these overwhelming experiences to be stored in the unconscious. Hopefully, they will be looked at again when we have the time, the sup-port and capacity to bring them back into consciousness. This rarely happens, however, and we continue through life accumulating more difficult and unexamined content in the unconscious. These memories remain repressed but active, and often grow stronger over time.

Adverse Childhood Experiences (The ACE Study)

There is ample research about difficult childhood experiences and the ongoing impact they have on a person's later life. One of the largest and continuing studies is the *Adverse Childhood Experiences* (ACE) study first published in 1998. Adverse Childhood Experienc-es are defined as,

> ... emotional, physical, or sexual abuse, emotional or physical
> neglect, and growing up in a household where someone was an
> alcoholic, a drug user, mentally ill, suicidal, or where the mother
> was treated violently, or where a household member had been
> imprisoned during the person's childhood. (2)

The study identified ten possible adverse experiences that would contribute to a difficult childhood. Each of these adverse factors is counted as one experience, and a person's score is determined by the number of these experiences encountered before the age of eighteen. The ACE test is included as an appendix at the end of this chapter and involves answering 'yes' or 'no' to ten questions about the ten possible adverse experiences.

Some of the more notable findings of the study were, that compared to persons with an ACE score of zero:

> **Those with an ACE score of four or more were twice as likely to be smokers, five times more likely to experience depression, seven times more likely to be alcoholics, ten times more likely to have injected street drugs, and twelve times more likely to have attempted suicide.**

The most sobering of all the findings is that 64% of the US prison population had an ACE score of six or more. (3) The study also demonstrates the cumulative effect of each adverse experience. A child who has one or two adverse experiences will be affected but the consequences will be less pronounced. Each additional adversity adds to the likelihood of grief-related consequences later in life.

These are very significant findings that prove beyond doubt the profound impact of childhood trauma. Each of the adverse experiences will be strongly associated with pain and grief for the child. In most cases, the grief will remain in the unconscious for the rest of their lives unless they can bring it into consciousness. It is this internalised grief that the child will carry forward into adult life that causes so much suffering and angst.

Vigilant Self-care

In Chapter 1 we identified how childhood trauma can have a profound impact on the development of the child. It is useful to revisit those ideas here:

Some insightful words from depth psychology highlight the profound impact of trauma, particularly in childhood: "With trauma play ends, and vigilant self-care begins." Children exposed to trauma lose their trust in existence. They no longer believe that the world is a safe or benevolent place. Therefore, they must take care of themselves — vigilant self-care. For them, vigilant self-care involves the premature development of strong coping strategies that cut them off from normal connections with the world and from the joys of life. Protecting themselves from further trauma becomes their priority and their protective shells become strong. They become disheartened and dispirited, as well as isolated from their feelings and the three centres. They are far removed from the experience of the Golden World.

They move to the lower Levels of Health of their Enneagram type and will want to stay there. Thus, childhood trauma can have devastating impacts on children for the rest of their lives; vigilant self-care becomes their life long priority.

The words above can be altered a little to make them relevant to all of us:

"With challenges and disappointments, play ends and vigilant self-care begins."

As we move through childhood and into adulthood, we seem to lose our ability to play, and become preoccupied with vigilant self-care. It is evident in the way adults play games that are meant to be for pleasure but have become serious and competitive affairs, devoid of any fun, spontaneity, or joy. It also shows in the way we, as parents, interact with our children. We could join with our children in playing games, but mostly we are too preoccupied with the challenges of parenthood and keeping our children safe. We live our lives from a position of vigilant self-care, and without trust in the benevolence of existence. We develop coping strategies which cut us off from existence and from our own being. It is the way to become 'grumpy old men and women.' As we focus on vigilant self-care, our experience of life becomes increasingly limited and dissatisfying. The joy of life can become a distant and foreign experience.

*   *   *   *

Trauma with a Little 't'

The ACE study is focused on children who have endured significant adverse experiences. This kind of trauma is sometimes referred to as big trauma or trauma with a capital T. Many of us may not rate on the ACE scale at all or, if we do, have low scores of one or two. However, most of us have had experiences throughout our lives that have been traumatic. They can include the trauma of absent, angry, or neglectful parents, the heartbreaks around loss of family, friends, pets, and other things we value. They can also be incidents of bullying, intimidation, exclusion, rejection, withdrawal, or the absence of love and support. For children, and even for adults, these experiences are hurtful, painful, and traumatic. They are sometimes referred to as trauma with a little 't'. (4) This trauma, while sometimes less obvious, can be destructive. Its classification as trauma with a little 't' should not be used as a reason to discount its importance.

The Inner Child

The difficult experiences we have as children, particularly with our parents, are acknowledged as having a profound impact on what is known as our Inner Child. Our Inner Child is a concept that represents the innocent state of the childhood psyche. If parents are abusive, angry, or never present, the person will have traumatic memories of these experiences that erode the innocence of their Inner Child. This abuse and absence of love results in what has been called the wounded Inner Child. These experiences are associated with strong feelings of confusion, grief, shame, and abandonment. The child struggles to make sense of them and often takes responsibility for the bad behaviour of the adults. The child blames themselves for what has happened, and this compounds the shame that they feel. They certainly don't have the capacity to deal with the experience in any conscious way. As a result, we don't want to bring the Inner Child into our conscious awareness. We don't want to experience the grief of those memories; they would be overwhelming and too much for us to handle. We would prefer to block it out completely and, in some cases, eliminate all memory of our childhood.

The wounded Inner Child is a useful metaphor that allows us to access the unacknowledged hurt that might still reside in the unconscious because of long-forgotten childhood experiences. There are simple processes that allow us to dialogue with our Inner Child. They allow the grief to be accessed in a gradual and safe way, so it does not become overwhelming. The processes also allow us to see what happened in those earlier experiences and to release ourselves from any misguided idea that we, as a child, were responsible for what happened.

The Shadow

'The shadow' is closest to the surface of the unconscious and contains the unwanted and disowned aspects of ourselves. Even in childhood, there were parts of ourselves that were not welcomed or approved of by our parents. Life went more smoothly when we repressed those aspects of ourselves and hid them in the unconscious. As we grew older, we had similar experiences with our friends and family, and in work relationships. We adapted to these messages from the world so we would be more acceptable and less threatening to other people. The shadow includes anything that is incompatible or inconsistent with the identity and persona we want to present.

We keep these unwanted aspects hidden in the unconscious. It can include aspects that we see as extremely unattractive. Our inclination to be selfish, wilful, unfeeling, controlling, and even stronger negative aspects can be found there. The more negative we think these aspects are, the more difficult it is for these aspects to be acknowledged and owned. As they are ignored or denied they will become stronger and more disruptive. It is often not until these aspects suddenly manifest in our behaviour that we have any idea that they are there. When we see behaviour oscillating between two extremes, as with Dr Jekyll and Mr Hyde, we usually know the shadow is involved. We are struggling to maintain an image of ourselves, but the disowned aspects of ourselves eventually break through. They can manifest in our behaviour in embarrassing and disruptive ways.

The shadow is supported and made larger by our ongoing scrutiny and judgement of our own behaviour. We have strong ideas about our inadequacies and shortcomings. This ongoing process of self-judgement is not helpful; it puts more unwanted content into the unconscious. Neil Donald Walsch offered some insight into this tendency towards self-judgement when he said:

> "Mastery is not measured by the number of terrible things you eliminate from your life, but by the number of times you eliminate calling them terrible."

The great price of concealment in the shadow is that we often remove and suppress the vital energies of life. Emotions like anger cannot be acknowledged and so we hide them. We then sit in frustration, hiding behind the meaningless mask we have made for ourselves. Our life becomes inauthentic and meaningless. As we grow older, we can become grumpy and bitter. We live behind a mask and struggle to have genuine heartfelt connection with anyone. We also spend significant energy trying to keep the mask in place. The work is to bring these unwanted aspects of ourselves back into consciousness — to claim our disowned parts. When there is nothing to hide there is no need to keep the mask in place.

Terminology — 'The Shadow'

The word "shadow" can be used in two ways. The first is the way it is used above, namely the aspects of ourselves that we don't want to own and that we have relegated to the unconscious. It can also be used in a much broader way to refer to all the contents of the unconscious. The phrase 'doing shadow work' usually means working with all the contents of the unconscious. We will continue to use the word in its narrow and specific sense of disowned aspects.

The Pain Inside

Each level of the unconscious can contain unconscious pain and grief. Sometimes the grief is related to just one level, but more often the various experiences of grief become connected in the unconscious. Hence the grief surrounding Basic Fear coalesces with memories of difficult childhood experiences. This can make it more difficult to identify the specific source of our pain; it can feel like a pool of amorphous grief that is just there and is difficult to feel. This pool of inner pain will be referred to as *the pain inside*. This is a simple label, but it gives insights into much of our behaviour. When we are triggered and begin to behave in defensive or reactive ways, we are wanting to get away from the *pain inside*. Our addictive behaviours are the ways we try to escape from, or alleviate, the *pain inside*. We keep returning to our addictions because they allow us to get away from the pain, even though the relief they provide is only temporary and often comes at a high price.

Eckhart Tolle talks about the pain-body, which he defines as "an accumulation of old emotional pain" that arises because of the human tendency to perpetuate old emotions. (5) This is a similar concept to the *pain inside*. He suggests that the pain-body is like a separate entity that requires food and periodically comes out to feed: "Any emotionally painful experience can be used as food by the pain-body. That's why it thrives on negative thinking as well as drama in relationships. The pain-body is an addiction to unhappiness."

Whether we call it the *pain inside* or the pain-body doesn't matter. Both concepts support and reinforce each other. They remind us that we all have pain within, and that our worst behaviour is an outer manifestation of inner pain. When we are hurt, we do things that we normally would not do. This is sometimes described as "the pain speaking". Most dysfunctional or cruel behaviour comes from people struggling with their own inner pain. It might come from some inner justification: if I am hurting, then it doesn't matter if I hurt other people. Maybe it provides some relief or distraction from their own pain. This behaviour can be summed up in two words: hurt hurts.

The sad consequence is that the pain and trauma keep being passed forward. The victims of trauma inflict further trauma on the people closest to them, particularly their children. The chain of pain continues. This underlies how important it is for all of us to do our own work and do what we can to release our own pain. We can break the chain, but it requires insight to see how our pain is causing pain for others. It is easy to see the pain in others; it is much more difficult to see it and own it in ourselves.

*   *   *   *

The Deeper Levels of the Unconscious – The Collective Unconscious

The four levels of the unconscious discussed so far are consistent with the thinking of Freud and Jung in the years of their collaboration. For Freud, this was about as far as he was prepared to go. However, Jung was finding there were deeper parts of the unconscious. He realised that with Freud he had been working with the negative content of the personal unconscious. Jung now discovered something which was much more inspiring and redemptive. He called it the collective unconscious because the contents were not personal but were shared by all humanity.

Jung saw that it offered the opportunity for complete healing and transformation of the psyche. His exploration began a period of many years of deep introspection that was his own journey into the depths of his unconscious. At times he felt he was bordering on the edge of insanity. What he discovered was revolutionary.

Hidden beneath the contents of the personal unconscious were the archetypes, the fundamental patterns of being that have been stamped on to the soul as part of the evolution of the human species. They have been encoded into the human psyche by hundreds and thousands of years of human experience. These patterns of thoughts and instincts are inherited and guide much of our behaviour. They manifest in the images that arise in the myths and stories of all tribes and civilisations and commonly appear spontaneously in our dreams. Jung was awed by the magnitude of his discovery. He felt his earlier work on the personal unconscious, and its negative content, "dwindled into insignificance beside his revelation" of what lay beneath it. (6)

And going further into the collective unconscious, past the archetypes of evolution, Jung discovered what we have been referring to as the three centres. He found the archetype of the divine, the experience of oneself as part of the One. He referred to this as the Self — the deep connection with the natural order and the expansion of the psyche to see itself as part of something much bigger. As he experienced these energies, he had the realisation that we are, indeed, part of God. This represented a profound change in his understanding of the unconscious. With Jung's insights, we can now see the unconscious as a healing and nourishing partner with consciousness. (7) His realisation was that,

> the psyche rests on a fundamental structure and this
> structure is able to withstand the shocks and abandonment
> and betrayal which threaten to undo a person's mental
> stability and emotional balance. This was the discovery of
> a deep, largely unconscious pattern of psychological unity
> and wholeness. (8)

The Healing Energies of the Divine

The energies of the divine are available to all of us. Jung was asked late in his life whether he believed in God. He answered "no," but after a pause, he added, "I know God." I believe he was referring to his experiences with the divine energies deep in the collective unconscious. On another occasion he said,

> I cannot define for you what God is. I can only say that my work
> has proved empirically that the pattern of God exists in every
> man, and that this pattern has at its disposal the greatest of all
> energies for transformation and transfiguration of his natural
> being. (9)

Jung's willingness to be with the negative contents of the personal unconscious led him to the redemptive and divine energies of the collective unconscious. He had found what we have been calling the Golden World. He had shown that we need to travel through the difficult energies of the personal unconscious to get to the divine. This parallels the journey described in Dante's *Divine Comedy*, where the beatific vision was only realised after the passage through hell and purgatory.

Jung's work gives us the reassurance to know that the energies of God are already within us. There is no need to put concepts around this; it is an experience available to everyone. We must remember that there is an infinite source of energy available to us for our own healing. We don't have to go through the extraordinary anguish that Jung experienced in his discovery. We also don't necessarily need the full-blown experience often associated with spiritual awakening. We can move towards freedom in a steady way, trusting those energies are there and allowing them to flow through us.

*   *   *   *

The unconscious is the terrain through which we need to pass to return to the Golden World. We need to discover and accept the parts of ourselves that reside in the unconscious. This gives an expanded and specific meaning to the instruction: 'Know thyself'. We must get to know the parts of ourselves we don't want to know. This is the most challenging and most important thing we can do in our lifetime. This is how we heal the *pain inside*. This is our Call to Adventure and our return to freedom.

Appendix to Chapter 10

Adverse Childhood Experiences (ACE) Survey
Please answer 'yes' or 'no' to the following ten questions.

Prior to your 18th birthday:

1. Did a parent or other adult in the household, often or very often ...

    Swear at you, insult you, put you down?
    or
    Humiliate you or act in a way that made you afraid that you might be physically hurt?

2. Did a parent or other adult in the household often or very often ...

    Push, grab, slap, or throw something at you? or

    Ever hit you so hard that you had marks or were injured?

3. Did an adult or person at least five years older than you ever ...

    Touch or fondle you or have you touch their body in a sexual way?
    or
    Attempt or actually have oral, anal, or vaginal intercourse with you?

4. Did you often or very often feel that ...

    No one in your family loved you or thought you were important or special?
    or
    Your family didn't look out for each other, feel close to each other, or support each other?

5 Did you often or very often feel that ...

> You didn't have enough to eat, had to wear dirty clothes, and had no one to protect you?
>
> or
>
> Your parents were too drunk or high to take care of you or take you to the doctor if you needed it?

6. Were your parents ever separated or divorced?

7. Was your mother or stepmother:

> Often or very often pushed, grabbed, slapped, or had something thrown at her?
>
> or
>
> Sometimes, often, or very often kicked, bitten, hit with a fist, or hit with something hard?
>
> or
>
> Ever repeatedly hit over at least a few minutes or threatened with a gun or knife?

8. Did you live with anyone who was a problem drinker or alcoholic, or who used street drugs?

9. Was a household member depressed or mentally ill, or did a household member attempt suicide?

10. Did a household member go to prison?

Add up your "Yes" answers. This is your ACE Score.

CHAPTER 11

Becoming Familiar with Unconscious Content

If you are still being hurt by an event that happened to
you at twelve, it is the thought that is hurting you now.
—James Hillman

Our coping strategies have formed to repress the contents of the unconscious and keep them away from consciousness. This results in
an ongoing struggle between the coping strategies (our identity) and
the contents of the unconscious. Inevitably, the difficult contents of
the unconscious do leak into consciousness, and we begin to be disturbed by them. The leakage can be slow and gradual, in which case
we feel it as a simmering background discomfort. There is a subtle
sense that something is not quite right; it could be described as low-
level disquiet that sometimes turns into anxiety. For some people it
is always there; for most of us, it is there a lot of the time.

When we are triggered, the unconscious content is activated, and
we can feel the energy much more strongly. There is an urge to react
to get rid of the disturbance. We feel the reactive energies building in
the body and they can turn into a full-blown shenpa attack.

The Theory of Complexes

The leakage of unconscious content can be explored using the theory of complexes developed by Freud and Jung. They saw complexes as bundles of psychic energy bound up around unpleasant memories or traumatic moments, buried in the unconscious. Two of the more common examples identified were mother complexes and father complexes, which may be familiar to many of us. They originate from difficulties or trauma that we might have experienced with either or both parents. However, there are limitless other possibilities based on real or imagined experiences with teachers, hospitals, places, air travel, animals, and particular objects. As we move through life, the complexes can be strengthened by avoidance and suppression, along with further experiences that replay or relive the earlier experiences. The pain and trauma associated with these memories remains in the unconscious.

Jung described the nature of the complex by comparing it to the energy of electrons in the structure of the atom. He suggested that the complexes "manifest a sort of electronic spin" that circles around the nucleus of the complex. (1) Their spinning accelerates when they are activated by a situation or a memory. The complex is energised, and it breaks through into consciousness. Their arrival is often awkward, embarrassing and sometimes even aggressive. At this point, the complex is controlling our behaviour and we act in irrational and inexplicable ways. The usual standards for acceptable behaviour no longer apply. We sometimes do and say things that are destructive. We go temporarily insane. It is reflected in comments like, "I didn't know what I was doing," "I seem to be possessed" or "I just lost control completely" This activation of the complex and its movement into consciousness was referred to by Jung as the "constellation of the complex." (2)

Complexes have an inner coherence and autonomy, and if they continue to be strengthened by our reaction to life's circumstances, they develop into sub-personalities. By this stage, the complexes have become frequent visitors to consciousness arriving of their own accord. In earlier times, they would have been referred to as "demons" and the behaviour explained as "being possessed by demons" or "being possessed by the Devil."

Basic Fear as a Complex

Jung lived before the modern Enneagram, so Basic Fear is not part of his psychology. However, in his terms, Basic Fear could be considered as being at the core of our complexes. It is a bundle of psychic energy bound up around an early painful belief about ourselves. It is something we have unconsciously believed about ourselves from the very beginning, and we don't want to acknowledge it. Many other negative unconscious beliefs and experiences are associated with it. For example, difficult beliefs about our parents often have their genesis in Basic Fear.

Jung noticed that the core or nucleus of a complex is made up of two parts. The first part is "an innate (archetypical) piece" which in Enneagram terms equates to Basic Fear. It is "inherited and not acquired, and belongs to each human being by virtue of being born." (3) The second part is the 'subsequent life trauma' that is often associated with our parents. "The dual core of the complex grows by gathering associations around itself, and this can go on over the course of an entire lifetime" (4). Jung's concept of the complex, adapted to include Basic Fear, is shown below.

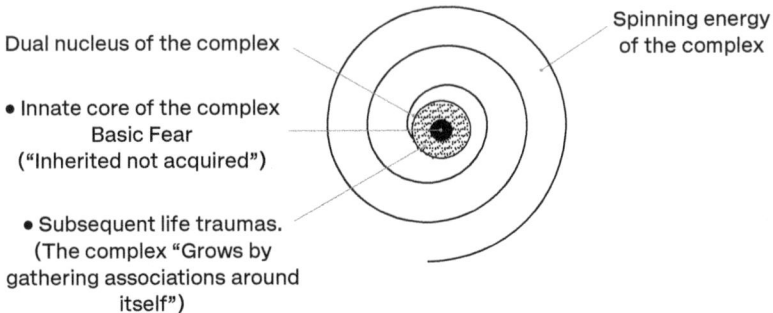

Dual nucleus of the complex

• Innate core of the complex
Basic Fear
("Inherited not acquired")

• Subsequent life traumas.
(The complex "Grows by
gathering associations around
itself")

Spinning energy
of the complex

The dual structure of the complex is probably why it was given the name 'complex'. It recognises there are two intertwined elements that complicate what would otherwise be a simple structure. The two elements make the complex more resilient, with the Basic Fear being reinforced by the subsequent life trauma and our beliefs about past trauma being reinforced by the underlying Basic Fear.

Keeping the Complexes Buried

We want to keep the complexes buried in the unconscious. To keep them there, we need coping strategies that counter the energy of the complex. Like the complex, they have a core that is made up of two parts. The first part is a belief that counters our Basic Fear. As we have seen, this is the Compensating Self-concept. It is a belief about ourselves that is the exact opposite of our Basic Fear. The second part is a belief or story that specifically tries to cover over the second part of the complex, the "subsequent life trauma." Hence, the coping strategy has a dual core that mirrors the complex but is opposite to it.

Each coping strategy can be seen as a bundle of psychic energy which is equal to, and opposite, the complex it is trying to conceal. It is formed around beliefs that are opposite to the complex. It has the same sort of electronic spin as the complex but spinning in the opposite direction. This leads to the perspective of two equal bundles of psychic energy spinning in opposite directions. One is in the

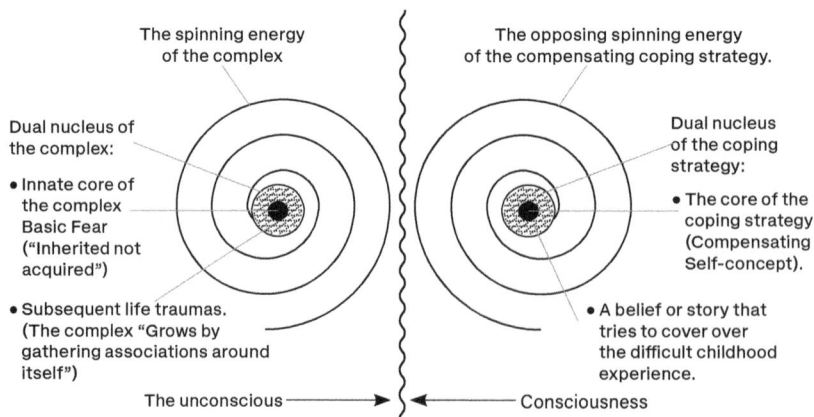

The spinning energy of the complex

The opposing spinning energy of the compensating coping strategy.

Dual nucleus of the complex:

• Innate core of the complex Basic Fear ("Inherited not acquired")

• Subsequent life traumas. (The complex "Grows by gathering associations around itself")

Dual nucleus of the coping strategy:

• The core of the coping strategy (Compensating Self-concept).

• A belief or story that tries to cover over the difficult childhood experience.

The unconscious ⟶ ⟵ Consciousness

unconscious, while the other, in consciousness, is trying to contain it. They are in equilibrium most of the time, with the coping strategy keeping the complex under control. Our effort goes into keeping the coping strategy in place, at all costs.

This perspective applies to all the complexes in the unconscious. Each complex is matched and blocked by a compensating bundle of psychic energy spinning in the opposite direction. At the centre of each complex, sitting next to the Basic Fear, is an unpleasant image or traumatic experience. At the core of the coping strategy, sitting next to the Compensating Self-concept, is a belief that attempts to neutralise the memory of that unpleasant experience.

For example, if a child is abused by a parent, the pain around that experience will be assigned to the unconscious. It will coalesce with the child's Basic Fear to form a complex. The unconscious conclusion about the experience might be that the parent doesn't love them and might continue to hurt them. The matching and blocking energy of the coping strategy has, at its centre, the Compensating Self-concept. It might also include a belief or story that the parent loves them and that they, the child, were responsible for the abuse. Believing "I must have done something to deserve it" is less painful than to acknowledge the parent does not love them.

When the Complex Is Triggered

When a complex is triggered, the spinning energy is activated and overpowers the coping strategy. Equilibrium is lost. The complex breaks into consciousness and takes over our behaviour. We feel strong discomfort and want to get relief in any way we can. Our behaviour becomes very erratic. Our aim is to get away from the grief that is associated with the arrival of the complex. We try to find ways of strengthening the coping strategy and scramble to restore equilibrium. We also try to find ways to escape from, or eliminate, the triggering event. All these efforts will have a desperate and irrational character. Each of them is an expression of our extreme discomfort. At best, they give us temporary relief.

The development of the complex and how we try to cover it over is illustrated in the following example. It is an inspiring account of how the pain of the complex can be used to move towards authentic and undefended relationships.

Allowing the Complex to Become Conscious
Colin is in his early thirties and is a Type Eight in the Enneagram. His mother disappeared at an early age and he and his two siblings were left with his father. His father was an alcoholic and absent much of the time. He was the oldest child and felt responsible for the well-being of his brother and sister. He found himself in circumstances that would have strongly confirmed his Basic Fear, "of being harmed or controlled by others." The response of the Type Eight child would have involved vigilant self-care at an extreme level. To alleviate his vulnerability, his Compensating Self-Concept: "I need to be strong, assertive and in control" would have driven his life. He became the virtual parent to the other children and did a credible job in raising them with only intermittent support from his father.

The painful experience for Colin was his father had consistently failed to protect or take care of him and had chosen alcohol over being with him and his siblings. This second belief had coalesced around his Basic Fear, forming the dual core of his complex:

Basic Fear: Of being harmed or controlled by others, and,

Subsequent life trauma: My father doesn't protect or take care of me.

Throughout his adult life, Colin had been reluctant to acknowledge the trauma and frustration he experienced around his father. He said that he loved his father and that his father really loved him. This was a more palatable story than having to look at the grief around his childhood experiences. In reality, of course, his unconscious experience was that his father didn't take care of him, but it would have been too painful to acknowledge this.

The two beliefs at the core of his coping strategy were:

Compensating Self-concept: I need to be strong, assertive and in control, and,

A story to cover over the life trauma: My father really loves me.

The combination of these two beliefs provided a strong containment of the underlying grief. On the surface it looked like everything was fine; he had survived a very difficult childhood through his own strength and resourcefulness. But the complex was still there, and it would remain unexplored and intact well into his adult life.

The great cost of the complex is that it remains alive and active in the unconscious. It can be triggered by any event that brings back memories of the childhood experience or touches on Basic Fear. The triggering event finds a way around the coping strategy and activates the energy of the complex. This can happen at any time, and when it does, it can have a disruptive impact on behaviour. The presence of the complex in the unconscious, and the opposing energy of the coping strategy in consciousness, is illustrated in the diagram.

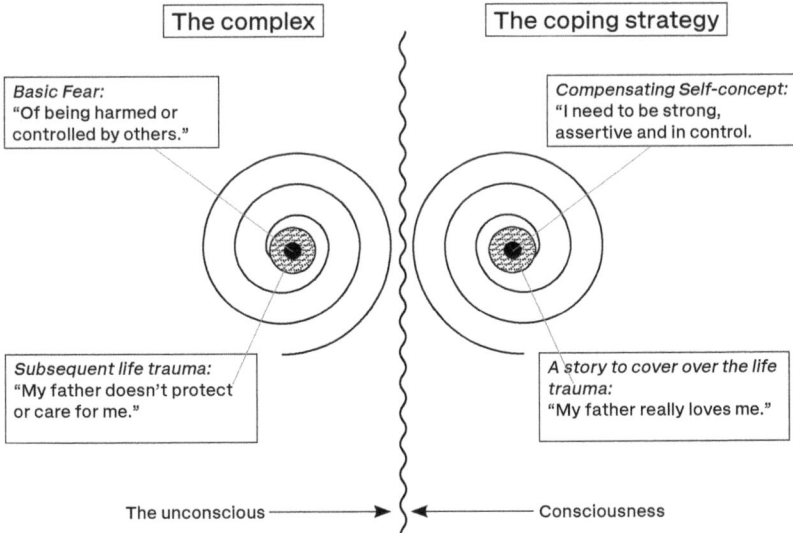

The complex | The coping strategy

Basic Fear: "Of being harmed or controlled by others."

Compensating Self-concept: "I need to be strong, assertive and in control.

Subsequent life trauma: "My father doesn't protect or care for me."

A story to cover over the life trauma: "My father really loves me."

The unconscious ⟶ ⟵ Consciousness

The other cost of the complex is the energy invested in keeping the coping strategy in place. Colin believed he had to take care of himself, and couldn't rely on other people. Unfortunately, this left no opportunity for intimacy and vulnerability, and little opportunity for an intimate life relationship that he desired. It also limited the relationship with his father. While he maintained the story that his father really loved him, it made it difficult to form an authentic relationship with him. If he became too close to his father, his story might be shown to be untrue. It was best to keep a measured distance from him and keep the story intact.

The first step in his enquiry was to explore the story that his father really loved him. He had to acknowledge the painful truth: he had been abandoned and neglected by his father. As he let go of the "he loved me" story, he gave himself permission to acknowledge his repressed feelings of anger and grief. He was able to accept these feelings and be with them; he was no longer investing energy in keeping them away. As is often the case, once the repressed feelings are felt, they are usually followed by genuine heartfelt feelings of compassion — firstly for oneself, but in time, for the other person. His constructed story to keep away from grief was replaced by compassion for his father, and the belief that he had done the best that he could. In time, this developed into an honest and authentic connection. There was now the space for the difficult memories of his childhood to move into his awareness.

Colin demonstrated how valuable it is to explore our coping strategies and be brave enough to feel the difficult feelings associated with the past. This exploration can be guided by Jung's idea of the dual core of the complex. In this, there are two parts to be uncovered. The first will be our Basic Fear. The second will be associated with some difficult life experience, usually in childhood, and it will have coalesced with our Basic Fear. In Colin's case it was his father's lack of protection and care. To cover this over, there will be a tenacious hanging on to the Compensating Self-concept. There will also be a belief or story we have made up to protect ourselves from the pain of what happened.

*   *   *   *

Complexes — Big and Not So Big

Colin's childhood experiences were profoundly difficult. His very survival and that of his siblings were at stake. Many of us had childhood experiences that were nothing like Colin's but were strong enough to develop into complexes. My own experience with my mother and tennis illustrates how these smaller complexes exist in the unconscious and how they affect our behaviour, even though, on the surface, they may not look that significant.

My Tennis — Mother Complex

My mother was a good tennis player and unfortunately, she decided I was going to be a tennis star. I started tennis lessons at five and by six was playing in local tennis competitions. I was okay at tennis, but I was never going to be a champion. The truth was, I wasn't that interested in tennis and didn't care whether I won or lost. This was a disappointment to my mother, but she didn't give up on her dream. She insisted I continue with my lessons and my weekly tennis routine. My tennis career continued until I was twelve when I went to boarding school. One of the few compensations of going to boarding school was I didn't have to play tennis. I kept my tennis skills secret for the next twenty-three years. For many years in my early adult life, the thought of playing tennis made me feel squeamish. I had my next game of tennis at the age of thirty-five.

Having to play tennis as a child does not rate highly on the scale of traumatic childhood experiences. On reflection though, I didn't enjoy tennis. I was resentful that I was being coerced to do something I didn't like. I remember the many hours and days spent playing tennis because of my mother's non-compromising attitude. More importantly, I concluded that my mother's connection with me was very conditional. She seemed determined to make me do what she wanted at all costs. This was where the grief resided.

In Jung's term, my dislike of tennis had developed into a complex. It was a minor complex, but it shows how the unpleasant experiences of childhood are carried through into adult life. My tennis complex had formed around my Basic Fear, and the ongoing behaviour of my mother.

Basic Fear for a Type Nine: Of being disconnected and cut off from everything including love.

Subsequent Life Experience: My mother will make me do what she wants; she doesn't really care about me.

To contain the grief around this experience, I developed a coping strategy around two beliefs:

Compensating Self-concept: I need to be peaceful, easy-going, and kind.

A story to cover over the life trauma: My needs are not important.

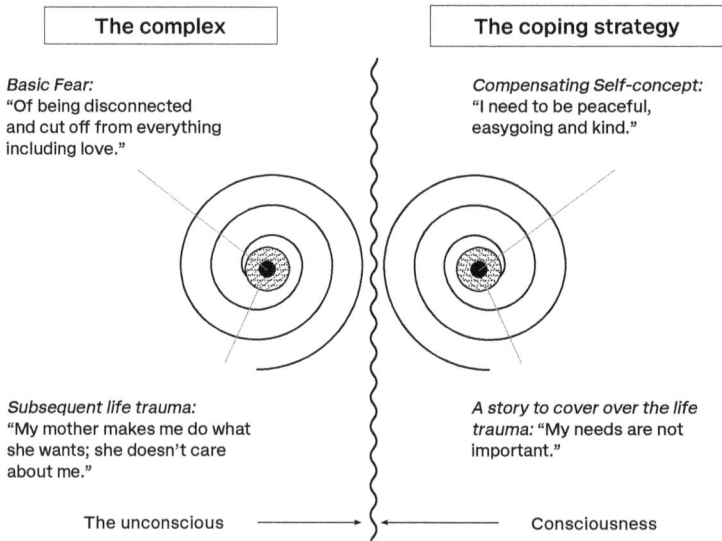

| The complex | The coping strategy |

Basic Fear:
"Of being disconnected and cut off from everything including love."

Compensating Self-concept:
"I need to be peaceful, easygoing and kind."

Subsequent life trauma:
"My mother makes me do what she wants; she doesn't care about me."

A story to cover over the life trauma: "My needs are not important."

The unconscious ⟶ Consciousness

Believing that my needs were not important was part of being easy-going. It was not worth standing up for myself and potentially losing connection with my mother. It also helped me minimise the grief I was feeling. My underlying experience was that my mother was determined to make me do something I didn't like over many years. I felt she really didn't care about me.

My experience with tennis and my mother shows that we can have smaller complexes, each one associated with a specific difficult life experience. At the core of each complex will be our Basic Fear. We develop a family of complexes, with the same underlying Basic Fear, but developing in different ways depending on our life experiences. The difficult life experiences will have a direct connection with Basic Fear. For Colin, the lack of protection from his father was closely aligned to his Basic Fear of being at risk. For me, my conditional connection with my mother, and the absence of love and care, was closely aligned with my Basic Fear of being disconnected and cut off from love.

Our response to each of the complexes will also have a consistent theme, all based around our Compensating Self-concept. The supporting coping belief will reinforce the Compensating Self-concept and deny or minimise what really happened. For Colin, it was the story that his father really loved him, aligned with the belief that he was strong and in control. For me, it was the belief that my needs were not important, aligned with the concept of being peaceful and easy-going.

These coping strategies become part of our conditioning and our identity. Through my tennis experience, and other experiences with my mother, I came to adopt a more general conditioned belief about myself: 'I don't matter'. This is probably a common coping strategy, particularly for Type Nines. If I believed this about myself, I didn't have to look at the underlying grief and sadness about my mother, stemming from the belief that she didn't really care about me. Unfortunately, these beliefs, such as 'I don't matter', can stay with us for the rest of our lives.

*   *   *   *

Understanding the complexes provides insights into the difficult content of the unconscious. It also reveals how we attempt to cover over this painful content with our coping strategies. And the coping strategies are part of our identity and reinforce our Enneagram-type behaviours.

As we come to know our complexes, we will recognise that they provide an opening for something important and beneficial to happen. They are disruptive, but potentially, in a positive way. They are calling us to begin our journey through the difficult terrain of the unconscious. When they are triggered, they present us with a moment of great opportunity. This is the topic of the next chapter.

CHAPTER 12

Allowing the Opposites
to Come Together

The conscious personality is brought face-to-face with
the counter-position of the unconscious.
The Transcendent Function, Carl Jung

A Moment of Great Opportunity

Whenever a complex is triggered, it can be seen as a moment of great opportunity. As it threatens to move into consciousness, our natural inclination is to defend ourselves and our identity. Our energy goes into sustaining this threatened, but false concept of ourselves. The arrival of the constellated complex, and our urge to push it back, is heralded by strong impulses in the body that may include contraction of the stomach, the overwhelming urge to physically react, tightness in the chest and throat, and so on. Jung described the experience as being "in the grip of ... a force stronger than one's will." (1) It requires courage not to react in our habitual way.

Sadly, our natural impulse is to prevent the threatened intrusion of the complex and to get rid of the discomfort as quickly as possible. We can then go back to 'business as usual' and our so-called 'normal lives'. We want to strengthen our identity and reassure ourselves that this idea of 'who we are' can be sustained. We can continue to "strut and fret our hour upon the stage." In doing so, we have missed the opportunity to access the enormous amount of psychic energy bound up in the complex as well as the energy we expend in keeping the complexes under control.

Our capacity not to react can be helped by adopting the perspective that something important and beneficial is happening to us. This is how unconscious content is revealed. If we can remain conscious and non-reactive in this moment of discomfort, then something quite different can happen. The psychic energy of the complex is allowed to move in and touch the structures of identity. The spinning energy of the complex is equal and opposite to the spinning energy of the coping strategy. As they are allowed to touch, they come together. The energy of the complex unites with the energy of the coping strategy.

The opposite energies are stripped of their oppositional character: they are now just pure energy. They are acting in concert, not in opposition. The union can be envisaged as the liberation of psychic energy. The energy being freed is strong enough to break down the tightness of the surrounding psychic structures. It blows apart the ideas and strategies we have been using to keep ourselves safe. What happens is akin to sexual union, where the opposite energies of male and female come together with the potential to create a new thing, a child.

Jung referred to this union of psychic energies, and the resultant transformation, as "the alchemical process". Joseph Campbell used the term "Sacred Marriage", which points to the idea of opposite energies being united. It also supports the idea that the union is creative; it leads to an offspring. Both Jung and Campbell recognised that the union resulted in something new and alive. In Jung's words:

> "it creates a living third thing ... a living birth, that leads
> to a new level of being."

The "new level of being" is our movement back to the three centres. This coming together of opposite energies is illustrated on the page opposite.

Vesica Pisces

The spinning energy
of the complex

The opposing spinning
energy of the
coping strategy.

Constellated complex
moving into consciousness

The unconscious ——————▶ ◀—————— Consciousness

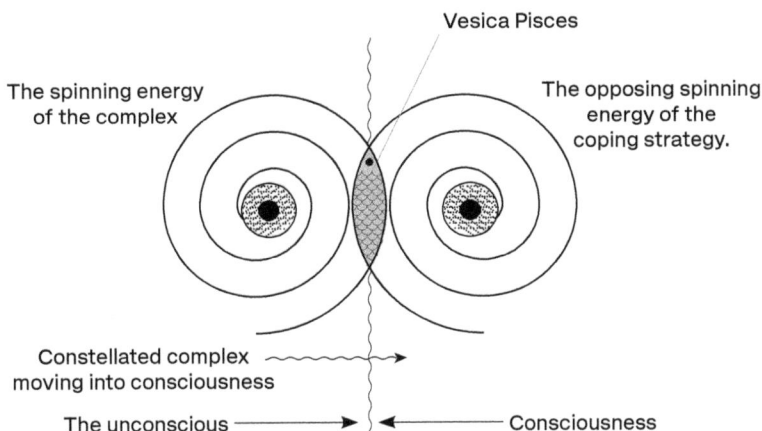

The Alchemical Process

Where the spinning energy of the constellated complex is allowed to unite with the opposite energy of the coping strategy, the two circles overlap to form the shaded almond-shaped space. It is a space of intense transformative energy, a space where opposites cannot be sustained. It is called *vesica pisces* which is Latin for "fish vessel". Jung believed it was the vessel in which the opposite energies were able "to cook". In allowing the uncomfortable energy of the unconscious to move into consciousness, the many opposing ideas of the psyche (good and bad, right and wrong, desirable and undesirable, and so on) can no longer be sustained. All the stories and beliefs we have made up to support our identity are released. In Jung's words,

> **"The conscious personality is brought face-to-face with the counter-position of the unconscious."** (2)

This process is sometimes accompanied by the physical experience of heat in and around the gut, which supports the idea of something being cooked. This is the alchemical process that was at the centre of much of Jung's later writing, where the unwanted 'lead' of the unconscious is the catalyst for the transformation of the psyche into gold. In our terms, it allows our entry into the Golden World.

The fish vessel or the fish was also the symbol of the early Christian Church and is still used today. The two circles overlapping represents the coming together of opposites. This idea is also inherent in the origins of the word "religion". It comes from the Latin word *ligare*, which is to bind together, so that "re-ligion" is to bind back together. It is affirming to see that this was the original purpose of religion. It is, in the first instance, a personal experience in which we allow the concepts of good and bad, and all the concepts we hold about our identity and the world, to be dissolved. We allow the discomfort to be there in ourselves without judgement. If any collective action is required at all, it is for some mutual support and encouragement to stay with, and experience, our own discomfort. The words from Jesus, quoted earlier, are a reminder that redemption can be achieved with this simple practice:

"What we bring forth will save us; what we do not bring forth will destroy us."

The Psychology Behind Alchemy

Jung believed there is an inherent healing capacity in the human psyche that is driven by the urge for unification. He called this inherent capacity "the transcendent function" and it is at the core of the alchemical process. The unification is achieved by the coming together of opposite psychic energies. The energy of the unconscious complexes meets the energy of the coping strategies and gives birth to a new perspective. This is how the movement towards wholeness happens. The struggle of the divided mind to sustain the false self is abating; ideas about good and bad cannot be sustained. The protective shells are united. They are like the unnecessary wrapping around the psyche; when the wrapping is taken away, we are simply left with the three centres. We return to a state of uncomplicated beauty and innocence. This is what we have always been. This is the Golden World.

As we move towards a state of pure awareness, we experience the world with an accepting, compassionate heart. The internal struggles of the psyche resolve themselves and inner peace can prevail. We begin to sense that there is more space. It is the freedom to simply experience life without agendas and judgements.

A Humbling Realisation

It is humbling to realise that the shells of our identity, are being dismantled without much input from us. We don't even have to know or understand what is happening. If we can catch ourselves early in our reactivity and feel the discomfort, the unification of the shells can happen. We no longer need to keep the coping strategies in place.

Our identity is being dismantled brick by brick. The encouraging aspect of this process is that most of us get triggered many times a day, in small and big ways. It doesn't really matter if we miss the first twenty or so; the opportunities will continue to present themselves. The triggers will range from minor irritations to moments of significant reaction. It doesn't matter how big or small they are; they all have something to tell us about the contents of the unconscious. Our challenge is to feel the discomfort as it arrives at the threshold of consciousness. We can also be curious about what it is in us that is being triggered. If we do anything more than that, we will interfere with the process. The keys to redemption are hidden under the stone of discomfort, but no one wants to look there.

These insights present an encouraging view on how we can use our complexes. When we realise that we have been triggered and our complexes have been constellated, our usual response is one of disappointment and regret. We get frustrated that we behaved in ways that were reactive and inappropriate. We want to get away from the disappointment and frustration as quickly as possible. We want to get back to normality. We want to put the stone back on the discomfort and hope that it will stay covered up.

If we want to use our complexes for our benefit and growth, we must sit patiently with the discomfort and feel what is happening in the body. We need to connect with the churning in the gut or the tightness in the chest or the jaw. As we focus on these physical sensations, we don't have to do anything. Eventually, the disturbing energies will dissipate, but that is not the goal. What is more important is to allow the complexes to do their work of transformation. With time, we will see the activation of complexes as a gift, which, when used well, takes us one step further towards freedom.

*   *   *   *

There are strong parallels between the complexes discussed in this chapter and Pema Chödrön's concept of shenpa in Chapter Six. They are different names for the same uncomfortable energy that arises when we are triggered. It is affirming that the psychological perspective provided by Jung's work confirms the perspective of a contemporary Buddhist teacher. And the conclusions are the same. We need to appreciate the potential benefits of shenpa just as we need to recognise the opportunities for growth when our complexes are constellated.

Complexes and the Levels of Health
Jung's idea of the complex can be incorporated into Don Riso's work on the Levels of Health (see Chapter Five). Riso proposed that our movement down the Levels of Health commences with an embryonic discomfort around Basic Fear. Riso's thesis is that this discomfort creeps into our awareness at an early age. We seek relief from it by trying to conceal it with a concept that is opposite to Basic Fear, the Compensating Self-concept.

Our attempts to cover over our Basic Fear are only partly successful and some discomfort leaks into our awareness. We then redouble our efforts to push it back by reinforcing the Compensating Self-concept. Our coping strategies get stronger, and our Enneagram-type behaviours become more pronounced. We are doing everything possible to strengthen our identity and sustain the false sense of 'who we are'. The protective shells get thicker, and we begin to move down the Levels of Health. Don Riso also showed that, by not reacting to the discomfort of our Basic Fear, we can retrace our steps and move up the Levels of Health.

Riso's model can be expanded by recognising that the movement down the Levels of Health is driven not only by Basic Fear, but also by the other painful content in the unconscious. In other words, the downward movement is driven by the activation of our complexes of which Basic Fear is a foundation part. Our coping strategies then respond to the activated complexes and the protective shells get thicker. This gives a more comprehensive understanding of the *pain inside*; it is not just Basic Fear that is causing the pain, it is all the challenging experiences that make up our complexes.

This interaction between our complexes and our coping strategies is essentially the same as that described by Riso but the idea of complexes has replaced the narrower concept of Basic Fear. This expanded model of the Levels of Health is shown in the diagram below: At Level One the influence of Basic Fear is minimal; it is only a glimmer of some distant existential discomfort. Also, at this level, the difficult experiences and trauma of life have not yet occurred. Or if they have occurred, they have been acknowledged and freed from the

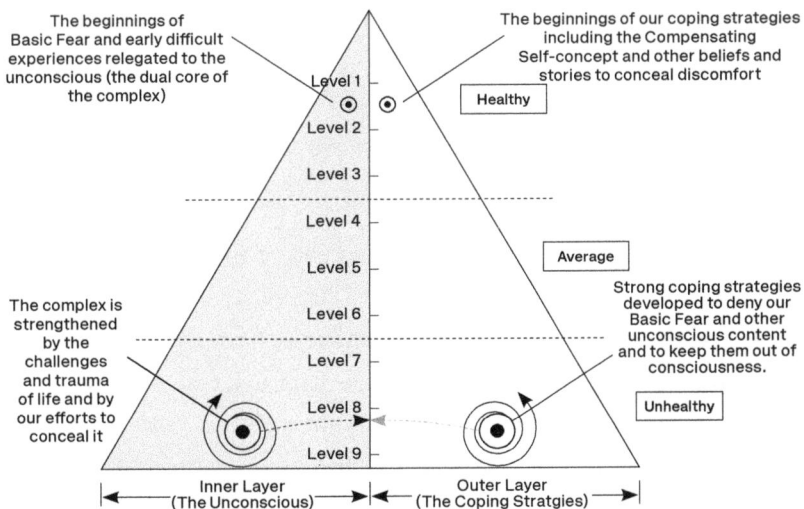

unconscious. At this level, the complexes are almost non-existent. Someone at this level has little need for coping strategies. They are fully open to the experiences of life and are connected to the energies of the three centres.

If they then encounter difficult life experiences, and try to conceal the pain of those experiences, the complexes begin to grow. Stronger coping strategies will develop to cover over the growing complexes. So begins the movement down the Levels of Health. The downward movement will only be interrupted by staying present with the arising discomfort and not reacting to it. By reacting to get away from the pain, the complexes will strengthen.

The movement down the levels was described in Chapter Five:

> The movement down from one level to the next comprises
> many thousands of reactive moments, and each moment can be
> envisaged as one small step. Our downward descent through the
> levels is a staircase of many small steps.

Each time we react in our habitual way, the complexes get stronger, and we go down a step. By the time we get to Levels 8 or 9, we have very well-developed and easily triggered complexes that we are desperately trying to contain. This struggle to cover over the complexes becomes our all-consuming mission in life. The protective shells have become thick, and we have lost connection with the three centres.

Alchemy and Moving Up the Levels of Health
In Chapter Five, we also explored how we can move up the Levels of Health.

> It is useful to envisage ourselves as 'sitting on the steps' between
> each reactive, downward movement. The trigger occurs and
> we feel the urge to react. In this moment we have an important
> choice to make. We can respond in the habitual, reactive way
> that takes us down another step. The alternative is to sit on the
> step and 'catch ourselves in the act'. It requires courage and our
> willingness to override years of conditioning. It is something we

have to learn slowly and practice with less important triggers, like having to wait in a queue. It helps to move our focus to our breathing, as this can break the momentum of the reactive energy, or at least slow down the reactive process. As we sit on the step, we can remember Eckhart Tolle's advice:

"Watch it, feel it, allow it."

'Sitting on the steps' is where alchemy happens. We are staying still and not trying to stop the movement of the complex into consciousness. The description in Chapter Five continues, although we can now substitute 'complexes' for 'Basic Fear' and 'coping strategies' for 'Compensating Self-concept':

> Each time we can 'sit on the steps' and not react, we move up a step. The psychic energy around the *complex* is allowed to move in and combine with the energy of the *coping strategy*. There is no attempt to push the *complex* back ... It is paradoxical, that the thing we try to avoid, namely discomfort, is the very thing that can lead us up the Levels of Health to freedom. It is our ability to be with discomfort that allows us to move to the freedom of Level One, and to reconnect with ourselves and the energies of the centres.

Jung's idea of alchemy gives insight into what is actually happening when 'we sit on the steps.' Each time 'we sit on the steps', the cooking process begins and the vesica pisces forms out of the opposite energies of the psyche. The complexes are uniting with the structures of identity and transformation happens. We move up the Levels towards freedom. Alchemy is the underlying concept that explains why we move up the Levels of Health. It doesn't change Riso's model at all; it supports and enriches it. It brings a rich psychological tradition from Jung to support one of the most important parts of Enneagram teaching.

*   *   *   *

Another perspective on what is happening is provided by Robert Johnson, a well-known Jungian author. He suggests the difficult thoughts and emotions arriving in our awareness can be viewed as animals walking out of the forest. They arrive of their own accord, often for no apparent reason, and there is nothing we can do to stop them. But these unwelcome and uninvited animals need to be seen for what they are. They are a manifestation of our own disturbing unconscious content coming into our awareness. And if we don't react to the animals, they will, in their own time, walk back into the forest and disappear. And so, with practice, we will become skilled in not reacting to our disturbing thoughts and emotions.

But there is an even bigger insight to be explored here. The animals, our unconscious content, can be encouraged to touch the structures of personality. And when they do, alchemy will happen. Each time we welcome these unpleasant animals, and be with our discomfort, the structures of identity will be dismantled, perhaps by just a little. As Rumi suggests, we need to greet all our difficult thoughts and feelings as they arrive in our awareness:

"meet them all at the door laughing and invite them in." (3)

*   *   *   *

The Obstacle to the Alchemical Process

Jung's alchemical process gives us insight into how the disturbing energy of a constellation can be used for our spiritual growth and liberation. The alchemical process is the inherent capacity of the psyche that makes our return to the Golden World possible. And the process can happen many times each day.

It can happen in small ways, usually beginning with some minor irritation or frustration. We feel mild discomfort in the gut or our jaw might tighten, almost imperceptibly. If we are alert enough to see our reaction, we can stop and be fully present with the disturbing energy. If we can simply watch our discomfort, the constellated complex will do its work. It has been given the space to move into consciousness. The alchemical process has happened, albeit it on a small scale. Or maybe it is bigger than we think. We might experience a momentary sense of more space, or perhaps a little glimpse of the Golden World. Or we might not. And if we do this often enough, it changes the way we experience life. Of course, there will be many times when we miss these opportunities completely, and we carry on with our usual patterns of behaviour. We just don't want to be with the unpleasant energies.

Sometimes we are triggered in more serious ways. We have been reminded of some significant loss or trauma from the past. Or maybe it is some difficult experience happening to us now. The disturbing energy is intense. Whatever is happening now or happened in the past, whether it be loss or trauma or both, is too overwhelming. At the time it is happening, now or in the past, we are unable to be with the pain, and seek relief by putting the painful experience into the unconscious.

Of all the centres, the Heart Centre is the one we protect the most; we don't want to feel the grief and be hurt again. So, we ensure the protection around the heart is as strong as possible. The protection not only stops us feeling grief, it cuts off from all our feelings, both pleasant and unpleasant. We live our lives in a protected state of numbness. Our determination not to feel grief becomes the fundamental obstacle to the alchemical process. We want to stop the grief of the unconscious ever coming into our awareness.

The challenge of dealing with overwhelming grief is captured in the illustrated fable "The Heart in the Bottle" by Oliver Jeffers (4).

The Heart in the Bottle
The Heart in the Bottle explores the way in which a young child might handle the overwhelming grief of loss. The little girl in the story has just lost her father to whom she was very close.

"Feeling unsure, the girl thought the best thing was to put her heart in a safe place.

Just for the time being.

So she put it in a bottle and hung it around her neck.

And that seemed to fix things... at first."

The little girl soon found that locking away the pain also locks away the capacity for love and aliveness.

"She forgot about the stars... and stopped taking notice of the sea.

She was no longer filled with all the curiosities of the world and didn't take much notice of anything..."

Many years later, now as a woman, she encounters a little girl on the beach who is filled with the same joy of life that had once been hers. She realises the cost of what she has done and sets out to liberate her heart from its glassy prison. The task was harder than she expected; the bottle couldn't be broken. There is a reluctance to give up the protective shells we have put in place. Eventually the woman seeks the help of the little girl she met on the beach. The little girl reaches into the bottle, finds the heart and puts it back in its rightful place.

*   *   *   *

Unfortunately, the story doesn't really explain how the woman was able to remove her heart from the bottle. This is the challenge for all of us. It is the accumulated grief in the unconscious that makes it so hard to let go the protective shells. As Marianne Williamson pointed out, we choose to live with "the dull pain of the unconscious that would last the rest of our lives, rather than feeling our unconscious grief."

With time, we all need to feel the grief that has accumulated in the unconscious. We need to allow the alchemical process to occur with each piece of accumulated grief. As long as the grief is there, the shells will keep us removed from the joy and innocence of life. Our life becomes difficult, limited and often bitter. Sometimes we choose to take our grief to the grave.

The work of Elisabeth Kubler-Ross (4), a Swiss psychiatrist, working in the 1960's and 1970's, can help us understand our grief and the obstacles to allowing it to be felt. It is fifty years since her findings were first published, but with ongoing amendments to her model, her work is still very relevant.

Kubler-Ross and the Five Stages of Grief

Based on her work with terminally ill patients, Kubler-Ross proposed that there were five stages of grief.

1. **Denial.** We want to deny the reality of what has happened and go numb; we might hope that the news we have been given is incorrect or we might simply refuse to believe what we are being told. In some cases, the denial can go on for decades. We chose to live in a false reality in spite of abundant evidence that this reality no longer exists.

2. **Anger.** We are angry that this happened to us. The anger can include thoughts like: "Why did this happen to me?", or "It's not fair." The anger will often manifest in finding someone to blame; a friend, a family member, a doctor or God.

3. **Bargaining.** It is common to want to undo by negotiation what has happened. The bargaining can include propositions like: "If I recover from this, I will live the best life I possibly can." Or even, "God, please take me, not them." It is an attempt to give ourselves hope that we can get back to our old life.

4. **Depression.** As we begin to take in the reality of what has happened, life can feel empty and meaningless. Our past life has gone. We might want to withdraw from life; it seems pointless. It can be difficult to get out of bed and we don't feel like talking to others. The world closes in and we feel powerless.

5. **Acceptance.** It is a recognition that this challenging experience has happened, our life has changed and 'here I am'. It is the acceptance of life as it is, even though it might be difficult. We begin to feel the grief and slowly it becomes less overwhelming. It comes like a wave; but, with time, the waves get smaller and further apart. We begin to see we can survive and we start to engage with life as it is now.

There was an underlying assumption in her work that we progress in a linear way from one stage to the next, and finally, after depression, we reach acceptance. Kubler-Ross came to realise that we don't move through the stages in this way; there wasn't a gradual progression from one stage to the next. They can happen in any order, and not everyone experiences all the stages. We can move from one stage, to any other stage, at any time. And we don't always get to acceptance. This more flexible framework is illustrated in the diagram opposite. On the left-hand side, is the original Kubler-Ross model. On the right-hand side, is the updated framework in which we can jump around the points of the oval, or sometimes just stay on one or two points. It is not until we feel the underlying grief that we can get to acceptance.

The points on the oval are the emotional and thinking patterns we use to protect ourselves. They serve a purpose in giving us time to process our grief, but we can get stuck in the oval for a long time. It is not uncommon to see people who have been unable to reach acceptance and remain with their repressed unconscious grief and sadness forever. The important question is how do we get to feel the grief, particularly when we are dealing with grief that has been there since childhood.

Kübler-Ross Stages of Grief

1   Denial

2   Anger

3   Bargaining

4   Depression

5a   Grief, sadness, sorrow
     (release)

5   Acceptance

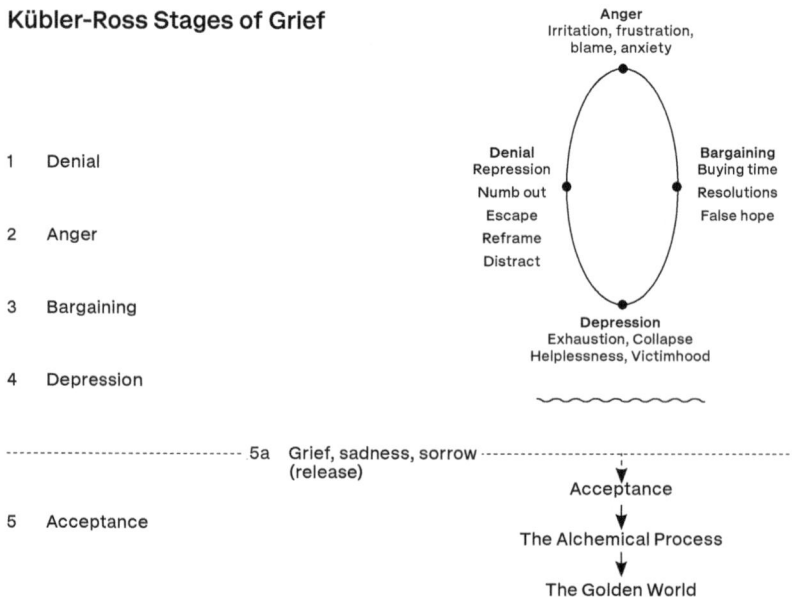

Anger
Irritation, frustration,
blame, anxiety

Denial
Repression
Numb out
Escape
Reframe
Distract

Bargaining
Buying time
Resolutions
False hope

Depression
Exhaustion, Collapse
Helplessness, Victimhood

Acceptance

The Alchemical Process

The Golden World

The Kubler-Ross model can help us become aware of what is happening. We can become familiar with the points of the oval and begin to be curious about what we are doing. If we can stay present with our feelings at each point of the oval, particularly with anger and depression, we can, with courage, begin to access the underlying grief. A good question to ask ourselves, particularly with anger is: "What is the feeling underneath the anger?" This will sometimes get us in touch with the underlying grief.

The value of the Kubler-Ross model is that it highlights our strong reluctance to feeling grief, both past and present. We prefer instead to keep moving around the points of the oval, slowly becoming bitter and disillusioned. The four points on the oval can be reminders to us that we need to pay attention. They represent important messages from the unconscious that there is underlying grief that still needs to be felt and freed. Our inclination is to ignore the messages, and find ways to treat the symptoms. We persist with the denial, or we get angry and frustrated and don't acknowledge how frequently this is happening. Or we hope that somehow, with time, our lives will improve. Or we become dispirited and depressed and seek remedies to make us feel better.

To break out of this pattern, it helps to recognise the magnitude and difficulty of what we are attempting to do. We need to follow a well-travelled path which takes us to where we are reluctant to go. It will hold us on course in spite of our urge to go back to the safety of the oval. This well-travelled path is the hero's journey, the focus of the remaining chapters of this book.

The Call to Adventure and the Hero's Journey

The challenge for all of us is to be willing to explore and acknowledge the contents of the unconscious. We have purposely hidden these unwanted parts of ourselves and the painful memories and grief of the past. The task now is to do the very opposite; how do we find them and bring them home? This goes against all our inclinations to avoid discomfort and grief. However, we now know these unwanted parts, specifically the complexes, are what makes alchemy possible.

As we begin this adventure, we can be encouraged by the words of Joseph Campbell:

"The cave you fear to enter has the treasures you seek."

The task is made easier when we view it in the context of the hero's journey. It is an inner journey of discovery that has been undertaken since the beginning of time. The story of the journey has been told and retold in the countless myths of all civilisations. The journey begins with the Call to Adventure described in the next chapter. The journey is often abandoned in its early stages; it is not for the faint-hearted. We need to steel ourselves for the adventure and remember it offers us the greatest prize of all. It is the healing of the *pain inside*, the undoing of identity and the return to the Golden World.

CHAPTER 13

The Call to Adventure

Many are called but few are chosen.
— Gospel of St. Matthew

Throughout the ages, there have been countless mythical stories of epic, life-restoring journeys. Joseph Campbell, a world-renowned author on mythology, found they are all essentially the same story, being told countless times in different ways. It is ageless and universal, spanning across all civilisations. He observed the same underlying theme in all myths regardless of race, geography, and culture. The myths that have been handed down from ancient Greece are the same as the North American Indians, the Aboriginal Australians, the tribesmen of the African continent, and so on.

The title of Campbell's classic work, *The Hero with a Thousand Faces*, reminds us of this reality. The stories describe the same striving by an individual, the hero, who is seeking something beyond the familiar life-horizons. (1) Campbell concluded that the similarity between the myths was not accidental. He also found that the same myths were being encountered by modern psychologists in the dreams of their patients. He observed that mythology and psychology had converged, and they were both "an expression of the unconscious desires, fears, and tensions that underlie human behaviour. They both point to the deep forces that have shaped man's destiny." (2) There is something inherent in the psyche of all men and women that is manifest in the legends of all people. Humanity has been engaged in the same pursuit for aeons, with the same challenges and shortcomings. If we can understand the fundamental elements of this one myth, it will give a map to guide us beyond our familiar horizons and onto our own hero's journey.

The stages of the hero's journey are outlined in the map below, adapted from *The Hero with a Thousand Faces*.

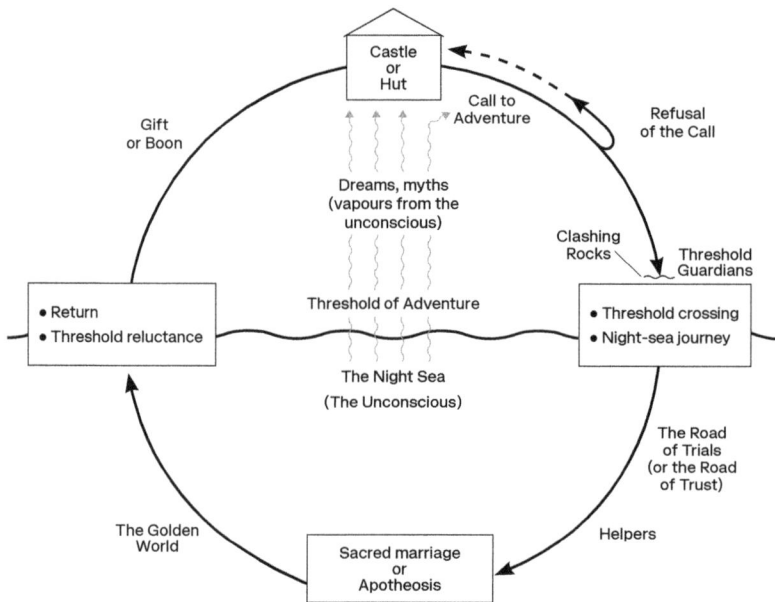

Castle
or
Hut

Call to Adventure

Gift
or Boon

Refusal
of the Call

Dreams, myths
(vapours from the
unconscious)

Clashing
Rocks

Threshold
Guardians

• Return

• Threshold reluctance

Threshold of Adventure

• Threshold crossing

• Night-sea journey

The Night Sea
(The Unconscious)

The Road
of Trials
(or the Road
of Trust)

The Golden
World

Helpers

Sacred marriage
or
Apotheosis

Stage One   The Call to Adventure (and Not Refusing the Call)

The story starts with the hero, residing in a hut or a castle, attending to the tasks and challenges of everyday life. Then something disruptive happens. It may be a disappointment, an irritation, a dream, a mistake, or an intuition. In mythology, the disturbance might take the form of a talking frog, a dragon, a witch, or some unusual herald from the underworld. Whatever its form, it disturbs the comfort of our hero's life. It challenges the coping strategies and the shells of identity that provide protection and safety.

Since birth we all have been struggling to sustain a false sense of intactness or adequacy. There is a low-level simmering anxiety that hints that 'something is not quite right'. We attempt to keep it together but the subtle, or not so subtle, anxiety continues. We distract ourselves by our striving in the world. We think we can find fulfilment and relief in the things of the world. It might be the pursuit of material success, or power, or relationships, or family, or self-improvement, or even peace. As worthy as these endeavours might be, we continue to know there is something deeper that needs to be explored.

The disturbing messages from the unconscious arise from beneath the floor of our neat little hut or the luxuries of our castle. They come from the part of our psyche that we don't want to own and don't know how to access. They can be painful memories of the past or some undiscovered potential within ourselves. The unconscious is the "Aladdin cave", where "not only jewels but dangerous *jinn*[spirits] abide." (3) The messages may be triggered by some challenging encounter in the present, a slight reminiscence that takes us back to an earlier, forgotten time, or some inkling that there is something more that is calling our attention. They are disruptive because they threaten the familiar structures we have built — our hut or our castle. But they are also exciting because they are the Call to Adventure. They are the keys that offer the possibility of dismantling our structures, our connection with the three centres, and our return to the Golden World. (Note: the term the Golden World was not used by Campbell; he used the more general expression, The Return.)

Leaving the Hut or the Castle
The foundations and walls of our hut or castle are beginning to tremble. The structures aren't quite as solid as we had hoped. Our dilemma is that we are sitting in the hut or castle and the walls are shaking. It is reminding us of the underlying sense of "not quite rightness"

in our lives. There is something coming from our unconscious that wants to be acknowledged. The urge is to do anything to alleviate the discomfort. How do we strengthen the walls? How do we make our coping strategies stronger? How do we restore peace and stability? None of these responses will help. We need to watch the walls shaking and do nothing to keep them in place.

This is the moment of truth; this is the call to leave the comfort of the hut or the castle. We can sense the futility of trying to keep the old structures in place; we have been doing that for a long time. This is the beginning of the journey. Each time we respond to this uncomfortable call, we begin to free ourselves from the habitual patterns of identity. It happens slowly at first, but we get better as we practice. Sometimes it doesn't feel like an adventure at all. But at other times, there is a sense of excitement or exhilaration. It doesn't measure up to the spectacular and epic adventures of someone like Jason and his search for the Golden Fleece. However, this is our call to adventure. It is an inward journey in which we explore the secrets of the psyche. It is our journey into the unconscious.

The Purpose of the Journey

All the great myths are set in the external world. They usually involve difficult journeys through unknown, and sometimes unfriendly, terrains. The purpose of the adventure is vague or difficult to describe. There is some metaphorical object that needs to be recovered. The object, such as the Golden Fleece or the Holy Grail, is recognised by the hero as being of absolute, life-restoring value. For Jason, the Golden Fleece "gave him the power to rest his rightful throne from a usurper." (4) The challenge for us is to convert the insights of the mythic stories into a way of understanding our own inner journey. We need to convert the stories from an exterior realm with ships and mountains and dragons and translate those objects into the challenges of exploring our own psyche.

The highly valued prizes of the Golden Fleece or Holy Grail have a fairy-tale quality to them. What is the prize on offer in our own

Call to Adventure? It is, of course, the recovery of the Self or the return to the three centres. The legend of Jason hinted at this in his search for the Golden Fleece. There was something of great value he had to recover. It was his own Self that gave him the power to sit on his own throne; he recovered his own sovereignty. Likewise, in his quest for the Holy Grail, Parsifal had to enter the castle of the Holy Grail and ask the ailing king, "Whom does the Grail serve?" If he did this, the king would recover, and the kingdom would return to abundant life. At an inner level, Parsifal is being asked to go within and to ask himself the question: "What do I serve? What is the meaning and purpose of my life?" With these questions comes the possibility of the unravelling of his identity and the false self he has constructed. The kingdom that is returned to abundant life is his own psyche.

One Momentus Step or a Steady Dismantling

The other translation to be made is that the myths present the adventure as a single, epic journey. Once it is completed and the prize achieved, there was no more to do. In Dante's *Divine Comedy*, there was the long and arduous journey through the Three Worlds, but it culminated in "the illumination of the voyager and his view of the one Eternal Light." (5) For most of us, it is different. We do not get to the prize in one momentous step. Rather, the adventure is the moment-to-moment opportunity for the steady dismantling of the shells of identity. Our identity is being dismantled brick by brick. We need to persist with the dismantling by repeating the adventure many times. Each time we respond to the call, a little more of our unconscious content is brought to consciousness.

This steady and repetitive view of the adventure can be frustrating. The adventure is often more uncomfortable than it is exciting. And when the adventure is over, we must hear the call once more and repeat it all again. It makes wrestling with a physical dragon seem like a more attractive option. This frustration is often manifested in the way we respond to the Call to Adventure. We can sense the futility in what we are doing and where our lives are heading. The temptation is to see our problems in the exterior world and to change the external circumstances of our life. We change our partners, look for a new career or explore a new interest. While some of these changes may be helpful, they do not really get to the opportunity that is on offer: the dismantling of identity and the recovery of Self.

The Refusal of the Call

We are often too busy or preoccupied to pay much attention to the call. We can be unhappy, depressed or disinterested in life for many years and still not feel we need to do anything about it. We reassure ourselves that this is normal. It is not that bad; it will get better, or this is not the time for change. We also don't know how to change. What is the first step? We are uncomfortable in even recognising our feelings of despair and deep dissatisfaction. It is often not until something seriously disruptive happens in our lives that we are forced to pay attention.

Campbell speaks strongly about the consequences of hearing the call and not responding:

> Often in actual life, and not infrequently in myths and popular tales, we encounter the dull case of the call unanswered; for it is always possible to turn the ear to other interests. Refusal of the summons converts the adventure into its opposite. Walled in boredom, hard work, or "culture", the subject loses the power of significant affirmative action and becomes a victim to be saved. His flowering world becomes a wasteland of dry stones and his life feels meaningless." (6)

"Walled in boredom" and "a wasteland of dry stones" are strong images. They could be used to describe the inner world of the four grumpy old men discussed in Chapter One. With each refusal, we return to our hut and its protective structures and cut ourselves off further from connection with ourselves and with life. It becomes our pathway to early senility. Each call is our opportunity to return to the abundant life of the kingdom promised to Parsifal in the quest for the Holy Grail.

King Minos – Distracted by the Affairs of State

Refusal of the call is often justified by our commitment and success in undertaking good works in the world. One of the most famous Greek myths is the story of King Minos of Crete. He was fighting for the throne that was rightfully his and asked the gods for a symbol of support. They acquiesced and sent a magnificent white bull on the condition that it was to be sacrificed when he assumed the throne. The throne was won, and the time came for the sacrifice. Minos, seeing the magnificence of the animal, decided to keep it for his own herd and substituted another in its stead. The return of the bull would have symbolised his submission to the rule of the gods. Instead, he chose to keep the bull for his own personal aggrandisement. It is often at the time of our greatest worldly success that we become engrossed in those affairs and lose sight of our higher purpose. It is a time when we start to believe in our own invulnerability and become convinced that we are in charge of our own destiny. We override our own inner wisdom and become arrogant and filled with self-importance. We start to believe our own deluded story.

Notwithstanding his ill-advised decision to retain the bull, Minos proved to be a good and noble king, much respected and loved by his people. Under his reign, the kingdom of Crete flourished, and his subjects enjoyed peace and abundance. However, he was busy and distracted with the affairs of state. In his absence, his wife became infatuated with the white bull. She conceived a child by the bull, a monster with a human body and the head and tail of a bull. The Minotaur, as the child was known, became troublesome and dangerous. Its origins were an embarrassment and a disturbance to the king and the good workings of the kingdom. To conceal the Minotaur, Minos had constructed an enormous underground labyrinth in which to hide the monster. With its blind passages and complex design, it proved effective in keeping the

Minotaur contained. However, the concealment was achieved at an enormous cost and energy, and there was a loss of innocence for the king and the kingdom. Each year eighteen young men and women from occupied lands were offered as a sacrifice to the Minotaur.

The labyrinth has become a symbol for the unconscious where we conceal what we don't want to acknowledge. We all have our little minotaurs that we would like to conceal. We try to deny them but at some level we know they are there. We receive unwelcome messages from the unconscious reminding us that they are still there. There is something concealed that needs to be acknowledged. We keep busy with our worldly endeavours and attend to our duties and obligations. Maintaining the hut or the castle becomes our life's work, even while the foundations are trembling from the rumblings of the minotaurs concealed beneath.

Stage Two   The Threshold Guardians and the Clashing Rocks
Even when we have responded positively to the call, the challenges of the journey have just begun. The unconscious is the area of the psyche in which we have put things we don't want to see or experience. We might realise that the external circumstances of our life are not working, and that provides the motivation for change. But there is a more difficult question: Do we really want to enter the inner world of the unconscious and explore the unknown parts of the psyche that we have been concealing all our lives?

Dante's *Divine Comedy* begins with the line: "In the afternoon of my life I entered into a dark wood in which there was no path." It expresses the confusion of many people as they approach middle-age: *Here I am in the afternoon of my life and nothing I have been doing makes any sense. My life has lost its meaning and it seems very dark.* It also hints at the trepidation and fear of the hero, and the reluctance to hear the Call to Adventure. *Do I want to enter the unknown inner world in which there are no paths, and I don't know where to go?*

The move away from the familiar and beyond our known life horizon is full of uncertainty. We are moving beyond the protected zone of our village boundary. We are also preparing to challenge the entrenched messages of our childhood conditioning that have been incorporated into the walls of our hut. (7) The internalised image of our parental figures is there, questioning the wisdom of moving forward and warning us of the perils that lie ahead. We are preparing to let go of the protective shells of identity that have kept us safe. It is not surprising that there might be some faltering in our commitment to move forward. There is an anxiety that wants us to stay in our "business as usual" world. Like King Minos, there is contentment in maintaining our kingdom exactly as it is. Even at this point, the hero might abandon the journey. This transition into the inner world is too difficult.

In many places of worship, the front portal is protected by fierce mythological carvings that serve as the threshold guardians. They are intended to "ward away all incapable of entering the higher silences within." (8) They question our willingness to leave behind the everyday world and all its distractions and enter the stillness and silence of the space within.

The Clashing Rocks

The risk of having to abandon the journey as we meet the threshold guardians is recounted in the story of Jason, in his journey to find the Golden Fleece. On his way, he encountered the 'clashing rocks' which stood astride a narrow passage through which Jason needed to pass. The clashing rocks were rock cliffs that smashed together and crushed anything that sailed between them. Jason had been warned of their existence by a friendly king who advised him to send a bird through first. They could proceed if the bird made it through, but without delay. Jason released a dove that made it through, losing only a few tail feathers. He followed, losing only the stern railing of his ship.

The story of the clashing rocks raises many issues for our own call to adventure. Are we able to listen to the advice of the friendly king who represents our own higher intelligence? When we are convinced that we know what we are doing, are we inclined to override our own intuition? Are we ever still enough to pass between our own clashing rocks? Watching "the bird fly through first" is our invitation to be the witness. The dove, which often represents higher guidance, needs to be our guide. In our own journey to the Golden Fleece, the shells of identity do not want us to proceed. We want to keep the defensive structures of the psyche in place. Yet there is a calling to go forward, and so we get trapped in a 'push and pull' dilemma; we don't know whether to stop or go forward. That is when we get caught by the clashing rocks and our journey ends. That the dove lost a few feathers and Jason lost the stern railing of his ship, suggests that the dismantling process has already begun. The clashing rocks provide a foretaste, in a small way, of what is to follow.

The clashing rocks is also a metaphor for the frenzied mind trying to find relief from its own inner discomfort. It jumps between ideas and possibilities to distract itself from the underlying unconscious pain. This relentless activity of the mind can manifest in our life in many ways. We might think that the dissatisfaction and frustration we are feeling is caused by the circumstances of our lives; by where we live, by our work or by our partners. So we change houses, jobs or partners and for a moment there is relief. But the relief is short-lived and the pain returns. The mind gets busy again and concludes that the change we made wasn't the right one. We try again and keep making changes to our life circumstances and all the while the underlying pain continues to be there. We can keep repeating this cycle of frustration for the rest of our lives and never get away from the underlying source of frustration.

Each time we fail to find any resolution or relief, the activity of the mind becomes more frenzied. It scuttles from one idea to the next and with each failed attempt, we become more anxious and depressed. Our searching for relief becomes obsessive, and we lose complete connection with our own inner guidance. It is our inheritance from our misguided concept of the Garden of Eden. We believed that we ate the fruit of the tree of the knowledge of good and evil. With that came our irresistible urge to judge. We began to divide the world into good and evil: *I want this, I don't want that; this is attractive, that is unattractive, and so on.* We took ourselves out of the Garden of Eden and our restless mind ensures we can't return. As long as we maintain the polarity of good and evil with our judgements, we can never quiet the mind. We can't get back to the Garden, and to the three centres. It is only when the frenzied activity of the mind subsides, we can watch the dove and pass through the clashing rocks.

The Threshold of the Adventure

We have now arrived at the threshold where the adventure can begin. The unsettling messages from the unconscious have brought us to this point. The messages may be arising because of some challenging life circumstance or the sense that something needs our attention. It might be coming from some difficult experience in the past we have concealed in the labyrinth of the unconscious. The temptation in these uncomfortable moments is to move our attention to "the affairs of state." Like King Minos, we can distract ourselves by taking care of our worldly affairs. We become pre-occupied with our careers, our interests, our relationships, our success and so on. We move back to our hut or our castle; our worldly endeavours strengthen the shells of identity. But all the while, at some level, we know that these are only distractions to keep away from discomfort. It is not that we don't take care of these worldly things, but they don't need to be our most important priority. We are never going to find fulfillment there. But the worldly endeavours are valuable; they provide us with the uncomfortable experiences with which we need to work.

As we sit in stillness watching the clashing rocks, we can reaffirm our commitment to move across the threshold and commence our journey into the unconscious. This is the subject of the next chapter.

CHAPTER 14

The Journey into the Unconscious

The very things we wish to avoid, neglect, and flee
from turn out to be the 'prima materia' from which
all growth comes. —Andrew Harvey

Once we pass through the clashing rocks, we move into the challenging terrain of the unconscious. This is the Road of Trials where we experience the unexplored content residing in the unconscious. Our resolution and courage will be tested. We might still decide that the pain of the past is too great to revisit; we give up and return to the safety of our familiar world. But there are also helpers along the way. If we can believe that the help will be there when we need it, the Road of Trials becomes the Road of Trust. It will deliver us to the realisation of the journey's purpose, the connection to the three centres and the return to the Golden World.

**Stage Three   The Road of Trials or the Road of Trust —
The Helpers**
There are no paths here, and we need to give up any idea that we are in control or can respond to the challenges that arise. We will be engaging with forces beyond our control and our identity we will not serve us here. The message to our identity is:

"Abandon hope all ye who enter here." (1)

We need to surrender as we move towards the slow dismantling of identity.

There will be discouragement, challenges, and the occasional dragon along the road. No matter how uncomfortable the journey, we have the support of a greater force. If we are truly willing to embark on the journey, then destiny will support us. The help will often come from unusual and unexpected sources. The existence of the support from a higher level is described in the love story of Amor and Psyche.

Amor, the son of Venus and Jupiter, has fallen deeply in love with Psyche. Although Psyche is a mere mortal, her beauty is so great that she is more venerated than Venus, and this angers Venus deeply. Venus tries to seduce her son and persuade him to destroy Psyche. Amor rejects his mother's advances and chooses to be with Psyche. This only increases Venus's jealousy, and she sets out to destroy Psyche by demanding tasks of her that she thinks will kill her. This includes sorting a barn full of different grains by dawn, and bringing a basket filled with "a day's worth of beauty up from the underworld". And to make sure that Amor is unable to help her, Venus ensures her son remains locked up and under guard. In desperation, Psyche turns for help to her future father-in-law, Jupiter. He remembers his own amorous experiences, accepts Psyche as his son's bride and helps her complete the tasks. In the end, Venus accepts her son's wishes. Amor and Psyche celebrate their wedding in the presence of all the gods. Psyche is made immortal, and Venus makes peace with her. (2)

From Mortal to Immortal
On the face of it, the story of Amor and Psyche looks like another love story, but it is much more. Psyche is the Greek word for "soul", and Amor the Greek word for "love". Psyche is a mortal; Amor is already a god. The story is then about a mortal soul and her movement towards divine love. The jealous behaviour of Venus towards her son's future bride is a familiar part of a mother's behaviour. While it could be judged as excessive and unfair, Psyche was able to use it for her own transformation and liberation. The remarkable thing about

the story is Psyche's ability to remain calm and non-reactive in the face of extreme provocation. She was dealing with forces far beyond her understanding. She could have chosen to become the victim, but instead, focuses on the tasks at hand, even though they must have seemed impossible. In the face of adversity, she surrendered and trusted that the help she needed would be provided.

The other insight from the story lies in the last task set for Psyche. She was asked to bring "a day's worth of beauty up from the underworld." This is really a request to bring the unknown contents of the unconsciousness into consciousness. It was her invitation to participate in the alchemical process. On completion of this task, her road of trials was at an end, and Psyche became immortal. It is encouraging for all of us to remember that whenever we are challenged by adversity, we are being asked to "bring a day's worth of beauty up from the underworld." It is our invitation to the alchemical process.

Psyche is an inspiring example of the hero's capacity to trust and to know that divine help may be at hand. It is when we surrender to what is happening and get out of the way, that something different can happen. As Campbell observed,

> "The hero is covertly aided by the advice, amulets,
> and secret agents of the supernatural helper ... Or it
> may be that the hero discovers for the first time that
> there is a benign power everywhere supporting him
> in his superhuman passage." (3)

We might discover a power within us that always supports us. Psyche, through her unwavering presence and trust in benign powers, realised the purpose of the hero's journey, to become immortal and to join the gods.

The Slender Threads
In reflecting on the forces that shaped his life, Robert Johnson, a renowned Jungian author, uses the term "slender threads". (4) For him,

this term describes the almost miraculous ways in which his life, both inner and outer, had evolved. At particular crossroads, opportunities arose when they were needed, and new directions appeared almost by accident. When he looks back with the benefit of hindsight, he can see how beautifully orchestrated his life has been. There has been a higher power that guided him through the stages of life. There were delicate moments of transition but, in the end, it was clear the slender threads informed them all, without his knowing. In our willingness to answer the call to adventure and explore the unknown inner terrain, we can trust that the same slender threads that Johnson found, will also guide us. Our compass will be our realisation that we know nothing and should listen; we only have to take the next step. We will be shown if that step was not the one intended for us. We also need to be alert to the little winks from the universe that encourage and inform us that we are on the path.

The hero's journey can be difficult and uncomfortable because we are trying to move beyond the familiar patterns of our lives. We have left the hut. We may lose a few feathers or even the stern railing of our ship, but that is no reason to lose our trust. When the journey becomes challenging, that is the time to give up our limited ideas of what we think should be happening and to surrender to a higher force. This wisdom is expressed in the first three steps of the Twelve Step Program (5), a program for recovering alcoholics:

1. We admitted we were powerless over ... — that our lives had become unmanageable.
2. Came to believe that a power greater than ourselves could restore us to sanity.
3. Made a decision to turn our will and our lives over to the care of God as we understood Him.

The challenge for all of us is to let go of our ideas of what we think should be happening. If we persist in trying to impose our ideas, we are setting ourselves on a collision course with reality. With this, we become disillusioned, fearful, and disempowered. We lose confidence and trust in life. Eventually it becomes too hard, we give up and go back to our hut.

Stage Four Allowing the Opposites to Come Together

As we come to the lowest point of our journey, we are moving close to the recovery of the Golden Fleece. The travails we have encountered along the way have tested our determination and courage and prepared us to take the last challenging steps to realise our purpose.

Joseph Campbell had two names for this moment of transformation and resolution occurring at the lowest point of the cycle. The simplest, and most powerful, is the Sacred Marriage, which refers to the same psychological process as Jung's alchemical process. But Campbell's term, the Sacred Marriage is a more potent term; it describes what is actually happening. The Sacred Marriage also supports Jung's idea that as the opposite energies unite, they 'create a new third thing- a living birth, that leads to a new level of being'. The living birth flows naturally from the Sacred Marriage. For Campbell, the 'new third thing' is a new perspective on ourselves and the world and the dissolution of identity. It is the natural offspring of the Sacred Marriage. Campbell refers to this next stage of the journey as The Return; in our terms it is the return to the centres and our entry into the Golden World.

The Sacred Marriage is the crux of the hero's journey; it is where transformation happens or where the wrappers of identity are removed. The framework Campbell has developed, and the myths he builds on, are simply there to support us in our reluctant journey to the Sacred Marriage. They reassure us that this path, with all its discomfort, has been walked by countless heros since the beginning of time.

Another term used by Campbell in describing the Sacred Marriage is *apotheosis*. Apotheosis in Greek means the elevation to the status of a god. This is reminiscent of the story of Psyche, who attended to the difficult tasks that had been set for her with such patience and grace, that she, too, was elevated to the realm of the gods. The "elevation to the status of a god" is not a description that is easy for us to comprehend.

It is not necessarily an outcome that sits comfortably for most of us. Perhaps if we revisit the idea, "The kingdom of heaven is spread upon the earth and people do not see it", it makes it more understandable. Apotheosis would then mean that we can experience and enjoy the kingdom of heaven while we go about our daily lives.

Both descriptions, the Sacred Marriage and apotheosis, hint at the profound nature of the transformation that is possible when we respond to the Call to Adventure in our daily lives. Apotheosis is a term that also recognises we are moving beyond our normal daily experience into a different realm, the Golden World, which is the next stage of the hero's journey.

Stage Five – The Golden World
The Golden World is the natural offspring of the Sacred Marriage. It follows on directly as an intrinsic and inevitable sequel of the Sacred Marriage. The difficult work of getting to the Sacred Marriage is complete and transformation has happened. A piece of unconscious content has been discovered and liberated. The tussle between unconscious content and the structures of identity has been resolved, at least in this moment. We are now in the Golden World. This might be a life-changing experience where our identity, or a big part of it, has been permanently dismantled. Or it might be a less significant transformation, where we experience the radiant beauty of the Golden World, perhaps only for a few minutes.

Some words from Chapter One describe how the Golden World might be felt:

> The body relaxes and surrenders; there is an absence of any need
> for action and the familiar boundaries of the body disappear.
> Our thinking stops and there is a knowing that everything is
> alright. We are being held and supported so there is nothing to
> fear. We relax into our own wisdom. And of course, the heart
> is happy beyond measure; it is overwhelmed by its intimate
> connection with life. We have connected with the three centres.
> We have returned to the Golden World.

The heart features prominently in our arrival in the Golden World. The grief that was being avoided has now has been freed. The protection around the heart falls away and our natural connection to the heart is restored, evidenced by strong feelings of intimacy and compassion. And there are particular heart experiences that each Enneagram type may encounter as they enter the Golden World. These type-related experiences, known as the Virtues, are one of the most beautiful parts of Enneagram teaching. They arise naturally as an intrinsic part of the experience of the Golden World. It affirms the power of the Enneagram when each type can experience their particular Virtue, without any guidance or direction. It just arises by itself without prompting.

For Type One, the Virtue is Serenity. Type Ones no longer need to react to the conditions of the world. They respond naturally to others and the world with acceptance and compassion. Serenity has replaced the One's Passion of Resentment.

For Type Two, the Virtue is Humility. Type Twos no longer need up to be seen as selfless or to sustain any concept of themselves. They surrender naturally to the vulnerability and delicacy of the heart. Humility has replaced the Two's Passion of Pride.

For Type Three, the Virtue is Authenticity. Type Threes no longer need to strive to impress others. They respond naturally to the world with purity and heartfeltness. Authenticity has replaced the Three's Passion of Vanity.

For Type Four, the Virtue is Equanimity. Type Fours no longer need to intensify or hold on to their emotions. They are naturally with whatever experience is presenting itself, allowing emotions to be in their awareness without being disturbed by them. Equanimity has replaced the Four's Passion of Envy.

For Type Five, the Virtue is Non-attachment. Type Fives no longer need to cling to their ideas and concepts. They are naturally allowing their hearts to be touched and seeing the preciousness of life as it really is. Non-attachment has replaced the Five's Passion of Avarice.

For Type Six, the Virtue is Courage. Type Sixes no longer need to be afraid and anxious about everyone and everything. They are naturally guided by the steadfastness of their hearts to do what their hearts desire. Courage has replaced the Six's Passion of Anxiety.

For Type Seven, the Virtue is Sobriety. Type Sevens no longer need to fill themselves up with experiences. They are naturally grounded in the moment and grateful for the experience they are having now. Sobriety has replaced the Seven's Passion of Gluttony.

Tor Type Eight, the Virtue is Innocence. Type Eights no longer need to "amp everything up" so they feel alive. They naturally respond freshly to each moment, knowing this is the vibrancy of reality. Innocence has replaced the Eight's Passion of Lust.

For Type Nine, the Virtue is Engagement. Type Nines no longer need to stay out of contact with their instinctual energies because they could disturb the peace. They naturally awaken to their true state and with an open heart, engage with the full experience of being. Engagement has replaced the Nine's Passion of Sloth.

We have now experienced the radiant beauty of the Golden World and have been touched by the exquisite qualities of our own Virtue. We have been reunited with the source that has always been within us. It is the "power that constructs the atoms and controls the orbit of the stars." (6). It is the same universal energy that Jung discovered as he travelled through the depths of the unconscious. Jung believed he had recovered the Self, a term that acknowledges its universal and divine origins, but also recognises that this is who we are. Other traditions have different words that describe this connection with something divine and beyond the realm of our daily lives. These include the Christ Mind, Buddha Consciousness, the Dao, Wu-wei, the Kingdom of Heaven and so on. They all recognise a state in which we are connected to our source, and free from the distractions of the world.

The Next Stage — The Return to the World

It is likely we might want to stop the journey here. Why would we want to leave the Golden World and return to the world? But the final task of the returning hero is to share the benefits of the journey with the world. The next chapter explores the challenges of the hero returning to the world.

CHAPTER 15

The Return to the World

When the hero's quest has been accomplished,
the hero must still return with his life-transmuting
trophy. The boon that he brings restores the world.
—Joseph Campbell

Stage Six — The Return and the Gifts to the World
The consistent theme of the countless hero myths is that the hero,
after his completion of the adventure, returns to the everyday world.
The hero's journey is a cycle; it follows a circular path in which the
end becomes the beginning of the new cycle. The hero returns to
the hut or the castle where the Call to Adventure was first heard.
However, something has happened; some transformation has taken
place. The protective shells have been dismantled, perhaps only
partially and not always permanently. But the hero has experienced
something that makes it difficult to return to the everyday world.
Like Jason's search for the Golden Fleece, the hero has recovered the
"thing of great value" that was the object of the search.

> Jason sailed through the Clashing Rocks into the sea of marvels,
> circumvented the dragon that guarded the Golden Fleece and
> returned with the fleece and the power to wrest his rightful
> throne from a usurper. (1)

For Jason, the recovery of the Golden Fleece represented his reconnection with Self and access to the divine energies. He gained the power to become master of his own kingdom and overcome the usurper, the divisive distractions of the material world.

Campbell suggests the hero's return to the world is often undertaken with some reluctance: "Having cast off the world, who would desire to return again?" (2) The Buddha, after his enlightenment, expressed some uncertainty about what he should do next: "The Buddha sat for four days enjoying still the sweetness of liberation. Then he doubted whether his message could be communicated, and he thought to retain the wisdom for himself." But after some intercession and persuasion from others, "he was persuaded to proclaim the path. And he went back into the cities of men ... bestowing the inestimable boon of the knowledge of the Way." (3)

For most of us, the hero's journey is not completed with a single round of the cycle. As we complete each round, we find ourselves back at the beginning, back in the familiar world with the same challenging conditions. The floor and walls of our hut or castle once again begin to tremble, but there is something different. We have had glimpses of a different dimension, and the irritations and frustrations we experience have lost some of their intensity. We are more able to be present in our world and the urge to move away from discomfort is more tempered. Each round of the cycle builds our trust in the benevolence of the universe. We know there will be further challenges, but we also know we will be supported. The supernatural and temporal helpers that supported us through the last round will also be there again. The terrain has become more familiar, and we negotiate each challenge with growing courage, encouraged by the little winks from the universe.

In each round we have explored parts of the unconscious content that has been the source of our inner pain, discomfort, and suffering. Each round has given us the opportunity to allow some of that disturbing content to move into consciousness. And each time we have allowed that to happen, the Sacred Marriage has facilitated a miraculous transformation. It has taken us to the Golden World. Each round of the cycle accomplishes a gradual bringing to consciousness the disturbing energies of the unconscious. We begin to experience, in some measure, the sweetness of liberation enjoyed by the Buddha.

The Life-transmuting Trophy – The Boon to the World

The final task of the returning hero is to share the benefits of the journey with the world. For Campbell, this is the other purpose of the hero's journey. The benefit is not just for the hero; it is to be shared with the world. It is for the good of all mankind.

> "When the hero's quest has been accomplished, the hero must still return with his life- transmuting trophy. The boon that he brings restores the world." (4)

Part of the life-transmuting trophy is the hero's new perspectives on his own reality and his life's purpose. It changes the way he lives in the world. Like Buddha, the hero has tasted, to some extent, the "sweetness of liberation"; hence, the reluctance to re-engage with the limitations and suffering of the world. The revelations of the deep inner journey make the old perspectives and beliefs irrelevant and meaningless. The structures and beliefs that have kept the world together no longer seem to have substance. This fraying of the world of ideas is described by Eckhart Tolle:

> "Past and future fall away. The timeless dimension of consciousness has come in." (5)

Apart from a changed perspective, the hero may bring back something of great value to the world. The Buddha is an obvious example in which the hero, after his return, becomes a world-renowned teacher. However, the example of the Buddha can create misleading and unrealistic expectations about the nature of the life-transmuting trophy. The trophy that any returning hero can offer is likely to be much more simple and subtle than the revolutionary insights offered by the Buddha.

In translating the hero's journey into our daily lives, the most important offering we can bring to the world is our capacity to be with our own pain. If, when we are disturbed or irritated, we can feel our own discomfort, and bring it into consciousness, this is the boon of great value. It ripples out into the world. We are not reacting to get relief for ourselves. We are not withdrawing, blaming, or projecting our discomfort on to others. We are staying present with it in a non-reactive way. The chain of reactive behaviour has been broken. Sometimes the people we are with will notice the difference. They will feel the change in the nature of the connection and will change their behaviour to align with the softer, receptive energy. This can happen in little ways in everyday situations: at the supermarket checkout, with the little interactions at work, or in our relating with our family. It looks simple and insignificant, but the energy ripples out and touches the world. It is just as important as the words and wisdom of the Buddha.

The second great boon is an extension of the first. When we don't react, we can be the space to listen to the other person. We saw the importance of this in Chapter Ten where Freud or Jung found they could treat their patients simply by allowing them to speak. In doing so, the patients were able to release the troubling contents of the unconscious. This gives an insight into the healing power of being able to listen while another person talks. It is one of the most important gifts we can give another person. We don't need to encourage them, give them good advice or interrupt in any way. This gift is particularly valuable when the content being shared has the potential to be challenging to ourselves. In a way, we are calling them to their own hero's journey and holding them as they move past the Clashing Rocks and along the Road of Trials.

The boons that we offer to the world are simple, but life transforming. As they ripple into the world, they will be passed on to others. The chain of compassion replaces the chain of reactivity. We are joined by an ever-increasing number of pilgrims moving around the cycle of the hero's journey.

THE RETURN TO THE WORLD

The Specific Gifts Unique to Each Enneagram Type

In Chapter Three we looked at the teachings of Richard Rohr and his exploration of the unique Gifts that each Enneagram might bring to the world. He proposed that the Gifts are a natural expression of the heart. They are the intrinsic qualities that manifest when we are connected to our heart centre. When, at the completion of the hero's journey, having experienced the Sacred Marriage and moved into the Golden World, it is not surprising then, that these type-related Gifts are likely to show up. The Gifts arise in innocence and happen without any attempt by us to make them happen. They are:

Type One	Integrity, fairness
Type Two	Caring, compassion
Type Three	Inspiration to get things done
Type Four	Creativity, beauty
Type Five	Innovation, clarity
Type Six	Warm-hearted dependability
Type Seven	Joy, optimism
Type Eight	Strength, truth
Type Nine	Acceptance, calmness

The boon that we can offer the world, therefore, has three components. The first is our ability to be with our own pain and not project our discomfort on to others; the second is our ability to be able to sit with another person, to be quiet and listen to what they are saying and not react to them or try to fix them. And the final component is our type-specific Gift. And in a way, they all connected to each other. As the protection around the heart falls away, all these beautiful capacities of the heart will be revealed. There will be a deep capacity to be with what is happening in our world and it will be flavoured by the Gift of our Enneagram type.

CHAPTER 16

Prospecting for Gold in the Unconscious

Can I give up all hope of a better past?
—Colin Tipping, *Radical Forgiveness:*
Making Room for the Miracle

The Small Practical Steps of the Journey

We can be seduced by the spectacular drama of the hero's journey that culminates in one esoteric moment of divine revelation. It is presented as an epic journey that ends in a single moment of revelation. In one way, this is encouraging; we can see the journey's end in such glorious and enticing terms that it becomes a powerful motivation to hear the call. In another way it is discouraging; it seems far beyond the possibilities and reality of our daily existence. The more modest and realistic alternative is to see the hero's journey as a moment-to-moment opportunity for the slow unification of the shells of personality. In this approach, we have to repeat the adventure many times. This perspective of the hero's journey helps us stay present with the challenges we encounter in our daily life.

There are things we can do right now that can start us on another round of adventure. It may be as simple as exploring the unconscious beliefs behind some of our actions or pondering on our reactions to situations that trigger us. Importantly, it can be our choice to 'sit on the steps' when we have been triggered, and feel the energies moving in the body. All these exercises offer the opportunity of allowing the opposites we have created to come together. We need the courage to stay in these exercises even as they become uncomfortable; they are an integral part of the hero's journey. It involves a shift in our focus to the small, practical steps in the journey, rather than anticipating a spectacular outcome. We can allow the dismantling of identity brick by brick, rather than hoping for a moment of psychological liberation.

The Truth Will Set You Free

The other pre-requisite for the hero's journey is our willingness to accept the truth about what happened. If we can look at the past squarely and honestly it allows the process of healing to begin. Until that happens, we are spending our energy trying to escape the truth. We are looking for excuses, trying to find someone to blame or becoming a victim and convincing ourselves we were powerless to make a different choice. They are all strategies to keep away from the unconscious pain or trauma associated with the past. What we deny, cannot be healed.

These strategies are the activities of the divided mind. We torment ourselves with our own inclination towards self-blame and scrutinising the past. We agonise about the past, and we get caught in the back-and-forth dilemma of the Clashing Rocks. Instead of resolution, we endure self-inflicted pain that can last forever. The only alternative is to be with the pain of the past. Can we allow ourselves to feel the pain and trauma that has been pushed into the unconscious? If what happened was painful, we can't change it or take it back. This truth is highlighted by Colin Tipping, the author of *Radical Forgiveness* (1) when he encourages us "to give up all hope of a better past."

With the opportunity for honest reflection, can we accept what happened? When we accept the truth of what happened, it means we can also feel the pain. This is the hard part, but it is where transformation occurs. Once we accept what happened, then the need for the cover-up disappears. All the strategies, stories and manipulations of the truth can be dropped, and we are left with the truth and access to the pain. This is a great relief; it is where freedom lies.

There is much value of being able to speak about what happened to another person. In sharing what happened with someone, it brings the truth out into the open. Once the words have been spoken, the secret is out, and we can't take it back. We give up any chance to further change or manipulate the story. This is also one of the benefits of counselling or sharing groups where there is the opportunity to speak about things we would prefer to keep secret. It is taking extreme responsibility for one's life and the things that have happened in the past or are happening now. It is a wonderful demonstration of the words,

"The truth will set you free." (2)

It also confirms the value of being able to hold the space for another person. If we can remain silent and listen with compassion to what they are saying, it can be the most effective way to get them to speak their truth.

Access to the Unconscious

There are many ways to discover the truth about the past and about ourselves. Some of them, like meditation and self-inquiry, are informal and organic. Others are more structured like counselling and the various depth psychology processes. These include dream analysis, active imagination, sand play, art therapy and dance. The common element in all these processes is to provide a space in which the unconscious is given equal authority and allowance for its expression. It is not the purpose of this book to explore all these possibilities; many excellent books are already available on these topics. However, there is one particular process that aligns closely with the stages of the hero's journey. It is called *Prospecting for Gold*. It is a process that is effective in finding the hidden content in the unconscious and allowing it to move into awareness. It is an extension of the ideas in Chapter Six when we looked at Pema Chödrön's concept of shenpa and the unusual ways we react when we have been triggered. It is also supported by Jung's insight:

> **"Everything that irritates us about others can lead us to an understanding of ourselves."**

The process seeks to explore the unconscious content that lies behind our reactive behaviour. In Jungian terms, it goes looking for the complexes that may have formed about the difficult experiences of the past. If Jung suggests that our irritations have something to teach us, we need to be curious about what that might be.

Prospecting for Gold — The Process

The process follows the same six stages of the hero's journey. To follow the process, it is helpful to recollect a recent situation or incident in which you were irritated, uncomfortable, triggered or in conflict with someone. Situations that have a recurring, difficult theme are particularly powerful. The exercise can be done by yourself but is much more valuable if you can work with another person.

(Some of the content in this process is adapted from material from The Centre for Attitudinal Healing in Canada and Costa Rica and my work with Claudette Thomas.)

Stage One: The Call to Adventure (and Not Refusing the Call)

- *Hearing the call*

- *Identify what happened in the current situation in which you were irritated or in conflict.*

- *Acknowledging that you are upset or in conflict*

  —This upset is gold

  —There are no small upsets

  —Denial is not helpful.

Often we will decide that the upset we are experiencing is not important or will go away by itself. Or we can blame it on the other person and decide that they are the ones who need to look at their behaviour. That might also be true, but it is not our business. We have to recognise that the irritation or conflict we are experiencing is there for a purpose; it is our way of exploring the unconscious. It is our Call to Adventure

---

Stage Two: The Threshold Guardians and the Clashing Rocks
Taking extreme responsibility for what is happening

- *Can you acknowledge that this is about you?*

- You need to take complete ownership and responsibility for this upset

  —Close all the exits

The concept of extreme responsibility is a potent one. In these situations, we are often inclined to slip away or mitigate the uncomfortable energies we are feeling. There is a tendency to explain the situation away or find someone to blame. Or we can tell ourselves that this situation is minor and doesn't deserve any further attention. Another common escape is to spiritualise what is happening. The spiritual bypass essentially moves us into a blissful state of dissociation away from what we are experiencing. We create an alternative reality that avoids the discomfort of the present experience. Of course, the discomfort continues to be there, and we feel it again as soon as we return from our dissociation and encounter the same experience.

A good summary of this stage is that "we need to close all the exits." In other words, we need to stand fully in the fire of our experience. Remember that we want to use this incident to find the illusive contents of the unconscious. We need to embrace it wholeheartedly, knowing it is happening for our benefit. It is our gold.

We have come to the threshold where we are preparing to move into the unconscious and experience the discomfort we don't want to feel. All our conditioning and our coping strategies are warning us of the perils of proceeding further. We can still return to the safety of our familiar world. Like Jason, we are preparing to sail through the clashing rocks. If we prevaricate and question the purpose of the journey, the mind will take over and we will be caught in its relentless machinations. We will, in our uncertainty and confusion, be crushed by the clashing rocks.

We need to stop and quiet the mind and listen to the "still small quiet voice" within. Then we can send "our bird through first" and be guided by our higher intelligence. It helps to stay with the physical experiences in the body and recognise we don't have to move away from the discomfort. It is getting past the protective mental activities that go into overdrive when we feel the discomfort. Those activities will be attempting to take us back to safety and have us abandon our adventure.

**Stage Three: The Road of Trials or the Road of Trust —
the Helpers**
Sitting on the Steps — Being With the Feelings - Surrender to
What Is Happening

"Watch it, feel it, allow it."

- What are the sensations in the body?

- What is happening in the gut?

- What is happening around the heart? In the throat?

- Is there an overwhelming emotion?

This is the road of trials; our resolution and courage are being tested. We have to focus on the feelings that are arising and surrender to the pain we might be feeling. There will be a temptation to argue with the unreasonableness of our current circumstances or think we can do something to alleviate our pain. But we need to surrender.

There will be helpers along the way; as Psyche found, some of them with divine powers. We need to be reminded of Campbell's words of encouragement:

> The hero is covertly aided by the advice, amulets, and secret
> agents of the supernatural helper ... Or it may be that the
> hero discovers for the first time that there is a benign power
> everywhere supporting him in his superhuman passage. (3)

This is the time to trust and surrender. Remember that we are seeking something beyond our comprehension. This is our journey to the Golden Fleece. It is what we desire more than anything else; it is the psyche's urgent longing for wholeness and unification.

Stage Four: Allowing the Opposites to Come Together — The Sacred Marriage

4.1 Moving Towards the Difficult Experiences of the Past

Associating this current feeling with feelings of a past incident

- Is this current feeling familiar?

- When did you first experience feelings like this?

- Can you remember an incident in the (distant) past when someone did something or said something that made you feel this way?

- Describe what happened in this earlier incident.

4.2. Feeling the past grief:

- Can you feel the grief that you must have felt in this earlier incident?

- Can you recollect what the feelings were around the heart?

- Can you surrender to these feelings?

This is the Sacred Marriage. We are allowing the accumulated painful feelings in the unconscious to move into consciousness. We have found the painful unconscious content we were trying to conceal, probably for a very long time.

Stage Five: The Golden World

The coming together of opposites, and the uniting of opposite energies, takes us into the Golden World. The beliefs and stories we have used to keep the pain away, are no longer needed. There is a spaciousness around what happened, both in the current situation and what happened in the past. We are naturally in our Heart Centre, with feelings of compassion for ourselves and for the other person. There is a sense of connection and oneness with everything. In this expanded spaciousness we can explore the misguided beliefs we made up to protect ourselves from the pain of that childhood experience.

5.1. What were the limiting beliefs you made up about yourself at the time of this earlier incident?

When these difficult experiences happen in childhood, we make up stories about ourselves, so we don't have to feel the pain. Often these stories include some element of self-blame, where the child assumes they were responsible or at fault. They can also include stories about shame, where the child assumes they must be unworthy and without value. Or they can include beliefs about being powerless and being unable to protect themselves or to take action. Some common examples of the beliefs we can make up are:

> * I am not worthy * I can't rely on love * I don't matter * It is
> safer not to have needs * I will lose the things I love or value
> * I can't get anything right (so it's best not to try) * I am flawed
> * I am alone (or I will remain alone so I don't suffer loss again)
> * I must do something to get love *I am unlovable * I don't

belong * I am at fault * I don't matter * I am at risk * I can't trust
anyone * I am disconnected * I have to get out of here * I need
space * I can't protect myself *I can't stop what's happening
* I am powerless *I must be easy-going *I must avoid conflict

Don't limit yourself to this list of possible beliefs. It is likely
that the beliefs you made up will be something specific to what
happened to you as a child.

5.2. Letting go of past beliefs?

- Can you see why you made up beliefs to protect yourself from
  the feelings of grief and hurt in this earlier situation?

- Can you let go of these beliefs and see that it was a misguided
  attempt to protect yourself from further pain?

- Can you see that these beliefs limit the possibilities for
  an authentic and empowered life?

- Can you see that in holding these beliefs you have
  unconsciously educated others to treat you in this way?

- Can you have compassion for yourself for hanging on to
  the beliefs that have limited your life for so long?

- Can you feel the freedom in knowing that these beliefs are not
  true?

We are using the feelings arising in the current incident to take us
back to difficult feelings of the past. It is taking us to the point where
we begin to feel the overwhelming emotion and pain of that earlier
experience. At that time, as children, we didn't have the capacities to
do anything else but push our pain into the unconscious and cover it
over with a story that denied what was really happening.

As we surrender, we stop resisting the arrival of the constellated complexes and the associated grief. They move into consciousness and touch the energy of the coping strategies. The unconscious

content and the protective shells come together and are united. This is the moment of alchemy and the Sacred Marriage.

The main concern for the child was to get away from, or minimise, the pain. The child made up misguided stories about what was happening as a way of getting relief from the pain. If the child's needs were constantly being ignored or over-ridden, it is not surprising the child would decide "I don't matter," "It's safer not to have needs" or "I am at fault." At least this reduces the threat of being disappointed in the future. Unfortunately, these become strong beliefs for the child as they are accepted as the most reliable way to avoid pain. In some cases, the beliefs could be critical to the physical and emotional survival of the child. Once these beliefs are formed, they will usually be carried into adult life. They have protected the child in their earlier years, so it is natural to keep them in place going forward. In fact, the beliefs will often be reinforced when, as adults, we experience similar challenges. We redouble our faith in the beliefs, even though they are not serving us.

We might also see, that now, as adults, we can have a different perspective on what happened. We might see why our parents behaved the way they did. We don't have to condone their behaviour, but we might see it was the best they were capable of at the time.

Stage Six: The Return and the Gifts to the World
The Gifts and the Boon

- Can you see that the current situation in which you were triggered, has allowed you to access difficult memories in the unconscious and let the grief and pain of the past come into consciousness?

- Can you feel the freedom in not having to conceal the painful experiences of the past?

- Can you let go of misguided beliefs you made up about yourself at the time?

- Can you feel the liberation in letting go the sad and limiting beliefs from the past?

- Can you take this freedom into the world and begin to relate to others in a different way?

The key to this process is that it uses the difficult feelings in the current situation to access the same difficult feelings and grief we experienced as children. Once we gain access to the grief and begin to feel it, its tight containing structures begin to unravel. The limiting stories we made up about ourselves to limit the grief can be released. This process can produce some intense feelings and needs to be embarked upon with care and compassion. It allows us to be with the grief that has been kept inside for a long time. Most people find the exercise to be liberating as they let go of the beliefs that have been limiting their lives in unconscious ways. It is a wonderful, practical example of how, if we can stay with the discomfort, the protective shells can be dismantled.

The following case studies demonstrate three actual, but disguised examples of this process. The descriptions have been shortened to focus on the critical steps.

Case Studies: Prospecting for Gold
a. "My family behaves badly."
Henry is a Type Two. He is a talented and intelligent man, married with children. He was to attend an Enneagram workshop away from home. At the last minute, he invited his family to travel with him, believing they could enjoy themselves while he attended the workshop. Once at the workshop his good intentions turned to disappointment and despair. His partner was frustrated that he was away during the day and the children were also unhappy. They were all complaining about being away from home and behaving badly towards him.

1. What are the feelings that arise when the family behaves badly?

"I feel angry and frustrated. I feel helpless in being able to do anything about it. I feel like screaming at them. I wish I had come to the workshop by myself and left them at home."

2. When did you first experience feelings like this? Can you remember an incident in the (distant) past when someone did or said something that made you feel this way?

"When I was about eight my older brother was punching me in the stomach. Finally, I yelled at him: 'I hate you.' My mother came over and slapped me across the face: 'Don't you every speak to anyone like that.' I felt angry, unfairly treated but powerless to do anything about it."

3. What were the beliefs you made up about yourself at the time?

His belief was: "I have to put up with bad behaviour if I want to get love."

Henry had been a good partner and father and had frequently put his family's wellbeing ahead of his own. They often took him for granted with no willingness to reciprocate. His belief from his childhood — "I have to put up with bad behaviour" — had limited his ability to call them into line and establish boundaries. In a way, he had unconsciously educated them to behave in a way that confirmed his belief. As he became conscious of this belief, he realised he didn't have to put up with bad behaviour. This changed the basis of many of his relationships, particularly those with his family.

This is also a good example how he had unconsciously educated his family to treat him badly, based on the belief: "I need to put up with bad behaviour to get love." This also aligns closely with his Type Two behaviour of needing to be thoughtful and selfless.

b. "I am alone (and I will always be alone)."
Alan is a Type Five. He is a warm and intelligent man. He has been in a successful career for twenty-five years but has never been in a long-term relationship. He is currently being triggered by a conflict

between his sister and his father. The sister is refusing to let his father see his grandchildren. Alan feels sad for the children and for his father, particularly for the father who has few other connections in his life.

1. What are the feelings that arise when you think about your father and the children?

> "I feel frustrated that the world has to be like this. I feel sad for my father who is struggling and is lonely. I feel sad for the children being denied connection with their grandfather. I feel angry with my sister for what she is doing."

2. When did you first experience feelings like this, particularly the sadness? Can you remember an incident in the (distant) past when someone did or said something that made you feel this way?

> "When I was six years old my mother died. I loved her deeply. She was my best friend. I felt absolutely distraught and very alone, as I was not close to the rest of my family. I was overwhelmed with loss and overcome with unspeakable grief. I couldn't talk to anyone; I didn't want to talk to anyone."

3. What were the beliefs you made up about yourself at the time?

> His belief at the time was: "I am alone, and I will always be alone."

Despite his warmth and intelligence, Alan had carried this belief about himself for forty-five years. He could now see how it had limited his life and his relationships. His unconscious belief had become his reality. His reluctance to get close to anyone arose from the fear of losing another loved one and re-experiencing the trauma he felt when his mother died. From that fear, he had created the protective shells that he thought would keep him safe. As he allowed the grief of his mother's death to become conscious it began to dismantle the protective shells. He recognised he did have a choice to move closer to the people he cared for, and to risk the possibility of loss.

c. "My boyfriend is too noisy."

Stephanie is a Type Three. She is an active, engaging, and successful woman. She is open to having a long-term partner. She likes her current boyfriend and there are many things that they share. However, when they are together, she feels he is "too noisy". She thinks it would be impossible to live with him in a long-term relationship.

1. What are the feelings that arise when your boyfriend is being noisy?

> "I feel anxious; I can't breathe; I feel at risk; there is not enough space; the noise is invading my space; I feel helpless."

2. When did you first experience feelings like this? Can you remember an incident in the (distant) past when someone did or said something that made you feel this way?

> "There were probably many times as a child I felt like this. My father was an alcoholic, and my mother had a very invasive personality. She wanted to control every aspect of my life. I remember her asking me what I wanted for my birthday, and I said I didn't want anything. I felt she would use the opportunity to try to get closer to me and control me. Eventually I told her: 'Just buy me a chocolate bar.' That felt like the safest option to limit her involvement in my life."

3. What were the beliefs you made up about yourself at the time?

> "The most important belief was: I have to protect my space. It was really important to me. My mother was constantly invading my space and I knew I had to fight to maintain some space for myself."

Stephanie clearly felt she had to protect herself from her mother; she probably had similar feelings about her alcoholic father, but to a lesser extent. Her dominant childhood belief was: "I have to protect my space." As a Three she needed the space to do outstanding things and to get validation from the people around her. This was not possible when she was being crowded out by her invasive mother. Stephanie carried this belief with her into adult life. It limited her capacity for intimacy and the ability to allow a partner into her life. As she brought this belief into her awareness, she could consciously navigate the challenges of allowing people to get close to her. She didn't have to compete with them for space.

Overview of the Three Case Studies

Prospecting for Gold is the invitation to travel into the unconscious to find the grief we have been trying to conceal, and to let go the beliefs and stories we made up to keep the grief away. Sometimes the beliefs will be small and subtle; other times, they will be significant, life-limiting beliefs that have affected our lives for decades.

In each of the three cases — Henry, Alan and Stephanie — they accessed experiences and feelings that had been very difficult for them as children. Those experiences had, to a greater or lesser extent, been placed in the unconscious and forgotten about. If any of them had been asked to recount details of their childhood, they may have been able to recall the facts of what happened. What they would not have been able to access were the profound feelings of grief associated with these experiences.

For Henry, it was the pain and trauma of not being able to defend himself and not being able to put boundaries in place to feel safe. It was also the hurt of being treated so unfairly by someone who was meant to love and nurture him. For Alan, it was the unspeakable trauma of losing the one person in his life that he loved and who loved him. For Stephanie, it was the unrelenting sense of invasion and suffocation she felt with her mother. Her struggle to find space to do outstanding things in her life would have been particularly challenging for a Three. For all of them, some misguided beliefs were being kept in place, so they didn't have to revisit the trauma. In the process they found the courage to allow their unconscious content to come into their awareness. This allowed them to remember what it was like for them when the trauma was happening. They were able sit in their pain and have compassion for themselves that this happened. With time, the pain abates. It won't ever be a pleasant memory, but at least it will be a conscious memory.

And as these deep unconscious experiences are touched and brought into consciousness, the shells of identity are dismantled. We no longer have to keep the unconscious pain away from our awareness. We can let go of the misguided beliefs we formed about ourselves to keep us safe. This is the culmination of the hero's journey.

Prospecting for Gold — Applying The Process As Soon As We Are Triggered

The myths on which the hero's journey is based are usually epic tales that often extend over many years. For us it is likely a round of the hero's journey might be completed in a much shorter period, even in minutes. All the stages of the journey will still be there: the Call to Adventure, the Threshold Guardians, the Clashing Rocks, the Road of Trials (or Trust), Allowing the Opposites to Come Together, the Sacred Marriage, the Golden World and the Return. However, it can take no time at all if we move through the stages without diversion.

Our progress in our journey will be helped if we use the Prospecting for Gold process to guide us through the stages. We can begin the process as soon as we realise we have been triggered. It might require us to step away from what we are doing or to excuse ourselves from a difficult interaction, just for a few minutes. When we have completed the process, we can come back to what we were doing, probably with a new perspective on what was happening and with something new to offer the world.

The short version of Prospecting for Gold is set out below.

Stage One

The Call to Adventure
We are triggered, irritated, frustrated, or afraid.

The Refusal of the Call
We see ourselves looking at ways of avoiding the call by
withdrawal, blame, projection and denial.

Stage Two

The Threshold Guardians
We feel the potentially overwhelming threats of continuing the
journey but we know we want to discover why this discomfort is
arising.

The Clashing Rocks
We prevaricate about the wisdom of continuing the journey but
remember that we need to stay present with what is happening.
We take extreme responsibility for what we are feeling and chose
to remain present and still.

Stage Three

The Road of Trials or the Road of Trust — The Helpers
We sit on the steps and feel what is happening in the body.
We identify which is the strongest feeling around this current
situation.

Stage Four

Allowing the Opposites to Come Together —The Sacred Marriage

We use our current feelings to find a time in the past when we
first experienced feelings like this. We focus on what happened
in that earlier incident. We find the feelings that would have

been arising in that earlier incident, particularly the grief. At that time, we didn't have the capacity to respond to what was happening. But now we have the time and resources to bring the grief into our awareness. We can feel it around the heart.

This is where we have to fully allow what is happening and what happened in the past. We do not resist the pain and discomfort as the unconscious grief becomes conscious. The opposing energies within the psyche are allowed to come together. The structures of identity are being dismantled and the beliefs and stories fall away.

Stage Five

The Golden World
We look for the limiting belief we made up about ourselves at that earlier time. We recognise we no longer need to hold on to that belief. A different and true perspective is available to us.

Stage Six

The Return and the Gifts to the World
We recognise that some transformation has occurred, we are offered a new perspective and, perhaps, experience a moment of "sweet liberation". We return to our worldly life to share the knowledge of the Way, often in simple practical ways.

From the moment of being triggered or irritated, the process can happen quickly. If we can stay with our feelings and allow the transformation to occur, the whole journey can be completed in ten minutes. Being able to use the process straight after being triggered will add to its potency. The material we are working with is fresh and we don't get a chance to forget, deny or minimise what just happened. With the feelings still in the body, we can become skilled in moving quickly to Stage Four, and linking those feelings to the distant feelings in the past. There we will find the unconscious experiences and memories which are causing us to be triggered in this current situation. We will also find the limiting beliefs we made up about ourselves at that time.

The possibility of moving quickly through the stages of the hero's journey is consistent with the idea that we need to keep repeating the cycle frequently until our work is down. In other words, we do many cycles rather than relying on one very significant journey that lasts for months or years and, in a single moment, offers profound transformation. While neither alternative should be discarded, the incremental, gradual approach fits more comfortably with the modern Western psyche.

Similar insights were found in the exploration of "the dark night of the soul" in Chapter Six. The traditional understanding of the dark night of the soul has, as its precursor, long periods of anguish and suffering. Eventually it culminates in a moment of surrender and ecstatic bliss. As with the hero's journey, we can adjust our understanding to include the idea of many small, dark nights of the soul. When we are triggered or feel fearful in our daily lives we are in the midst of a small dark night of the soul. Our moment of surrender is to stay in the discomfort as it arises. It is worth repeating the lines of St John of the Cross describing the potential for transformation of the dark night:

> **"One dark night, fired by Love's urgent longings,**
> **I went out by a secret ladder, unseen."**

These lines describe the same potential for transformation that is on offer every time we complete a round of the hero's journey.

CHAPTER 17

The Most Important Round
of the Hero's Journey

*Each time we repeat a round, we build the courage
to sit in the grief a little longer. This is how
transformation happens. Being in discomfort
is the doorway to freedom.*

The hero's journey is a cycle, and the hero always returns to where the journey began. We commenced our journey in this book with an exploration of the Enneagram. In particular, we explored the Passions that were the seminal idea in early Enneagram development. And so, we should now return to where we began and to a deeper exploration of the Passions. This offers the opportunity to make one more cycle of the hero's journey, focused directly on the unconscious material that can be accessed through the Enneagram.

Evagrius saw the Passions as distorted human motivations and obstacles to true union with God. With the benefit of the intervening chapters, we can now understand how we use the Passions to keep away from grief and trauma accumulated in the unconscious. They are the nine ways we distract ourselves from the underlying grief; they are the coping strategies we use to keep the grief from touching our hearts. They lead to habitual patterns of behaviour, which we hope will keep us safe or distracted. The Passions keep us locked in the hut or the castle not wanting to hear the Call to Adventure.

The Grief Underlying the Passions

To be able to move to the freedom we all desire, we must bring the grief underlying the Passions into awareness. The grief comes from our Basic Fear and will be different for each Enneagram type. It will be remembered that Basic Fear is an existential belief that we have held about ourselves from the beginning. It is an idea that we are inadequate in some way; that we are flawed, unloved, worthless, insignificant, and so on, depending on our type. This may have been an embryonic belief at birth, but the belief has been reinforced by subsequent life challenges. Inevitably, this belief becomes a major source of grief; we are believing in our inadequacies and finding evidence to support the belief. It is grief that we don't acknowledge, and we don't really accept that it is there. It is placed in the unconscious and, for the most part, it stays there. Our best hope of gaining access to the grief is to start with the Passions of each Enneagram type and explore what they are trying to conceal.

- For a Type One, Resentment towards themselves and others avoids the grief of believing that they are flawed.

- For a Type Two, Pride, and the belief that they are doing selfless work supporting others, avoids the grief of believing they are unwanted and unloved.

- For a Type Three, Vanity, and their presentation to the world as someone who has it all together avoids the grief of believing that they are worthless.

- For a Type Four, Envy, and melancholic fantasising that they should be more or have more, avoids the grief of believing they are insignificant and their life has no meaning.

- For a Type Five, Avarice and the withdrawal from life and any heartfelt connection with others avoids the grief of believing that they are helpless, that there is not enough of them to go around and that have no place in the world.

- For a Type Six, Anxiety and their fear that something terrible will happen, avoids the grief of believing they have no support or guidance and are unable to survive on their own.

- For a Type Seven, Gluttony and the need to keep reaching for the next experience, avoids the grief of believing that that they are deprived and trapped in pain.

- For a Type Eight, Lust and the need to amplify experience to create a false sense of aliveness, avoids the grief of believing they are at risk of being harmed or controlled.

- For a Type Nine, Sloth and the need to avoid conflict and disharmony in themselves and the world by disengaging, avoids the grief of believing that they are disconnected and cut-off from everything including love.

These are specific insights into the unconscious motivations that underlie the Passions. The challenge is how do we move closer to the grief around Basic Fear and allow the heart to be touched. We have spent our whole lives using the Passions to keep our heart safe. It is difficult to stop protecting the heart even when we want to. To help us do this, we can be guided by the insights and inspiration of the hero's journey. We want to walk past the Threshold Guardians and stop using the Passions to keep away from grief. We can allow the unconscious grief to move into consciousness, and let the transcendent function move us towards freedom.

Getting to Know Our Passions – Moving Closer to Our Unconscious Grief

Our Passions are a self-created state-of-mind that distract us from the grief of our Basic Fear. They keep us away from being present with ourselves and with our experience. We mistakenly believe the protection provided by the Passions is needed for our wellbeing and survival. For this reason, there is an unrelenting tenacity associated with the Passions; the protection is going to be kept in place, even when we want to move beyond it. That might be why Evagrius, when he observed how fiercely he and his fellow monks clung to these behaviours, gave them the name "Passions". They are not something we can easily let go. We choose to stay absorbed in this distracted state-of-mind so the unconscious grief cannot leak into our awareness.

We can use the Prospecting for Gold process to explore the Passions in detail and what they are trying to conceal. Unlike the previous exercises using Prospecting for Gold, we are not relying on any triggering event to lead us into the exercise. We know that Basic Fear is there all the time, so we can do this exercise at any time.

Sometimes it is difficult to know when the Passions are at work; they can operate unconsciously and mostly remain under the radar. As we get to know the Passions, we can sense the grief they are trying to conceal. With this understanding, we can now move into this important round of the hero's journey.

Stage One. The Call to Adventure (and Not Refusing the Call)

Becoming Familiar with Your Passion — Acknowledging How You Protect Yourself
Review the behaviours associated with your Passion in the list below. You may not relate to all of them but some should be very familiar to you. Concentrate on the behaviours that you recognise in yourself. Recall situations in the last few months where you have behaved like this. Reflect on the behaviours and notice the familiar theme underlying all the behaviours. Be curious about them, but don't judge yourself for behaving in these ways. Recognise that this is how you have been protecting yourself since the very beginning.

Type One: **The Passion of Resentment**

- I am resentful that I and others are not perfect.

- I am frustrated that others don't support the high standards I try to bring to the world.

- I feel nothing ever quite attains the ideal; nothing ever quite comes up to the standard.

- I am frustrated because I need to suppress my unacceptable feelings of resentment and this makes me feel even more resentful.

Type Two: **The Passion of Pride**

- I am constantly manipulating my heart to support a concept of myself that I think is worthy.

- I am filled with ideas about how worthy and selfless I am.

- I am not willing to feel my own hurt and acknowledge that I have needs.

- I have ideas that I am being in service, but it blocks the natural expression of the heart.

Type Three: **The Passion of Vanity**

- I need to present myself to others as someone who has it all together.

- I need to stand out from the crowd and I need to give a great deal of attention to my performance.

- I need to suppress personal feelings that may reveal I don't have it all together.

- I become impressed with the identity I have created and want to believe it is really me.

Type Four: **The Passion of Envy**

- I believe I am missing something other people seem to have.

- I believe that something is wrong with me and I am acutely aware of what is not working in my life.

- I feel I fail to measure up to how I ought to be.

- I want to be with the truth but I suspect this identity of who I think I am is getting in the road.

Type Five: **The Passion of Avarice**

- I feel small and helpless and there is not enough of me to go around.

- I feel I lack the ability and capacity to be open and generous with myself and others.

- I sustain an image of intellectual competency and at the same time I try to minimise any heart connection with others.

- I accumulate every potentially significant piece of information, believing that eventually I will know enough to feel confident.

Type Six: **The Passion of Anxiety**

- I feel the world is scary and I don't have the inner strength to deal with it.

- I feel afraid; it is how I might feel alone and frightened in the jungle at night.

- I wouldn't know who I was if I wasn't anxious and afraid.

- I sense that something terrible happened in the past and that it will happen again in the future.

Type Seven: The Passion of Gluttony

- I have an insatiable desire to fill myself up with experiences that arises from a deep sense of emptiness.

- I try to create a sense of abundance and excitement that masks the underlying pain.

- I distract myself by anticipating and planning what is next.

- With my mind being revved up with exciting options, the experience I am having now cannot be satisfying.

Type Eight: The Passion of Lust

- I want to feel intensely alive and I love the sense of being fully engaged in life.

- I feel my desire for intensity can degenerate into a need to constantly push against the world.

- I want to "amp up" experience so it becomes bigger, louder and stronger but this can lead to a sense of false aliveness.

- I sometimes become agitated and reactive to get a false sense of being alive.

Type Nine: **The Passion of Sloth**

- I want to stay out of contact with my instinctual energies because they could disturb the peace.

- I don't want to be affected; I don't want to experience reality or feel disconnection.

- I want to maintain the status quo and avoid the need for personal action or change.

- I try to create an identity that appears to be about love and connectedness but is really about avoiding conflict.

(The descriptions of the Passion-driven behaviours come from a Russ Hudson training workshop.)

Stage Two. The Threshold Guardians and the Clashing Rocks

Extreme Responsibility. Closing All the Exits
You are coming to the threshold where you are preparing to move into the unconscious and feel the feelings that you don't want to feel. The Passion-driven behaviours are a central part of your identity and your protection. As you start exploring these behaviours you will feel that your identity is being challenged.

- Can you acknowledge and take responsibility that you behave in these ways? This acknowledgement is how you 'close all the exits'.

You don't want to refuse the call and go back to where you were.

Stage Three. The Road of Trials or the Road of Trust — The Helpers

"Sitting on the Steps" — Being With the Feeling
Imagine that you are sitting in your little hut reflecting on these behaviours. What are the feelings that arise? They may include:

- Sadness about the compromises and limitations.

- Frustration at putting safety ahead of joy.

- Embarrassment about the lack of authenticity in interacting with others.

- Regret for missing out on a much richer life.

- Shock about the extent of denial of your true feelings.

- Disappointment about not moving beyond these limiting behaviours.

As you acknowledge your behaviours, it is common to feel frustrated that you have limited your life in this way. You begin to see the fearful and futile ways you protect yourself. It is a very small and miserable hut you have constructed for yourself. Do you want to inhabit this hut for the rest of your life? If you stay with these habitual behaviours, you might only be living half a life. Or even less than half.

Continue to sit with these feelings. Feel them in the body and around the heart. Keep going back to the feelings that are strongest for you. Just let the feelings be there. Observing your behaviours has led you into this moment full of sadness, frustration, and regret.

Stage Four. Allowing the Opposites to Come Together — The Sacred Marriage

4.1 Using the Feelings to Take Us Back to the Grief Around Basic Fear
As you stay with the feelings of sadness, frustration, and regret, do they remind you of earlier feelings of grief that have been with you

from a very early age? Is it possible that this deep underlying grief is connected to your Basic Fear? Slowly read the words describing your Basic Fear to yourself.

Type One	Fear of being flawed or defective
Type Two	Fear of being unloved and unwanted
Type Three	Fear of being worthless
Type Four	Fear of having no personal significance
Type Five	Fear of being helpless and unable to find a place in the world
Type Six	Fear of having no support or guidance and being unable to survive alone
Type Seven	Fear of being deprived or trapped in pain
Type Eight	Fear of being harmed or controlled by others
Type Nine	Fear of being disconnected and cut off from everything including love

- How familiar are the deep existential feelings of grief associated with this fear?

- When did you first experience feelings like this?

- Have they always been there?

Basic Fear is the mother lode of grief; it is the grief that arises from beliefs about your inadequacies. These are deep existential beliefs that say there is something wrong with you. They have been there from the beginning. They originate from fear, but they are felt around the heart as deep sadness and hurt. It is Basic Grief. You have been resisting feeling this grief for a lifetime. You have done everything possible to keep away from the pain and have relied on your Passion to keep you safe. You have developed a collection of protective behaviours that you think will keep you distracted. But now you can see how limiting they are.

Know that if you can stay with this grief, something different will happen. Remember Psyche and the impossible challenges that were set for her. And her final challenge was an invitation to bring up a "day's worth of beauty from the underworld." Also know, you are travelling around a path that has been trodden by thousands of pilgrims before you.

4.2 Feeling the Past Grief

This is the moment to feel the grief that has been there for a lifetime. Repeat the words of your Basic Fear. Allow the meaning of the words to fully touch you. You are saying and believing something deeply painful about yourself. This is the moment when you must stay with the grief of your Basic Fear and feel it deeply. It is heartbreaking that you would hold on to this belief of inadequacy.

- Can you feel the grief that has been with you all your life?

- Can you feel the pain that this grief caused you as a child?

- Can you also recall all the difficult experiences in your life that have strengthened this belief?

These experiences have confirmed to you that this belief about yourself is true. Now is the time to sit quietly and feel the energies moving in the body. This is where the grief of the unconscious is allowed to move into your awareness. It meets the structures of identity. It comes face-to-face with the Passions and all the beliefs and stories you have used to defend yourself from this grief. This is the moment of alchemy and the formation of the Vesica Pisces.

This is the Sacred Marriage. The Basic Fear sits beside the Passion and they are allowed to come together. As they meet, the opposite energies unite with each other. In their meeting, your identity begins to be dismantled. The beliefs and stories begin to fall away. You are offered a true perspective on reality. This new perspective is free of the struggle between them. The Sacred Marriage is doing its work. This is the natural movement of the psyche towards wholeness and the Golden World.

Stage Five. The Golden World

You no longer need to keep the structures of identity in place. You now have the freedom to look for some of the limiting beliefs you made up to cover over the grief of your Basic Fear. The central belief we have all made up is our belief in our Compensating Self-concept.

For example, a Type One has made up a belief that: "I am, good, have integrity and am beyond reproach." A Type Two has made up a belief that: "I am loving, thoughtful and selfless." And so on for all the types. These beliefs become a central part of our identity and a significant restriction on the way we lead our lives. Our life becomes focused on being "good" or being "loving" or whatever the Compensating Self-concept wants us to be. Trying to conform to these beliefs limits us in everything we do.

5.1 What Were the Limiting Beliefs You Made Up About Yourself Around Basic Fear

- Can you see that you developed a belief about yourself, your compensating self-concept and thought it would protect and distract you from the grief of Basic Fear?

- Can you now see how limiting this belief has been?

5.2 Letting Go of Past Beliefs

- Can you see that just behind the compensating self-concept lies the truth of who you really are?

As the unconscious content moves into consciousness, there is no need for further struggle. The protective shells are being dismantled. You feel the energies of the three centres and that becomes your reality. You know you are part of something much bigger than identity. Your belief in Basic Fear, that has been with you since birth, loses its power. As this belief disappears, so does the grief around the heart. You no longer need the compensating self-concept and the Passions to protect the heart. There is a new perspective and a spaciousness.

You return to the energies of the three centres and realise the magnificence of your own soul.

Stage Six. The Return and the Boon

- Can you feel the freedom in not having to conceal this life-long grief?

- Can you feel the sweet liberation in your new spaciousness?

*   *   *   *

The consequences of this most important round ripple out into the world. Your release from your Passion-driven behaviours will be noticed and will be a call to others to begin their own hero's journey.

Working with the Most Fundamental Belief — Basic Fear

This round of the hero's journey is the most challenging round we can undertake. In the earlier exercises, we commenced the journey after being triggered by some challenging circumstance. The Call to Adventure was loud and the purpose was clear. In this latest exercise, there was no compelling call. We set out to explore the grief coming from our Basic Fear. Basic Grief is a difficult concept to grasp and even more difficult to feel. We might accept that it is there, but often it just remains a concept. It has been there since birth. It is so familiar it is accepted it as an intrinsic part of our reality. But it is not.

This round is also important because it takes us to the core of the protective shells and challenges our most fundamental belief, our Basic Fear. It is the underpinning belief that keeps our identity in place. It is unseen and subtle but is the source of much of our suffering and our angst. Bringing the Basic Fear into consciousness offers a revolutionary step in moving towards freedom. We can then realise that we have always been connected to the three centres. This is the recovery of the Golden Fleece or the Holy Grail.

*   *   *   *

It is unrealistic to think that one round of the hero's journey is going to yield a prize of such magnitude. This round of the hero's journey needs to be repeated many times. It is getting to the core of the unconscious content and past a lifetime of conditioned behaviour. It is not going to be done easily. But each time we repeat this round, we build the courage to sit in the grief a little longer. This is how transformation happens. Being in discomfort is the doorway to freedom.

CHAPTER 18

Freedom from Our Unconscious Pain

I am the sky, everything else is the weather.

Each time we complete a round of the hero's journey, we uncover a little more unconscious content. We learn to be with our grief and allow it into our awareness. We become familiar with our Basic Fear and as we do, it begins to lose its power. We begin to realise that it couldn't be true. We touch the *pain inside*, and we learn that we can feel it and survive it. With each round, there is a little less to protect and the need for coping strategies begins to fall away. Our identity is being dismantled brick by brick, and all the beliefs and stories we thought were important, no longer matter. With this, we gain access to the vulnerability and delicacy of the heart. Our hearts begin to open, and we connect to the fullness and beauty of life.

But this can only happen when we have done the challenging rounds of the hero's journey. We need to have done our work to clear the difficult content in the unconscious. And when this is done, we can take our prize, the Golden Fleece, or in our terms, the return to the Golden World.

Beyond Identity

And with this prize comes a different experience of ourselves and the world. As we are freed from our unconscious pain, there is nothing to conceal and nothing to protect. We no longer seek comfort and relief in our identity and all the Enneagram-type behaviours that are part of it. Our identity fades away because it is not needed. It no longer has a purpose. We no longer struggle to hold together all the self-constructed beliefs and stories about ourselves. We don't put energy in trying to sustain our identity; we no longer believe that this is who we are. The blocks to the awareness of our true nature have slowly been removed. We are now connected to the deep life force energies of the three centres.

And then the question arises as to 'who are we without our identity'. This is the most fundamental of all questions and has been the subject of enquiry and speculation since the beginning of time. There is no direct answer to this question; it is something we need to experience in ourselves. However, there is some guidance as to what we might experience as our identity begins to be dismantled.

Robert Johnson (1) suggests that our true self is a vessel of awareness. It is not a vessel for thinking or doing: it is a vessel of being aware. It is where things rise into consciousness. This definition encourages us to distinguish between the vessel of awareness, and the contents of awareness. The contents of awareness, our thoughts, emotions and the ideas we have about ourselves, can come and go. Johnson suggested they are like animals walking out of the forest. They wander into our awareness, and, with time, will wander away again. After they have gone, we realise the only thing that has always been there, and continues to be there, is our awareness. We become aware of ourselves as awareness. And that is what we are. We are putting some distance between 'who we are', the vessel of awareness, and our thoughts and emotions.

Johnson's idea of the vessel of awareness is similar to Eckhart Tolle's idea of the Deeper I. "Your inner most sense of self, of who you are, is inseparable from stillness." (2) He suggests that stillness is our essential nature and with stillness we can connect with an inner space of awareness. "You are that awareness disguised as a person". He suggests a question to help us find the Deeper I: "What is it that allows every experience to be experienced?" (3)

These ideas suggest we are something less fearful than the transient ideas of 'who we think we are'? There is something deeper in ourselves that doesn't change over time. We watch the procession of changing thoughts, ideas and emotions all our lives, but the awareness that watches them doesn't change. The same awareness that was there when we were seven will still be there when we are seventy-seven. If we can sense the consistency and continuity of awareness, we begin to get a sense there is something about us that continues to be there regardless of what is happening. This is 'who we are'. It does not change with the changing flow and flux of ideas. It is always there as the awareness of life and our experiences.

An Eastern Perspective
Recognising the suffering that comes from believing in our identity is a large part of the teaching of the East. The prevailing message of many Eastern teachers is to drop all ideas of ourselves. As Nisargadatta says:

> **"Stop imagining yourself being or doing this or that and the realisation that you are the source and heart of all will dawn upon you. With this will come great love." (4)**

Nisargadatta also points to the transient stream of thoughts that has become our pre-occupation:

> **"The stream of mental states is endless, meaningless and painful."**

When the mind is still, we have the opportunity to experience our true nature. We will remember ourselves simply as awareness. The state of awareness, which is free of thoughts and ideas, is known as a state of "I am". Nisargadatta explains:

> **"When the mind is quiet, we come to know ourselves as the pure witness. We withdraw from the experience ... and stand apart in pure awareness." (5)**

When We Have Done the Challenging Rounds of the Hero's Journey

We may not achieve the state of pure awareness attained by Nisargadatta. Or we might. It is the same state described by Johnson's vessel of awareness and Tolle's Deeper I. It is, of course, the experience of the Golden World. In this place we can distinguish our true nature from the thoughts, emotions and stories that make up our identity. In seeing this distinction, we are taking the backward step, away from our belief in identity. In this state of unprotected awareness, we are guided by the three centres of intelligence discussed in Chapter One. We are informed by the deep knowing and wisdom of the Head Centre; we feel compassion and connection at the Heart Centre and experience intense aliveness and vitality at the Gut Centre.

This realisation can be expressed in the words:

I am the sky, everything else is the weather.

We can watch the difficulties and challenges pass through our awareness, but ultimately, they are like the clouds passing across the sky. We can see the clouds, but we know our awareness, the centre of our being, is not threatened. In time, the clouds will pass, and we will still be experiencing ourselves as awareness, or, as the sky. The weather will always be changing. At times it will be pleasant; at other times it will be threatening. It doesn't change the underlying nature of the sky. As we become aware of ourselves as the sky, the comings and goings of the clouds are no longer important.

Acknowledgements

My love of the Enneagram was born in a workshop taught by Russ Hudson seventeen years ago. Since then, I have continued to be inspired by his profound teaching. The Enneagram has been a life-changing gift delivered by Russ and has become a fundamental part of my life and my teaching.

I am indebted to the many courageous people who have attended the Academy workshops over the years. Their willingness to honestly explore their behaviour has been a source of inspiration to me and a demonstration of the growth that is possible through using and applying the insights of the Enneagram.

Mackayla Chalmers who taught the Enneagram workshops with me for many years has been a major influence on my understanding of the Enneagram and contributed to the development of many of the experiential exercises that make the work so powerful. Andree Evans, who continues to teach with me, brings a depth to teaching the Enneagram and has offered many new insights on how it can be presented. Chad Beckett, another Academy teaching partner, has always inspired me with his unique ability to access the wisdom of the Enneagram through movement and voice. David Andor has been tireless in his creative work for the Academy and has been an important contributor to the development of the workshops.

Silvia Roos over many years has created beautiful diagrams which have helped bring life and clarity to some of the more challenging Enneagram concepts. Many of those diagrams have been incorporated into this book and they add enormously to its value.

Barbara Ivusic had the unenviable task of transforming the first chaotic manuscript into something that approached its current form. It was a herculean task that drew on her great editing skills, and which she delivered with gentleness and patience.

I was fortunate to be supported by two dear friends, Andrew Hughes and Peta-lyn Farwagi who were brave enough and dedicated enough to read the first draft of the manuscript. They were able to offer much needed guidance, and at the same time, give me the encouragement to persist with the project. Chris Siegert, Rachael Carter and James Bruce all offered invaluable contributions in the editing process.

John Hale, an experienced author in his own right, went way beyond the call of friendship and read the final manuscript twice. The book has been greatly enhanced by John's involvement, both in its content and expression. He gave me the discernment to leave out the parts of the book that needed to be left out.

One of the joys of the project has been working with Akiko Chan who has been responsible for the design of the book and its beautiful cover. I fell in love with her work and her amazing aesthetic sense when I first saw it. She has continued to provide beautiful design options, the only challenge being to choose which is the most beautiful.

Notes and References

Introduction

1. The term, the Golden World, was first used by Mircea Eliade, a Romanian professor of religious history. It was made popular by the Jungian author, Robert Johnson in his book *The Golden World: Our Search for Meaning, Fulfillment, and Divine Beauty*.

Chapter 1   *The Three Centres*

1. Gospel of Saint Thomas. Logion 113
2. Maxon B and Daniels D.N. *Personality Differentiation of Identical Twins Raised Together*.

Chapter 2   *The Nine Enneagram Personality Types*

1. Kadloubovsky E. and Palm G.E.H., *Early Fathers from the Philokalia*, eighth edition
2. The unwillingness of Pope Gregory to acknowledge the negative consequences of vanity and fear have continued to be repeated down through the centuries by many spiritual and religious teachers.
3. Alexander and Chess. *Temperament and Development.1977*
4. Daniels D.N. *Nature and Nurture*. IEA.1996
5. Riso D.R and Hudson R. *The Wisdom of the Enneagram*.
6. Palmer H. *The Enneagram*

Chapter 3   *Finding Your Enneagram Type*

1. A short questionnaire can be found on our website www.enneagramacademy.com. A longer questionnaire, known as the RHETI, can be found on the Enneagram Institute website. A small charge applies.
2. Howe-Murphy R. *Deep Coaching Using the Enneagram*.
3. Rohr R. and Ebert A. *The Enneagram, A Christian Perspective*
4. The descriptions of the Essence Qualities come from a Russ Hudson workshop
5. Chestnut B. *The Complete Enneagram. 27 Paths to Greater Self–Knowledge.* 2013

Chapter 4   *What Each Enneagram Type Tries to Conceal*

1. Riso D.R. and Hudson R. *The Wisdom of the Enneagram*.

Chapter 5   *Basic Fear and the Levels of Health*

1. Riso D.R. and Hudson R. *The Wisdom of the Enneagram*.

Chapter 6   Allowing the Protective Shells to Be Dismantled
1. Don Richard Riso D.R. and Hudson R. *The Wisdom of the Enneagram*.p.10
2. Stein M. *Jung's Map of the Soul*. p.114.
3. Tolle E. *The Power of Now*. p.1.
4. Gospel of Saint Thomas. Logion 70
5. Williamson M. *The Return to Love*. p.116

Chapter 7   Using Relationships to Uncover Unconscious Content
1. Riso D.R. and Hudson R. *The Wisdom of the Enneagram*.
2. A Course in Miracles, For They Have Come, p.617
3. Ibid. Lesson 121

Chapter 9   The Challenges and Opportunities of Close Relationships
1. Collins, N. L. *Working models of attachment: Implications for explanation, emotion, and behaviour. Journal of Personality and Social Psychology, 71*, 810-832. 1996
2. Peck M.S. *The Road Less Travelled*. p.114
3. Campbell J. *Pathways to Bliss*.
4. Jett Psaris and Marlena S. Lyons. Undefended Love. p.193

Chapter 10   Exploring the Unconscious
1. Van der Post L. *Jung and the Story of Our Time*, p.115
2. *ACE Reporter*. April, 2003.
3. Horstman F. Step Inside the Circle. Video. Compassion Prison Project
4. The distinction between trauma with a "capital T" and a "little t" was shared with me by Andree Evans, my Enneagram co-teacher and clinical psychologist.
5. Tolle E. *A New Earth: Awakening Your Life's Purpose*, p.140
6. Van der Post L. *Jung and the Story of Our Time*, p.208
7. Ibid. p.208
8. Stein M. *Jung's Map of the Soul*, p.153
9. Van der Post L. *Jung and the Story of Our Time*, p.216

Chapter 11   Becoming Familiar with Unconscious Content
1. Stein M. *Jung's Map of the Soul* p.44
2. Ibid. p.43
3. Ibid. p.52
4. Ibid. p.52

Chapter 12   Allowing the Opposites to Come Together
1. Stein M. *Jung's Map of the Soul*. p.43
2. Jung C. G. *Letter to A. Zarine*, 1939. C.G. Jung, Letters Vol. I, p.267
3. Rumi. *The Guest House*.
4. Jeffers O. *The Heart in the Bottle*

5. Kubler, Ross E. *On Death and Dying*. 1969

Chapter 13   The Call to Adventure
1. Campbell J. *The Hero with a Thousand Faces*. p.51
2. Ibid. p.256.
3. Ibid. p.8.
4. Ibid. p.30.
5. Ibid. p.181.
6. Ibid. p.59.
7. Ibid. p.62.
8. Ibid. p.92.

Chapter 14   Journey into the Unconscious
1. The inscription at the entrance to hell in Dante's Divine Comedy.
2. Bettelheim B. *Freud and Man's Soul*. p.13.
3. Campbell J. *The Hero with a Thousand Faces*. p.97.
4. Johnson R. *The Golden World. An audiobook*. Sounds True
5. The Twelve Step Program is the core program of Alcoholics
    Anonymous, an organisation dedicated to the personal recovery
    of people challenged by addiction to alcohol. It is also used in
    other programs focused on addiction.
6. Campbell J. *The Hero with a Thousand Faces*. p.191.

Chapter 15   The Return to the World
1. Campbell J. *The Hero with a Thousand Faces*. p.30.
2. Ibid. p.207.
3. Ibid. p.33.
4. Ibid. p.193.
5. Tolle. E. *Through the Open Door*. Audio recording.

Chapter 16   Prospecting for Gold in the Unconscious
1. Tipping C.C. *Radical Forgiveness, Making Room for the Miracle*.
2. Gospel of St. John 8:31.
3. Campbell J. *The Hero with a Thousand Faces*. p.97

Chapter 18   Freedom from Our Unconscious Pain
1. Johnson R. *The Golden World. An audiobook*. Sounds True
2. Tolle E. *Stillness Speaks*. p.3.
3. Ibid. p.3.
4. Nisargadatta M. *I Am That*. p.3
5. Ibid. p13.

Milton Keynes UK
Ingram Content Group UK Ltd.
UKHW010634260923
429382UK00014B/382/J

9 780646 858371